The Earl and Countess Howe by Gainsborough:

a bicentenary exhibition

English Heritage looks after over 350 historic buildings and ancient monuments throughout England which are open to the public.
You can support the work of English Heritage, and enjoy special privileges and benefits, by becoming a member. Your membership card grants free admission to all English Heritage properties where an entrance fee is charged. You will receive the comprehensive *Guide to English Heritage Properties* when you join, together with a map of England to help you plan your visits, and a regular Newsletter to keep you in touch with special events and activities. Ask for details at any of our staffed properties, or, by post only, from English Heritage Membership Department, PO Box 43, Ruislip, Middlesex HA4 0XW.

The Earl and Countess Howe by Gainsborough

a bicentenary exhibition

edited by
Anne French

with contributions by
Aileen Ribeiro and Viola Pemberton-Pigott

English Heritage

1988

The Earl and Countess Howe by Gainsborough: a bicentenary exhibition.

Published for the exhibition held from
3 August to 30 October 1988 at The Iveagh Bequest,
Kenwood, Hampstead Lane,
London NW3 7JR

ISBN 1 85074 222 7

Designed by Two plus Two Design Partnership and printed by Traynor Francis Wood Ltd.

The costume section of this catalogue (section B) has been supported by a grant from the Pasold Research Fund.

Front cover: *Mary, Countess Howe* by Gainsborough (detail)
The Iveagh Bequest, Kenwood (cat. A1)

Back cover: *Richard, Earl Howe* by Gainsborough (detail)
The Trustees of the Howe Settled Estates (cat. A25)

Contents

Foreword

The Kenwood exhibition this year marks something of a departure; for the first time we are concentrating on just two paintings, rather than the whole *oeuvre* of an artist, but at the same time celebrating, with other galleries, the bicentenary of one of England's greatest painters: Thomas Gainsborough, who died in London on the second of August 1788.

The two paintings are his famous full length portraits of Countess Howe and her husband Commodore Earl Howe, the future victorious Admiral of the battle of 'The Glorious First of June' in 1794. This is only the third time since they were separated in the 1880's, when Lady Howe was acquired by Agnew's, and later purchased by the Earl of Iveagh, that they have been brought together. The portrait of Lady Howe formed part of Lord Iveagh's Bequest to the Nation in 1929, and has ever since been one of the glories of the Kenwood collection. The companion portrait of her husband remained with the family, and we owe a special word of thanks to the present Earl Howe, who has not only allowed us to borrow the magnificently nonchalant portrait of his forebear for this exhibition, but has permitted us to submit it to the most searching photographic and X-ray examination. Lord Howe has also generously lent several other items from his collection, and at all times has been as enthusiastic and co-operative over the project as the Kenwood staff itself. We could not have wished for a more helpful lender, and I know that Anne French, whose tireless work has resulted in this informative and scholarly catalogue, is immensely grateful.

The pose of the young Commodore may be marked by an easy nonchalance, owing as much to the becoming naval uniform as to the powers of Gainsborough's early maturity in Bath, but Lady Howe in contrast, conveys an image of fashionable *hauteur* which is almost unique in British Art. We are indebted to Aileen Ribeiro for her masterly analysis of the costume, and for selecting the costume items in the exhibition, as well as for arranging for the splendid reproduction of Lady Howe's dress to be made by Margaret Dobbie, Conservator in the Textile Department of the Victoria and Albert Museum, complete with fichu and apron. The two (not three!) replica shoes were made by Francis Wilson, and the gloves were supplied by Dents. The hat has been recreated by Miss Jenny Adey, and the jewellery by Christina Rowley. We are extremely grateful to the Pasold Research Fund for their generous grant towards the costume section of the catalogue.

The rare proximity of the two portraits has made possible a detailed technical examination of the paintings by Viola Pemberton-Pigott, who was responsible for the sensitive and very successful restoration of Lady Howe in 1976. She has contributed the fascinating report on her findings to the scientific section of this catalogue, for which we are also grateful to Christopher Hurst of the Hamilton Kerr Institute for his infra-red and X-ray photographs. It remains for me to thank our colleagues in the national and regional museums, and the County Archive Officers, all of whom have answered our numerous enquiries with good humour, and willingly undertaken the extra burden involved these days in processing our loan applications.

John Jacob
Curator, London Historic House Museums

Acknowledgements

First and foremost, I should like to thank my two contributors, Aileen Ribeiro, and Viola Pemberton-Pigott, who have given so much time and enthusiasm to this project, in the midst of a host of other important commitments. Aileen Ribeiro has not only provided an absorbing introductory essay, but has selected, as well as written, the section on costume – which involved her in a literally exhaustive search of British costume collections for surviving items of dress. She has also provided the paragraphs on costume for the portrait entries in Section A, several of which, again, she helped to select, while her enthusiasm has been the motivating force behind the recreation of the *Countess Howe* costume.

Viola Pemberton-Pigott's essay on the design and technique of *Countess Howe* is the culmination of many years knowledge of this painting, which began when she cleaned and conserved it in 1976. The hours we have spent examining Gainsborough's two paintings have been among the most rewarding of this exhibition, and have greatly increased my own understanding of them. As well as supervising the X-ray and infra-red photography, and the taking of paint samples (the information from these sources is incorporated on a display board for which she has provided the text) she has also surface cleaned the two Gainsborough portraits specially for the occasion.

This exhibition would not have been possible without the support and help throughout of Lord and Lady Howe, whom I should like to thank most warmly for so patiently answering a multitude of enquiries, and for allowing us the privilege of borrowing the portrait of *Earl Howe* before the exhibition, so that it could be fully examined, photographed and X-rayed at Kenwood. They have also kindly allowed me to consult and photograph the many other items relating to the first Earl Howe at Penn House.

A particular debt is owed to Christopher Hurst of the Hamilton Kerr Institute, who so expertly and patiently arranged the X-ray photography of two such large canvases at Kenwood, under less than ideal conditions, and who took the infra-red photographs of *Countess Howe*. With Sally Jeffery he also produced the display boards used to illustrate these in the exhibition. We are most grateful to Ashok Roy of the National Gallery for taking the paint samples of *Countess Howe*.

The replica items of costume have been made for us by leading specialists in the field, who are credited individually in the *Costume Note* on p. 76. However, I should like here to pay tribute to the expert re-interpretation of the *Countess Howe* dress itself by Margaret Dobbie, of the Textiles and Dress Conservation Department at the Victoria and Albert Museum. From her own expertise, and that of Madeleine Ginsberg, she has created as authentic a likeness as is possible on the evidence available to us. Happily, the dress will have an 'after life' in education projects at Kenwood, and I should like to thank English Heritage's Education Department for funding this project.

I have received invaluable support in my research into the Howe family history from the many local libraries and record offices in the counties with which the Howes are connected, and I would like to thank the staff of the National Archive Register, Nottinghamshire Local Studies Library, and the record offices of Derbyshire, Devon, Hertfordshire, Leicestershire, and the City of Bath, for their co-operation. Among the many lenders, private and public, the staff of museums, libraries and other institutions, and the individuals who have helped in so many different ways are the following: John Baskett; Megan Boyes; Duncan Bull; Margaret Christian; Stephen Deuchar; Ellen D'Oench; Joan Dormer; Elizabeth Einberg; Christopher Kingzett; Ann de Lara; Colin Johnston; Rica Jones; Raymond Lea; Rodney Merrington; Mr. Liddle; P. H. McKay; Evelyn Newby; Richard Ormond; Nicholas Penny; the Rev. C. B. Perkins; Janice Reading; Imogen Skirving; Lindsay Stainton; Miss J. M. Swann; Lady Walley; Neil Walker; Arthur K. Wheelock; Sarah Wimbush; Kai Kin Yung; and the staff of the British Museum print room who, as always, have helped at every step of the way in tracking down a large mass of disparate material. Aileen Ribeiro and Anne French would also like to thank the costume curators who have assisted in identifying and photographing 18th century articles of dress which relate to *Countess Howe's* costume, and in particular P. J. Boughton, Penelope Byrde, Elizabeth Earle, Madeleine Ginsberg, Anthea Jarvis, Josie Sheppard and Santina Levy.

Viola Pemberton-Pigott would like to thank Sir Oliver Millar and Lindsay Stainton for reading and commenting on her manuscript, and also her colleagues Amelia Jackson and Rupert Featherstone for their help and many useful suggestions.

As always, I am grateful to my colleagues at Kenwood for their help and support over the last year. In particular I should like to thank Georgina Mersh for coping so expertly with the major part of an always difficult manuscript; Christine Higgs for her assistance over typing and for orchestrating much of the photography; Sandy Salt for compiling the transport schedule; and Peter Cross for mounting so many of the prints and drawings. Julius Bryant, Christine Mathez and Gill Nock have all assisted in a variety of ways, while I should like to thank the Curator, John Jacob, for his encouragement and support of this project from its inception and the custodians at Kenwood for their work on hanging the exhibition.

As in the past, we are grateful to *Two plus Two* for designing this catalogue so proficiently in the face of a very tight timetable. The photographs of Earl and Countess Howe, of Earl Howe's tomb, and of the Penn House loans, have been taken by Rodney Harrigan and A. C. Cooper's.

Lastly, I should like to thank my husband, William Monroe, for temporarily deserting the Middle Ages to give me so much advice over the research and writing up of this exhibition, and for finding time to consult the rate books for the Howes' home in Grafton Street; for searching the Visitor Lists in Bath local papers for references to Lord and Lady Howe's visits to the city; and for nobly deciphering Countess Howe's seemingly interminable will.

A. F.

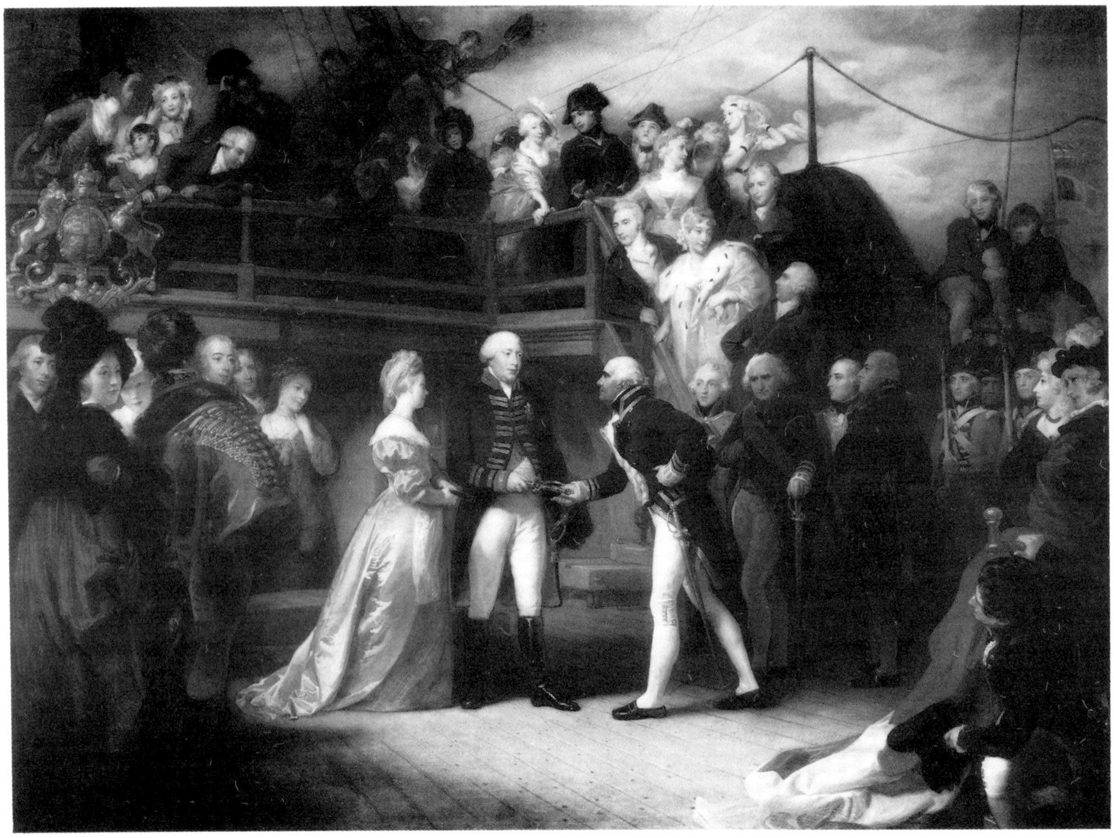

Fig. 1
H. P. Briggs
George III presenting a sword to Earl Howe on board the Queen Charlotte, 1828.
The National Maritime Museum.

Anne French

The Earl and Countess Howe: a biography

This exhibition centres around the lives of two people, Richard, 1st Earl Howe (1726–99) one of the foremost admirals of the generation before Nelson, and his wife, Mary Hartopp (1732–1800). Husband and wife were probably painted by Gainsborough in c. 1764, six years after their marriage in 1758, in companion full-length portraits which are among the very finest productions of Gainsborough's years in Bath, or indeed, of his entire career. The exhibition focuses principally on the portraits themselves, both on the circumstances surrounding their commission, and on the paintings' sources, iconography, costume, design and technique. It also seeks, however, to provide a context for the portraits by examining the lives of Gainsborough's two sitters, and the naval career of the future Admiral Lord Howe, who is shown in Gainsborough's portrait as a young Commodore.

When Richard Howe, then in command of the *Magnanime* and Mary Hartopp, daughter of the Governor of Plymouth, Chiverton Hartopp, were married at Tamerton Foliot Church, on the outskirts of the city, on 16th February 1758,[1] they were uniting two landed families who had been near neighbours on the Nottinghamshire, Leicestershire borders for generations. Whether they had in fact known each other in this connection is uncertain, but their near-neighbourhood in the country must have formed a bond between them when they met again in naval circles in Plymouth.

The Scrope Howe family were large landowners in the Vale of Belvior, and had been lords of the manor of Langar since the mid 17th century when John Howe married the natural daughter of the last of the Scropes, Annabella[2]. The Scropes, in their turn, had married into the powerful local medieval family of Tiptoft. The family politics were firmly Whig, and its members had played their part on the national stage. Scrope Howe, Richard's grandfather, was a Member of Parliament from 1672–98, and became Groom of the Bedchamber to William III, who created him in 1701 Viscount Howe in the Irish peerage. The family managed, however, to face both ways simultaneously, for Scrope's youngest brother, Emmanuel, had married Ruperta, natural daughter of Prince Rupert. Richard Howe's father, Emanuel Scrope Howe, 2nd Viscount (c.1669–1735), however, managed to ally the family's fortunes very nearly to the Hanoverians, when he married Mary Sophia, daughter of Baronness Kielmansegge, mistress of George I. The family resemblance between the Howes, and the Royal Family and their princely German relations, was remarked on by contemporaries (Horace Walpole, referring in 1762 to a visit from the Queen's brother reported 'he is like her, but more like the Howes'),[3] and this family tie was probably one of the reasons for the close friendship which came to exist between Richard and Mary Howe, and King George III and his family. There was a strong tradition of national service in the Howe family. Emmanuel Scrope Howe was Governor of Barbados, and of his three sons the eldest, William Augustus, and the youngest, William, went into the army, while the middle son, Richard, entered the navy.

Mary Hartopp was descended from the cadet branch of a family which, since the late 16th century, had owned several estates in the area of North East Leicestershire around Melton Mowbray, a few miles from Langar which was just across the Nottinghamshire border. The senior branch of the family lived at Little Dalby Hall, but Mary's family was decended from the cadet line of the family formed by Valentine Hartopp of Burton Lazars. In 1684, this estate had to be sold because of debt, and Thomas Hartopp, Mary's grandfather, began to purchase property in the Woodhouse area, just south of Loughborough.[4] Here the future Countess Howe was born; she was baptised in Woodhouse church on July 20th 1732.[5] Twenty years later, in 1752, her father, Chiverton Hartopp, inherited the estate of his aunt, Elizabeth Bennett, at Welby (a tiny hamlet on the outskirts of Melton, now almost totally submerged in the desolate landscape surrounding Asfordby mine), together with a smaller estate at Cottesbach. Evidently Welby was now his principal estate, since he is described in the memorial tablet to him in Melton Church as 'Chiverton Hartopp Esq. of Welby',[6] but in 1745 he had moved to Devon, and his official duties as Governor of Plymouth must have taken him largely from the area. His wife, Catherine Mansfield, again came from the local landed gentry; her father owned the manor of West Leake, in Nottinghamshire.[7]

Chiverton Hartopp, too, was an enthusiastic supporter of the Hanoverian succession. In June 1745 he was given the freedom of the City of Nottingham for his 'eminent services' against the Jacobites; he not only served as a major in the Duke of Kingston's Light Horse regiment, but also provided it with forty-one horses, and served on the Nottingham Committee against the invasion.[8] If the family was of local, rather than, as with the Howes, of national prominence, Mary Hartopp became a very considerable heiress when, on her father's death on April 2nd, 1759, she and her sister Catherine inherited his estates. There can be no doubt that, taken altogether, these were substantial.[9]

The early naval career of Richard Howe

Richard Howe may have been educated from 1731–5 at Westminster School. Certainly he was at Eton from about 1735, and it was probably while still there that he was entered on his first ship, the *Pearl*, in 1739. The following year was his first actually at sea, in the *Severn*, when he sailed in Anson's fleet on a voyage round the world. He first saw action in the West Indies in the attack on *Le Guayra* in 1742–3, when his captain, Lushington, was killed. Two years later, on 8th August 1745, he was made Lieutenant. In November of the same year he obtained his first command, of the sloop *Baltimore*, in the North Sea and around the coast of Scotland, under Admiral Smith.[10]

Howe now provided the first example of his 'persevering intrepidity' when he 'fell in with two French frigates of 30 guns, with troops and ammunition for the service of the Pretender', and 'instantly attacked by running between them. In the action which followed, Capt. H. received a wound in his head, which at first appeared to be fatal. He, however, soon discovered signs of life and... continued the action, if possible, with redoubled spirit',[11] obliging the French ships to sheer off. The engagement led to his promotion to Captain. By 1750–51, Howe was already playing a prominent role in naval affairs, settling disputes between English and Dutch settlers on the Guinea coast. Then, after two years in the *Dolphin* in the Mediterranean and on the Barbary coast, he leapt to national fame in 1755 when, in Admiral Boscawen's fleet of the St. Lawrence river, he fired the first shot of the Seven Years War in an encounter with the French ships *Alcide* and *Lys*, both of which were captured.[12]

In 1757, when he was elected, *in absentia*, Member of Parliament for Dartmouth, which he would represent until he went to the House of Lords in 1782, Howe served under Admiral Hawke in attacks on the French port of Rochefort. Although the expedition was a failure, Howe again won applause for his reduction of the battery on the Island of Aix when, under heavy fire, he kept on course 'with the greatest coolness and bravery, not firing a shot till he was within his ship's length of the walls'. He then dropped anchor and 'poured such a torrent from his whole broadside, as drove every man from the guns in the fort'.[13]

It was, however the year of his marriage, 1758, which was the year of Howe's greatest early triumph. William Pitt the elder had decided to put the young Commodore in charge of an expedition against the French coast, and Howe now set out in the *Essex* with 150 sail under his command. The target was St. Malo, but the troops, under the command of the Duke of Marlborough and Lord George Sackville, went on shore only to re-embark again a few days later, when Howe 'with the expedition of Harlequin as well as the taciturnity' re-embarked the whole force in seven hours... with the loss only of one man'.[14] Bad weather finally forced the fleet to return to St. Helens. Howe was disgusted at what he saw as a costly farce, and did not trouble to disguise his contempt, giving an early example of his famous taciturnity when he replied to Lord George Sackville, who had put to him several questions without a reply, 'I don't love questions'.[15] However, on 1st August the force re-embarked and took Cherbourg, as Walpole reported in high excitement: 'Taken Cherbourg! – yes, he has – he landed within six miles of it on the 6th saw some force, who only stayed to run away; attacked a fort, a magazine blew up, the Guards marched against a body of French... and then, and then, why then we took Cherbourg'.[16] Howe and the new commander, Lieutenant-General Bligh, made such an effective job of destroying the new and costly fortifications that Cherbourg would not be reinforced again by the French for another fifty years. The expedition was not, however, destined to end as well as it had begun. Further hesitations ensued, and a second attack on St. Malo proved abortive. Howe had now, in Dunkirk-like circumstances, to evacuate troops under heavy fire: on seeing his sailors' reluctance,'he went in person in his barge, which was rowed through the thickest fire, to save the retreating soldiers'. The fleet followed his example, and over 700 men were saved.[17] In the inevitable post-mortem, Howe was entirely absolved of blame.

Marriage and a change in circumstances

During this busy year, which effectively established his fame, Howe managed to obtain leave to get married. According to his biographer, George Mason, 'February 16th 1758 was an auspicious day indeed in our hero's calendar. Being allotted a cessation for a few months, amidst the career of his glorious actions, he married Mary, one of the two daughters and co-heiresses to Chiverton Hartopp Esq. of Welby in the County of Leicester'.[18]

The next few years were to be filled with incident for the Howes, and were largely to determine the course of their future lives. At the time of Howe's marriage, he was dependent on his officers' pay, but on 5th July 1758 his elder brother, George Augustus, 3rd Viscount, was killed at the battle of Ticonderoga and Richard Howe now inherited the Viscountcy, together with the Howe estates at Langar and at Clenawley in Ireland.[19] This event was followed, as we have seen, by the death of

Countess Howe's father in 1759. From now on, Lord and Lady Howe would be able to live on a substantial scale, and the history of their married life is an astonishing success story in purely worldly terms. By the time of their deaths, they owned no less than five major properties in Nottinghamshire, Leicestershire, Derbyshire, Hertfordshire and London, while Howe's personal fortune was also increased through bequests from Sir Gregory Page in 1775, and through the death of his ward, Miss Lepine, in 1798,[20] on which he inherited her Bedfordshire property. It was probably the former inheritance which led his detractors to suggest he had profited irregularly from the American War of Independence.[21] While Lord Howe's wealth and position were undoubtedly a permanent asset to him in his rise to ascendency in the navy, there can be no doubt that he also earned it by his high personal courage, by his management of his seamen, who adored him, and by his pioneering of a new code of signals. If he was not the greatest of naval strategists, this was not appreciated by his contemporaries, who held him in the very highest regard.

While the years 1758–9 were years of trauma and change, more cheerful events would soon overtake the Howes. On February 19th, 1762, their eldest daughter, Sophia, was born; as Mason tells us, there was all the more reason for celebration, since 'the marriage was productive of no living child for the first four years'.[22] The births of two other daughters now followed: Mary Juliana, born on April 17th, 1765, and the youngest, Louisa Catherine, on December 9th, 1767. During the earlier part of these years, Lord Howe was almost constantly at sea. His success at Cherbourg in 1758 was followed by his leading role at the Battle of Quiberon Bay in 1759 (see p. 81 and cats. C1–C2), in which he was largely responsible for disabling the French ship, the *Formidable*, and for sinking the *Thesée*. Afterwards, his commander, Hawke, presented him to the King, who thanked him with the words: 'Your life, my lord, has been one continued series of services to your country';[23] this might stand as a fitting epitaph to Howe's entire career. In 1762 Howe's relationship with the Royal Family was cemented when Prince Edward, Duke of York, became rear-admiral on board the *Amelia*. At his special request, Howe became his flag-captain. Walpole's comment was that 'Prince Edward is bound 'prentice to Mr Howe'.[24]

In 1763 the Seven Years War with France came to an end, and with it Howe's seemingly endless commitments at sea. He had in fact come ashore the previous year, and was now appointed a Commissioner of the Admiralty. This office he held until August 1765, when he was appointed to the highly lucrative post of Treasurer of the Navy. To his great credit, he is said to have refused to profit by a system which allowed him the use of the funds which passed through his hands.[25] As we shall see, it was during these years ashore that Lord Howe and his wife sat to Gainsborough for their portraits (pp. 19–20). Almost certainly, this took place on an early visit to Bath in 1763–4, to seek a cure for the gout from which Howe had already begun to suffer.

The American War of Independence, and Gibraltar

The next few years saw Howe's promotion to Rear-Admiral (18th October 1770), and then to Vice-Admiral on 7th December 1775. He now became involved, in 1776, in what was to prove the least satisfactory episode of his career, on the outbreak of the American War of Independence (discussed in detail on p. 81 and in cats. C3–C8), when he was appointed Commander in Chief of the naval forces in North America. Howe's younger brother, Sir William Howe, was already there in command of the army, and he now sailed for America to join him. Unfortunately for Howe, who was also appointed, jointly with his brother, as peace negotiator, he arrived after the signing of the American Declaration of Independence on 4th July 1776. This left him with no other option than to prosecute a war which would be considered by many contemporaries a 'disastrous' one[26], and which, with hindsight, could not be won. While at home the Howes were attacked for their inaction, the inconclusive nature of their campaigns, and their failure to send regular despatches – Walpole writes at various times of the 'the loquacious Howes', or complains that 'the Howes and the war are so dumb'[27] – they, in their turn, felt that they were being starved of resources and subjected to a barrage of criticism in the British press which was inspired by government sources. In 1778 both resigned, but the Committee of Enquiry which they now demanded should investigate their conduct adjourned in 1779 without reaching any definite conclusions.

On his return from America, Howe refused to serve any longer under the present administration, and the next three years were spent at home with his family at Porter's Lodge in Hertfordshire, the estate which he had purchased in 1772 from the writer George Mason, who later became his biographer.[28] However, in 1782 a change of ministry led to his appointment as Commander-in-Chief in the Channel, together with his promotion to Admiral of the Blue,and the award of an English peerage, as Viscount Howe of Langar. Howe spent much of the year 1782 trying to keep the Channel open for merchant shipping against the allied threat of the French and Spanish fleet. On 11th September he set sail for Gibraltar, which he relieved on 11th October in one of the most important actions of his career (see p. 83 and cats. C9–C11). 'It was the action', Mason tells us, which Lord Howe 'always spoke of to his dying day, as the greatest he had ever performed, and as the only one, of which he claimed the sole merit to himself'.[29]

First Lord of the Admiralty: on shore and at home

In January 1783 Lord Howe was appointed first lord of the admiralty, an office he held, with one brief interruption,[30] until July 1788. This was a period of retrenchment, and despite Howe's reforms in dockyard administration, and the technical improvements he introduced, he was bitterly attacked in print as 'a man universally acknowledged to be unfeeling in his nature, ungracious in his manner, and who, upon all occasions, discovers a wonderful attachment to the dictates of his own perverse impenetrable disposition.'[31]

With his constant commitments at sea, Howe can rarely have been at home during the early years of his marriage, and we catch a revealing glimpse of the peripatetic existence of a navy wife in the diaries of the Hon. John Byng, who met Countess Howe in August 1782 when she was staying at a boarding house in Dorset during her husband's absence at sea. He tells us that she 'brought with her a store of good humour and talkativeness'.[32] Now, however, Lord Howe was able to spend more time with his wife and family and in the pages of Mason and Barrow we can glimpse their family life at their Hertfordshire estate, Porter's Lodge. Here, following the marriage of their youngest daughter, Louisa, to the Irish Earl of Altamont (later 1st Marquess of Sligo) on 27th May, 1787, and Sophia's marriage, two years later, on July 31st, 1788 to Penn Asheton Curzon of Gopsall, Lincolnshire, the Howes lived with their middle, and favourite daughter, Mary Juliana. This seems to have been a family which revolved around the person of the Admiral himself; Barrow tells us that 'Lord Howe was quite the idol of his family',[33] and that 'The Countess was a most affectionate wife, watching over her lord in all his illnesses, accompanying him wherever he went, and when employed afloat, it was her special care that everything was provided for his convenience and comfort'.[34] On a more humourous note we learn that, on one subject at at all events, husband and wife did not see entirely eye to eye: Countess Howe was 'a lady rather particular with regard to the keeping a good table, and at one time had a French cook',[35] who was, however, entirely unable to understand the simplicity of Lord Howe's taste in food.

From the correspondence of Lord Howe's sister, Caroline, with the King and Royal Family,[36] it is clear that the Howes were on very intimate terms with the Royal Family, and the Queen and Princesses often came to visit Lady Howe and her daughter at Porter's Lodge. Lady Mary, who, we are told, had a strong taste for learning, and in particular for natural history and zoology, was a particular favourite with the young Princesses, who in 1791 appointed her their Lady of the Bedchamber. A few years later she was obliged to resign the post 'through natural tenderness of frame',[37] and returned to her parents at Porter's Lodge, amusing herself there with the creation of a menagerie. Countess Howe herself also seems to have been a candidate for a vacancy in the Queen's bedchamber in 1791, although in the event the post went to Viscountess Sydney[38].

The Howes were not always at Porter's Lodge, however. The Admiral's naval commitments must have meant that he, at least, frequently stayed at their London houses, at Nos. 3, 10 and 11, Grafton Street. From the rather confusing picture of these properties to emerge from the rate books, and from Countess Howe's will, it seems likely that No 3 Grafton Street formed the Howes' principal London home; Nos 10-11 were probably purchased additionally, towards the end of their lives.[39] The main family seat at Langar they appear to have visited only rarely, and the antiquarian Throsby notes that it was rather neglected although the new classical portico, shown in an engraving of Langar in 1792, must date from their time (see cat. A39). Their town house in Nottingham, at 19, Castlegate, was occupied in 1789 by a Mr. Stanford, and it seems likely that the heyday of the house was at an earlier period in the family ownership when, from the Restoration onwards, the local gentry were attracted to Nottingham by its vigorous social life.[40] The Derbyshire estate is mentioned only in Lord and Lady Howe's will, but it must have been relatively substantial, since Lord Howe bequeathed it to his daughter, Lady Mary, as an alternative to Porter's Lodge.[41] The Irish estate at Clenawley is not mentioned by Howe's biographers, and one suspects that there was little time for journeying to Ireland.

There was one other place, however, with which the Howes were closely associated, and this was the city of Bath, which, as Lord Howe was increasingly incapacitated by gout in his later years, now became almost their second home. Howe's letters to the Admiralty are full of repeated requests to go and take a cure there, and from 1780 to 1797 there were only three years (1781, and 1788–9) in which he did not visit Bath to take the waters.[42] Often he stayed for months at a time. On their later visits, the Howes lived at 71, Great Pulteney Street, one of the finest residential streets in Bath, which was completed in 1789.[43] Lord Howe was not the only senior naval officer to be a frequent visitor; Lord St. Vincent and Lord Duncan both had houses there and Lord Bridport and Lord Hood both retired to Bath. Nelson, too, was a visitor to the city, while only a few years later Jane Austen gives us a delightful insight into naval circles in Bath in the company of her hero, Captain Wentworth, and his brother-in-law, Admiral Croft, who also sufffered from gout. Like Howe himself, her characters came here not only to take the waters, but also to indulge in some of what Howe called 'rural dissipation'.[44]

The last years

The decade of the 1790's saw Lord Howe loaded with further honours, and brought him the post of Commander-in-Chief in the Channel in 1790, and again in 1793–4. On the death of Lord Rodney in 1792 he now became Vice-Admiral of England, a post he considered 'superior to all other naval ranks except that of Lord High Admiral.'[45] There now followed, in 1794, Howe's greatest victory, of 1st June, 1794, when, in the first decisive battle of the newly opened Revolutionary Wars with France, he defeated the fleet of Admiral Villaret-Joyeuse off Ushant (see p. 85 & cats. C15–C37). Tactically, the battle was not a total success for Britain, since Howe failed to stop the arrival in France of the grain ships from America which the French fleet had put to sea to protect. However, the capture of six ships, the sinking of the *Vengeur* and the dismasting of ten more, raised popular enthusiasm to record levels, as the mass of commemorative material on canvas and in prints, coins and medals clearly shows (cats. C15–37). We learn from Lady Elizabeth Foster how 'Lady Howe received the account at two this morning – heard the sound of horses – the messenger called out "Glorious news, my lady". She, quite out of breath with agitation, called to the servant to open the door and bring her the letter. "I can't, my lady, I am naked". "Well", says Lady Howe, "I will get into bed again. Don't stay to dress but lay the letter on the table and get away".'[46]

From this period on, Lord Howe's health began to decline. Although he remained nominally in charge of the fleet from 1795–97, it was really Lord Bridport who was in command, while Howe increasingly spent his time in Bath being treated for gout. His last act, which followed just after his official resignation, was to quell the seamen's mutiny at Spithead in May 1797. His personal popularity was such that the mutineers accepted his promises of improvements in pay and conditions, and only five days after his arrival the English fleet was able to put to sea.

Fig. 2
John Flaxman
Tomb of Richard, Earl Howe,
in St. Paul's Cathedral,
1803-11.

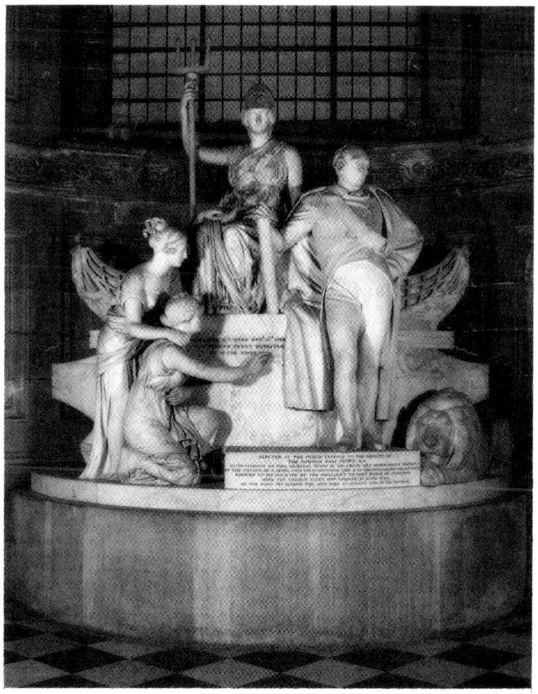

Mason tells us that for the two years prior to his death, Lord Howe was in a valetudinarian state.[47] In a touching postscript to a letter from Lord Howe to Sir Roger Curtis, Lady Howe writes that 'My dear Lord has had so very severe a return of the fever. . . that I really avoided writing to you. . . I am thankful I can say he is now recovering, but though he has written the above, he is infinitely more reduced in strength and flesh than when you saw him last. God keep him from another relapse!'[48] Lord Howe now had to depend on crutches, and one can sense the man of action's frustration in Mason's comment that this 'perpetual memento of his infirmity suited not his genius.'[49] In 1799 he 'grew so impatient of his weakness and pains in his knees, that he could not forebear trying electricity', which for a time apparently helped his mobility. However, supposedly as a consequence of this treatment, 'the gout had seized upon his head; and by August the 5th he was no more'.[50]

Lord Howe had died at his London home in Grafton Street, and the body was now carried back to Langar, stopping at Stevenage and Newark on the way: 'His Lordship's bays drew their venerable master to the grave; the cavalcade was attended by three mourning coaches, with the domestics in his service, the family carriage bringing up the rear'.[51] The burial which was in the family vault in Langar Church, 'was conducted in a private manner, without vain pomp or parade; the coffin in which (his remains) were inclosed was of English oak, covered with crimson velvet, and ornamented with gilt furniture'.[52] An elaborate tomb in St. Paul's, designed by John Flaxman, and erected in 1811, would later provide a more public memorial (fig. 2).

Almost immediately after Lord Howe's death, Lady Howe's health began to give cause for concern. In a touching letter, which reveals much of the close affection which bound husband and wife, their daughter Lady Mary Howe wrote: 'I would flatter myself she has no positive complaint, but she is thinner and more altered than imagination could suppose, but not more than those who have known the interior of this family will easily comprehend'.[53] More cheerful news, Lady Mary's engagement to Lord Morton, was followed, shatteringly, by her sudden death from a fever on April 9th, 1800. The King wrote to Mrs. Caroline Howe on the occasion to express to the Countess 'how sincerely he participates in her grief', and to hope that 'she and the Baroness Howe will not too strongly struggle against the real feelings of nature: tears are the necessary indulgence on such an occasion.'[54] In reply, Mrs. Howe wrote that 'my accounts from Porter's Lodge are, that she sleeps better for the air, and that upon the whole there is a trifle of amendment; but that she can ever feel happiness in this world again is not to be expected, but time, of course, will bring composure and resignation'.[55] In the event, however, the Countess outlived her daughter by only four months, dying, apparently at her home in Grafton Street, on 9th August 1800.[56] 'Her death was an easy one. Her two affectionate and dutiful daughers never left her till the last scene was closed',[57] Mrs. Howe told the King, who responded: 'It is impossible for any one who saw how deeply the late Countess's heart was affected, as well as the weakness to which her frame was reduced, could look on her exit but as a release'.[58]

A Brief Portrait

Lord Howe's contemporaries were not slow to set down their opinions of his character and abilities, and from his early biographers, as well as from commentators like Horace Walpole, we can picture the sort of man he was. Perhaps inevitably, it was Walpole who penned the most famous comment on Howe, when he described him as 'undaunted as a rock and as silent',[59] thus encapsulating both his almost legendary bravery and his silence, not only in sending home despatches, but also in ordinary conversation. He was, in fact, a man of few words: 'His speaking resembled his fighting; no idle prelude; close action was his aim'.[60] However, this 'taciturnity' as Walpole called it, was perhaps not carried over into his private life, if Mason's attractive pen portrait of Howe is to be believed: 'though most deservedly popular with seamen, he had no spice of the tar in his personal behaviour anywhere. His domestic manners were unassuming, candid, and friendly; they evinced too that he was habitually attached to Piety and Temperance. Justice swayed all his dealings; and his fortitude was blazoned over the world'.[61] This account is confirmed by Barrow, who quotes Sir Roger Curtis, a close friend of Howe's, as saying that 'although to a stranger he appeared to present a rough outside and a coldness of manner, it contained a warm heart.' Indeed, Barrow, whose sources appear to be Howe's friends Sir Roger Curtis and Sir Roger Barlow, stresses the warmth and evenness of Lord Howe's temper, saying that there were 'few instances when his temper was ruffled in the smallest degree.' 'His manner, it is true, was reserved, but had no tinge of haughtiness', and Howe possessed the ability to divest himself in a remarkable manner of 'every approach to a state of anger or resentment'; he would, always take the good natured and favourable side of every question.' Also praised are Howe's generosity in sharing his prize money with his fleet, his extensive private charities, the 'deep personal interest he took in the officers who served under him', his 'patient endurance under adverse events', and his high sense of honour[62]. While there were plenty of detractors to find him instead 'haughty, morose, hard-hearted, inflexible',[63] Howe lived constantly in the public gaze, and any public figure must expect such verdicts to be levelled by opponents. Certainly, the contemporary journalistic accounts of Howe's life largely bear out his biographers' portraits, telling us that professionally he was 'intrepid, active, determined and collected', and that his manners were 'easy, accessible and friendly'.[64] While all are agreed on his popularity with his seamen, there is some disagreement as to his methods of discipline. Whereas the *European Magazine* tells us that 'though a rigid disciplinarian, he has acquired the regard of his sailors, who look upon him as a protector and confide in him as a commander', other accounts suggest that his discipline may, instead, have been rather lax.[65] Everyone agrees, however, on the excellence of morale among the men under his command.

Lord Howe was known familiarly to his troops as 'Black Dick' on account of his rather swarthy complexion, and Barrow comments that 'his countenance (was) of a serious cast, strongly marked and dark; at the same time there was a shyness and awkwardness in his manner, which to a stranger at first sight gave rather an unfavourable impression; that, however, is said to have soon worn off, and the expression of his features to have assumed a very different and an animated character, assuming that benign aspect which corresponded with his disposition.'[66] The earlier part of this description is perhaps borne out by the portraits of Howe in later life by John Singleton Copley (cat. A31). Mather Brown and Henry Singleton (cat. A32). In Gainsborough's portrait, by contrast, Lord Howe is depicted as having a plumper, fresher face, which seems somewhat at variance both with Barrow's account and with the later portraits, even allowing for the effects of age. Gainsborough is, however, known for his accuracy in the depiction of facial features, and we must assume this to be a faithful, if perhaps slightly idealised, likeness of the young Commodore.

Of Countess Howe we know so little that it is impossible to draw any satisfactory conclusions as to her character. While a mass of Lord Howe's correspondence survives to speak for him, we are not so fortunate in her case, and her husband's biographers portray her only as a loyal wife, supporting his naval career. From the occasional glimpses of her we receive elsewhere, we hear only that she was good-humoured and talkative, that she kept a good table, and that she looked after her dying husband with genuine devotion. Nothing in this pen portrait prepares us for Gainsborough's portrait, which is among the most forceful he ever painted of a woman, and which we know to have been a strong likeness from a comparison with a miniature of the Countess in later life (cat. A37). One is left with the feeling that here was a much more determined and decisive character than Howe's biographers would suggest, but, unfortunately, the evidence to support this is lacking.

1. The original parish registers for Tamerton Foliot survive only from 1794, but the Bishop's transcript (a contemporary copy returned to the Diocesan authorities at the annual Archdeacon's visit) records their marriage on February 14th 1758: 'The Honorable Richard Howe & Miss Mary Hartopp by license February the 16th'. The license was issued by the Bishop of Exeter and describes Richard Howe as Captain of H.M. Ship 'Magnamine' and Mary as of Tamerton Foliot, spinster. There is no record in the rating records for the relevant period of the Hartopps living in this parish. Information kindly supplied by Devon County Record Office.
2. For the Scrope Howe family, see G.N.B. Huskinson, *Transactions of the Thoroton Society of Nottinghamshire,* Vol. LVI, 1952.
3. Walpole, *Letters,* Vol. 10, p. 10. (To Montagu, 6 February 1762).
4. For the Hartopp estates at Little Dalby, see the records of the Hartopp family in the Leicestershire Record Office. (8D39). These papers refer briefly to Thomas and Chiverton Hartopp, Mary Hartopp's grandfather and father (Introduction, pp. XIV-XV). Thomas Hartopp's estate at Woodhouse is given in an undated survey as consisting of six houses and 190 acres of land (4D 31/140).
5. Nicholls, 1795-1810/11, Vol. III, p. 118.
6. For the Hartopp estates at Welby and Cottesbach, see Nicholls, Vol. II, p. 285 and Vol. IV, p. 148. Only the church and a few isolated farmhouses at Welby survive. The tablet to Chiverton Hartopp and his wife can still be seen in Melton Church; see Nicholls, Vol. II p. 254.
7. Thoroton, Vol. I, p. 53.
8. Robert White, Dukery Records, 1904, p. 173 and vi, p. 199 and Thoroton Society Transactions, 1934, p. 57.
9. We know from Nicholls, IV, p. 148 that Cottesbach passed to Lady Howe's sister, Catherine, wife of James Modyford Heywood 'by agreement between the two heiresses', but how the other estates were divided between them is unclear.
10. For his schooling, see Mason, p. 4; for his early years at sea, see Mason and DNB.
11. *Gentleman's Magazine,* Vol. 69, September 1799, p. 805.
12. There is a painting of the *Capture of the Alcide and Lys,* by an unknown artist, in the National Maritime Museum (32-63).
13. Walpole, *Letters,* Vol 37, p. 506. (From Conway, 26th September 1757; and *European Magazine,* October 1782, p. 144.
14. Walpole, *Letters,* Vol. 37, p. 536. (To Conway, 16th June 1758).
15. Walpole, *Memoirs of the Reign of George II,* Vol. III, p. 125n.
16. Walpole, *Letters,* Vol. 21, pp. 225-6 (To Mason, 12th August 1758).
17. *Gentleman's Magazine,* Vol. 69, September 1799, p. 806.
18. Mason, p. 19.
19. There is no reference to this estate, beyond its name, in any of the books or papers on Howe consulted for this exhibition, nor does it feature in Lord or Lady Howe's wills. It seems likely that they rarely visited it. This estate may be Clenawney (also spelt Clannawney or Clanawley) in Co. Fermanagh, Ulster; see S. Lewis, *A Topographical Dictionary of Ireland,* I, 1837, p. 338.

20. Walpole confirms that Howe inherited £8,000 from Page in 1775 (*Letters,* vol. 39, p. 252: to Conway, 9th August 1775). Howe was related to the Pages through his aunt, Juliana Howe (1701-80), who married Thomas Page, Sir Gregory's brother. For the inheritance of Miss Lepine, see Countess Howe's will in the Public Record Office (PROB11/1346).
21. Mason is almost certainly correct in his assertion that Howe inherited the money (see note 20 above) rather than profiting from the war.
22. Mason, p. 19.
23. *Gentleman's Magazine,* Vol. 69, September 1799, p. 806.
24. Walpole, *Letters,* Vol. 37, p. 549 (To Conway, 21st July 1758).
25. Barrow, p. 77.
26. *Gentleman's Magazine,* Vol. 52, October 1782, p. 245.
27. Walpole, *Letters,* Vol. 28, p. 327 (To Mason, 18th September 1777) and Vol. 28, p. 337 (To Mason, 5th October 1777).
28. *The Victoria County History,* Vol. 2, p. 155 confirms the date of purchase, as mentioned by Mason, as being 1772. The mansion was rebuilt after a fire in 1901; it was sold to the former Middlesex County Council in 1928, and is now a psychiatric hospital.
29. Mason, p. 50.
30. DNB, p. 97. In April he gave place to Keppel, but was reinstated in December 1783.
31. DNB, p. 100 and see also Barrow, p. 404.
32. The *Torrington Diaries of the Hon. John Byng,* Vol. I, ed. C. B. Andrews, London, 1934, p. 93.
33. Barrow, p. 375.
34. Barrow, p. 360.
35. Barrow, p. 376.
36. See, for example, Barrow, p. 387 ff.
37. Mason, p. 93.
38. Walpole, *Letters,* Vol. 11, p. 367. (To Mary Berry, 16 October 1791).
39. The earliest reference to Lord Howe and the 'Honble Mrs. Howe' paying rates in Grafton Street is in 1771. (St. Georges, Hanover Square, Poor and Highway Rates (Collectors Book), 11, iv, 1771, Dover Street Ward (Westminster City Archives, C. 314, Victoria Reference Library). Unfortunately the earlier rate books for this street, which was renamed, have not survived. In the *Fashionable Court Guide* for 1792 (ed. P. Boyle) and in Boyle's *New Fashionable Court and Country Guide and Town Visiting Directory* for 1796, Earl Howe is listed at no. 3. Later edition of Boyle from 1800, however, list first the Dowager Countess and then her son and daughter-in-law, Lord and Lady Sligo, at nos. 10 or 11. In 1796-98 nos. 10 and 11 belonged to L. Concannon and J. M. Heywood; James Modyford Heywood was the husband of Countess Howe's sister and co-heiress, Catherine. Mrs. Caroline Howe is listed consistently as having lived at no.12.
40. A. C. Wood, *A History of Nottinghamshire,* 1947, pp. 221, 266. The house as it survives today is of the late 18th century and in the Adam style. See also *Transactions of the Thoroton Society.* Vol. XVI, 1912, pp. 54 ff.
41. Kent County Archives, Abstract of the Will and Codicil of Rt. Hon. Richard, Earl Howe (5th October 1796 and 26 July 1797 (C268/1)).
42. Cotterell, 1931, p. 12.
43. Cottrell, p. 21.
44. Barrow, p. 203; 'I promise myself to have done with professional concerns for some length of time, in the enjoyment of rural dissipation'.
45. Barrow, p. 311.
46. Dorothy Margaret Stuart, *The Life and Times of Lady Elizabeth Foster, afterwards Duchess of Devonshire,* London, 1955, p. 72.
47. Mason, p. 87.
48. Barrow, p. 368.
49. Mason, p. 87 ff.
50. Ibid.
51. *The Naval Chronicle,* Vol. 2, 1799, p. 263.
52. *Gentleman's Magazine,* September 1799, p. 807.
53. Barrow, p. 391.
54. Barrow, pp. 393-4 ff.
55. Ibid.
56. The family letters would suggest that she spent her last days at Porter's Lodge, but the *Gentleman's Magazine* records that she died in Grafton Street (Vol. 70, 1800 p. 805).
57. Barrow, p. 394.
58. Barrow, p. 395.
59. DNB, p. 100.
60. Mason, p. 102. See also *Anticipation,* cat. C8; Mason tells us that this pamphlet imitates Howe's manner of speaking.
61. Mason, p. 110.
62. Barrow, pp. 401-418.
63. Barrow, p. 404.
64. *European Magazine,* Vol. 27, April 1795, pp. 219-20.
65. Op. cit., p. 220; see also DNB, p. 100.
66. Barrow, p. 402.

Anne French

Gainsborough's portraits of Earl and Countess Howe

The Commission

The question is often asked as to whether Gainsborough's portraits of Earl and Countess Howe can be seen as marriage portraits. Technically, of course, they cannot, since, as we shall see, they were almost certainly painted in 1764, six years after the Howes' marriage in 1758. Indeed, it seems possible that this event may have been commemorated, not by Gainsborough, but by Arthur Devis, whose lost 'Portrait of Commodore and Lady Howe' may date to around or shortly after 1758.[1] It is tempting to suggest that the young naval officer, still making his way in the world, might have turned to Devis for one of the small conversation pieces (or, perhaps, two pendant, small-scale portraits) which were Devis's stock-in-trade. By 1764, however, Howe was able to afford something on an altogether grander scale.

As we have seen, the period from 1758–64 was one of rapidly changing circumstances for the Howes. It included the deaths of Howe's elder brother, George Augustus, on which Howe succeeded to the Viscountcy, and of Countess Howe's father, Chiverton Hartopp, and also the birth of the Howes' eldest child, Sophia. These were also the years of Howe's early successes at sea, his harrying of the French coast and capture of Cherbourg in 1758, and his leading role at the Battle of Quiberon Bay in the following year. For the next three years Howe was fully occupied at sea and there would have been no time or opportunity to think of sitting for a portrait. However, in 1762, just before the end of the Seven Years War with France, he came ashore, obtaining a post at the Admiralty.

By now Lord Howe had the wealth and position to enable him to commission a pair of large-scale portraits such as these, and Gainsborough's full-length canvases of husband and wife can surely be seen, not as a celebration of the marriage itself, but of the birth of their first child, and of Lord Howe's brilliant achievements at sea. The Howes had, in fact, arrived on the national stage, both in terms of social position, and of Lord Howe's career. Gainsborough's portraits, painted soon after Howe's return from sea, surely commemorate this moment.

Gainsborough's companion portraits of Lord and Lady Howe have been dated by John Hayes to the years around 1763–4[2], during Gainsborough's early years in Bath. Not only are there strong stylistic reasons for accepting this dating. John Hayes' discovery of a payment from Howe in Gainsborough's bank account for 21st July 1763, 'By Lord Howe £32 11'[3] must surely represent a part payment for one or both portraits. To this can now be added the fact that Lord Howe, who suffered from gout even as a fairly young man, can be shown, through an examination of the visitor lists in the Bath papers[4], to have visited Bath with Countess Howe in the winter of 1763–4. They arrived by 15th December 1763, presumably staying over Christmas, and Lady Howe was there again on 27th September 1764. She must have stayed several weeks, since on October 25th she attended a ball given to mark the anniversary of the King's accession to the throne. Although the Howes later became regular visitors to the city, this was only the second time they had visited Bath since Gainsborough's arrival here in 1759 (the first was in April and May 1760), and there seems every reason to suggest that this was when husband and wife sat to Gainsborough. As Viola Pemberton Pigott has pointed out, Gainsborough's serious illness in the summer and autumn of 1763 (he wrote to James Unwin on October 15th of having 'kept my bed 5 weeks to morrow excepting two hours sitting up for the last 3 days of a most terrible fever') is yet another reason for prefering a date in 1764 to one in 1763.[5]

Although the portraits were presumably intended as pendants, the general conception of the two is in fact markedly different, and one wonders if they can have been painted concurrently. *Countess Howe* is an exercise in the manner of Van Dyck, painted in a shimmering harmony of pastel pinks, whereas her husband's portrait, which relies on the tried and tested formula in English portraiture of the cross-legged pose is, of necessity, restricted to the darker, richer palette of naval blue. Whereas the Countess stands in a hilly landscape, the Earl is positioned beside a coastel inlet, a setting in keeping with his profession. If Gainsborough has made some attempt to link the paintings compositionally – the prominent birch tree on the right of *Countess Howe* is intended to counterbalance the rocky cliff on the left of *Earl Howe*[6] – there is no further integration of the two designs. And while Gainsborough clearly took tremendous pains with *Countess Howe*, altering the figure, as his composition developed, in a positive network of different ways, and working over every inch of the surface to bring the canvas to a high degree of finish (see pp. 37–39), *Earl Howe* is laid in much more directly, with few apparent changes of mind; large areas of the background are left almost empty. Rather more concrete evidence as to the portraits' separateness[7] is provided by the fact that whereas *Earl Howe* is painted on a twill canvas, with an orange-red ground, for *Countess Howe* Gainsborough has used a plain canvas, and has selected the lovely warm reddish ground so favoured by Italian 18th century artists.[8] One possible reason for the differences between the two portraits is that Lord Howe, with his commitments at the Admiralty, probably had less time available for sitting for his portrait than his wife; certainly he does not appear to have accompanied her on her visit to Bath in the autumn of 1764. However, the explanation may simply lie instead in that rare empathy between artist and sitter which resulted, in *Countess Howe*, in one of the most magical of all Gainsborough's creations.

Whatever the differences between them, the two portraits remained together as pendants for over one hundred years, first in the collection of Lord and Lady Howe themselves, and then at the home of their daughter, Louisa, Marchioness of Sligo. Where they were hung is, however, less certain. At the time of the commission the Howes had no regular home in Bath. Langar, their principal estate, was a house they seem to have visited only infrequently, while Porter's Lodge in Hertfordshire was acquired only in 1772. On balance it seems likely that the portraits were destined for their London home at No. 3 Grafton Street, although the rate books for the relevant years on this property are lacking, and their ownership of the house by 1764 cannot therefore be confirmed.[9]

Gainsborough in Bath

As John Hayes has pointed out, Gainsborough may have painted a small number of full-length portraits during his Ipswich years.[10] It was, however, on his arrival in Bath in 1759 that he encountered a new clientele, whose demands for ambitious, full-length portraits he now set out to satisfy. Almost immediately, the three-quarter length canvases of the late Ipswich years were converted into a string of grand full-lengths. In his portraits of women, beginning with *Mrs. Thicknesse* (1760), *Lady Alston* and *Countess Howe*, Gainsborough fell under the fertile spell of Van Dyck, whose canvases he now saw for the first time in the collections at nearby Wilton and Corsham Court.[11] At the same time the informality of male portraits like *William Poyntz* (Society of Artists, 1762) or *Thomas John Medlycott* (Society of Artists, 1763) represents an equally radical departure for full-length portraiture.

Gainsborough's arrival in Bath almost coincided with the opening in London, in 1760, of the Society of Artists, with its first regular exhibitions of contemporary British art. It is clear from his submission to the Society, from 1761 onwards, of his finest full-length portraits of these years, that Gainsborough realised these were the paintings on which his reputation would depend. They stand apart, not only in scale, but also in quality, from most of the other portraits of the early Bath years; as Waterhouse points out, Gainsborough's output during the years 1760–64 was greater than for any other period in his career, and included 'more thoroughly dull pictures' than are found at any other time![12]

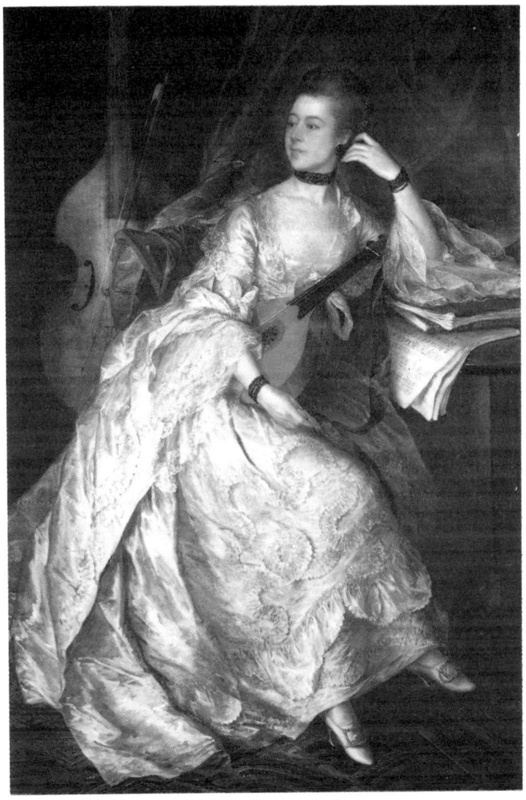

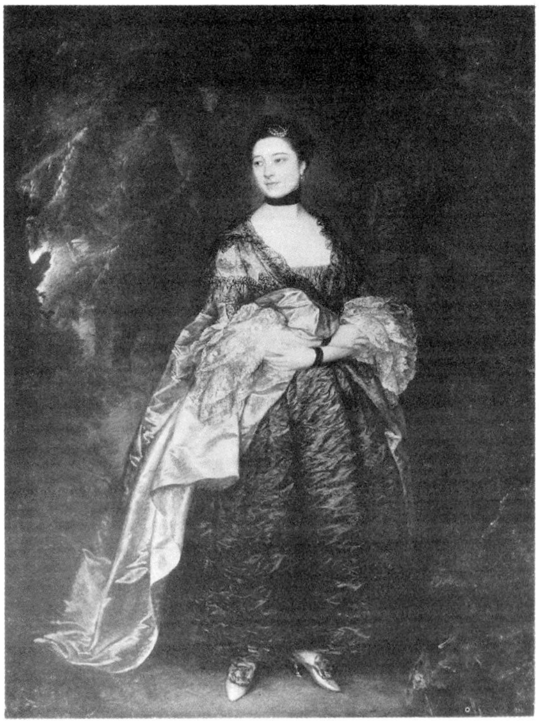

Fig. 3 (far left) Thomas Gainsborough *Ann Ford, later Mrs. Philip Thicknesse,* 1760. Cincinnati Art Museum, Bequest of Mary M. Emery.

Fig. 4 (left) Thomas Gainsborough *Lady Alston,* early 1760's. Musée du Louvre.

The artist's submission of full-lengths to the Society of Artists paid immediate dividends. By 1769 Gainsborough was as well known in London as in Bath, and in that year he became the only painter outside the capital to be invited to become a founder member of the Royal Academy. Although *Earl and Countess Howe* were not among the exhibited works – Gainsborough did not show at the Society of Artists in 1764 – they undoubtedly rank among the finest portraits of these years. *Countess Howe*, in particular, is a highly 'public' picture, and one which was surely calculated to attract the maximum amount of attention when on display.

Mary, Countess Howe

Countess Howe was the third great full-length portrait of Gainsborough's early years in Bath. The first of this series, *Ann Ford, later Mrs. Philip Thicknesse*, (fig. 3), painted in 1760, showed the sitter arranged in a spiralling seated pose that created something of a sensation: the bluestocking Mrs. Delany found the portrait 'a most extraordinary figure, handsome and bold, but I should be very sorry to have anyone I loved set forth in such a manner'.[13] Gainsborough learnt rapidly from comments such as these, and the portrait's two successors are both, in their different ways, more restrained in manner. In *Lady Alston* (fig. 4), which probably dates to a year or two after *Mrs. Thicknesse*, Gainsborough evidently set out to meet the challenge provided by Reynolds and Allan Ramsay, who had each produced, in 1759, his first full-length portrait in the open air: the *Duchess of Hamilton* and *Lady Louisa Connolly* (see cat. A20). He turned for inspiration to Van Dyck, but his sitter's figure, arms crossed rather awkwardly across her waist, is rather static, and only partially successful, while the elaborately ruched dress, complete with train, is hardly suitable attire for walking. The portrait is, however, more than redeemed by the almost Venetian richness of colouring, and by the twilight world of shadowy garden bowers in which Lady Alston stands.

In *Countess Howe*, Gainsborough offers a much more convincing outdoor portrait; his subject has stepped fully out of the boudoir and into her own landscape park, arrayed in a dress which, fashionable though it is, is nevertheless correct attire for walking (see p. 32). Gainsborough defines every aspect of his sitter's environment with care. At first sight the Countess appears to be standing on a patch of grass, but she is in fact positioned on a narrow pathway. Evidently she has just turned back after reaching the fence which demarcates the boundary of the estate; inside are the deer – a marvellous cameo touch – and the cultivated parkland scenery with its groups of trees, while beyond stretches a wilder, mountainous prospect which is a response to the 'sublime' scenery Gainsborough now encountered near Bath. 'Take Bath & 20 miles round it', he wrote to Farington, 'and there is not in the world anything superior to it. Rocks of the finest forms for a painter. . . Wyck and Hampton Rocks, Cheddar Cliffs, most picturesque. . . '.[14] Whether Gainsborough intended to suggest one of the Howes' own estates is highly doubtful. As we have seen, Langar – well stocked with deer in their predecessors' time – was a house they rarely visited, while they only bought Porter's Lodge in 1772. While it is always possible that the landscape could refer to their Irish estate at Clenawley, it seems much more probable that the parkland is intended to be symbolic of ownership, rather than representing a specific estate.

Although the subject of a lady or gentleman enjoying a walk in their own landscape park had long been a favourite theme of the conversation piece, which specialised in showing this act of ordered possession,[15] the subject was new to full-length portraiture. As we shall see, Gainsborough and Reynolds arrived at it almost simultaneously; *Countess Howe* probably post-dates by less than a year Reynolds's *Mrs. Riddell*, which almost certainly belongs to the year 1763 (see p. 24 and cat. A23). Gainsborough is, however, alone in depicting convincingly the effects of wind and weather, and *Countess Howe* is surely the first English portrait to do so. The sky behind Gainsborough's sitter suggests a rather stormy evening light, and one can see that the wind has risen, blowing the Countess's muslin apron sideways in the breeze. Gainsborough has allowed for even the subtlest effects of movement on his sitter's costume; as her left foot advances, her skirt is trailed back by the thistle which strays across her path. Not even Van Dyck had tackled the effects of climate, or thought through so completely the impact of his sitters' movements on their environment.

Sources: Van Dyck and others

If Gainsborough had paid tribute to Van Dyck before, *Countess Howe* is perhaps the most deliberate, and surely the most perfect, of his early tributes to his 17th century predecessor.[16] Unlike earlier 18th century imitators, with their predilection for 'Van Dyck' dress, Gainsborough had studied his subject with exhaustive care;[17] no other 18th century artist penetrated, as he did here, to the very essence of Van Dyck's portraiture, or so succeeded in capturing the sense of distance, aloofness, even hauteur, which Van Dyck and Gainsborough alike intended as the expression of an inherent aristocratic reserve.

The starting point for Gainsborough's composition was the type of female full-length portrait which Van Dyck evolved during his second stay in England from 1632 until his death in 1641. In these portraits he frequently posed his richly clad sitters, imbued with all the elegance and refinement of the Stuart court, against the backdrop of an open-air terrace, with a fragrant garden setting glimpsed beyond. More rarely, as in *Anne, Countess of Clanbrassil* in the Frick Collection, he actually set them in the open-air, and it was surely from a portrait such as this that Gainsborough learnt how to make use of a strongly accented group of trees to offset the figure in *Countess Howe*. The *Countess of Clanbrassil* is, however, shown in profile, and it is from a more frontally-arranged portrait like *Elizabeth Howard, Countess of Peterborough* (cat. A11) that *Countess Howe* in most important respects derives.

Gainsborough did not look at the composition alone; he also studied, and reproduced on his own canvas, the care which Van Dyck lavished on every detail of his sitters' costume, his understanding of how movement and light play across the surface of a dress. Every crease, every highlight, is depicted, and one can almost hear, in both artists, the gowns rustling in movement. In the *Countess of Peterborough* Van Dyck shows his sitter lifting the hem of her dress with one hand, to prevent her skirt trailing on the floor as she walks. Gainsborough, likewise, has *Countess Howe* gather up the heaped wispy folds of muslin apron under her arm, but whereas Van Dyck's gesture suggests incipient movement, Gainsborough's Lady Howe actually takes a step forward. If Van Dyck manages to convey the almost liquid quality of a string of pearls, each single stone luminous in its refinement, Gainsborough's pearl choker, although painted with a more energetic and dazzling brilliance, is equally fine. He also reproduces his mentor's fluid painting of lace, although with a more flickering touch which lends to his portrait a sense of vibrancy and flux, in contrast to the perfect equilibrium achieved by Van Dyck. Lady Howe's plain kid gloves, one of which is held so loosely in her grasp that it could easily slip to the ground, are also a popular Van Dyck conceit; see, for example, his portrait of the *Countess of Bedford* (cat. A12). The gloves may well have been a late addition to the portrait (see p. 39), and one would like to think that Gainsborough may have included this 'signature' as a deliberate reference to the source of his portrait as a whole.

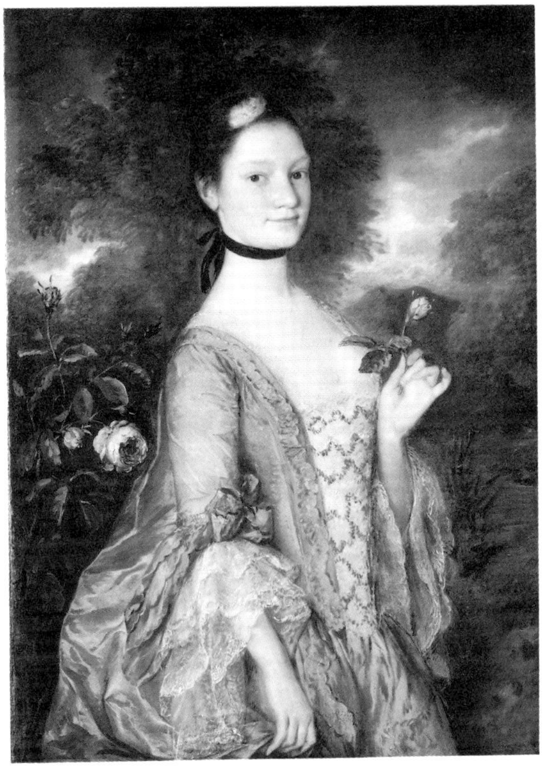

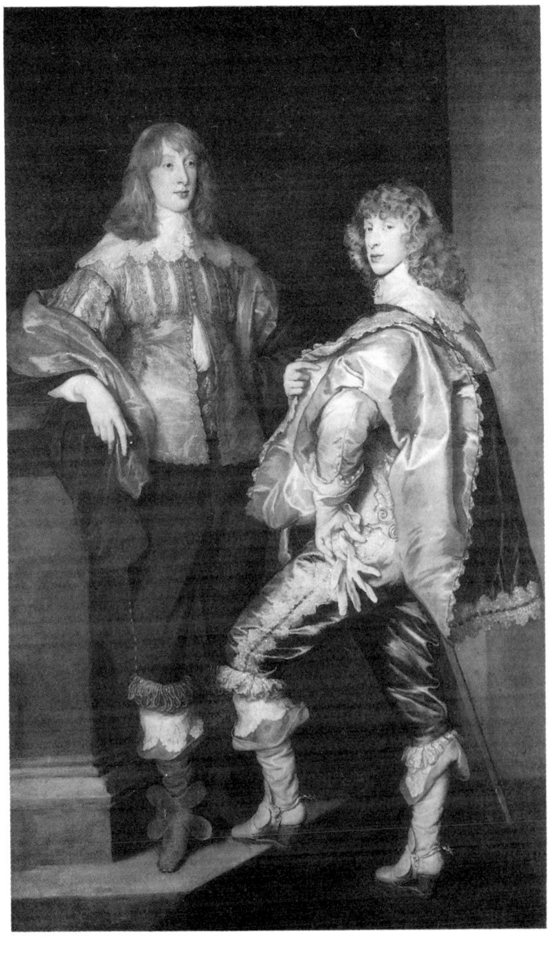

Fig. 5
(far left)
Thomas Gainsborough
Lady Innes, late 1750's.
The Frick Collection, New York.

Fig. 6
(left)
Sir Anthony Van Dyck
Lord John and Lord Bernard Stuart.
The Trustees of the National Gallery, London.

Although there can be no doubt that Gainsborough's likeness of Countess Howe is an accurate one (compare, for example, cats. A1 and A37), Gainsborough may not have been uninfluenced by the ideal of feminine beauty proposed by Van Dyck: Lady Peterborough and Lady Howe share the same long, straight noses, pursed lips and hooded eyes. It is possible that Gainsborough also learnt from Van Dyck's full and sensitive modelling of faces, since the rather curious, hatched brushwork found in his late Ipswich portraits, and which still appears to some extent in *Mrs. Thicknesse* and *Lady Alston*, is now replaced by an almost porcelain-like finish for the complexion.

Gainsborough also borrowed freely from Van Dyck's male portraits. The hand on hip pose from which much of his sitter's imperiousness derives is found, for example, in Van Dyck's great double portrait at Broadlands of *Lord John and Lord Bernard Stuart* (fig. 6), or in the lyrical *Sir Thomas Hanmer*; like Reynolds some years earlier in *Mrs. Bonfoy* (cat. A21), Gainsborough evidently realised the dramatic possibilities inherent in applying this forceful pose to the portrait of a woman where, by tradition, the gestures tend to be softer and more relaxed. Gainsborough also studied Van Dyck's use of plant forms to fill the awkward wedges of foreground space created in a full-length to left and right of the figure's feet. The thistle which occupies the left corner of *Countess Howe* is a direct descendant of the plants found in Van Dyck's late male portraits, for example *James, 1st Duke of Hamilton* or *Lord George Stuart, Seigneur d'Aubigny* where the plant is, similarly, a thistle.[18]

Gainsborough's achievement in re-interpreting Van Dyck in contemporary terms cannot be over-estimated; if his portrait is a reincarnation of a Van Dyck portrait, containing all the refinements which make Van Dyck one of the greatest of all portrait painters, it also breathes the air of a new and different age. Nevertheless, it is important to realise that *Countess Howe* did not emerge fully fledged and in isolation; in Gainsborough's study of Van Dyck not only Reynolds, but several earlier 18th century artists, have been there before him. A portrait in the collection of the Earl of Harrowby of *Lady Mary Wortley Montagu*, attributed to Jonathan Richardson (c. 1725), shows the sitter promenading, in Turkish finery, in a landscape setting; Lady Mary even adopts the same hand on hip pose as Countess Howe. Thomas Hudson would later experiment with the presentation of richly dressed ladies in open air settings, as in the fine *Lady Frances Courtenay* or *Miss Hudson*.[19] And *The Hon. Rachael Hamilton and her brother* of 1740 finds Allan Ramsay applying the hand on hip pose to the portrait of a woman long before the motif had been considered by Reynolds or Gainsborough.[20] Moreover, if it was Gainsborough and Reynolds who finally established the full-length portrait of a sitter in a landscape setting, as representing one of the principal themes of English portraiture in the age of the exhibition picture, Gavin Hamilton's remarkable neo-classical portrait of the *Duchess of Hamilton* (1752-3), still in the family collection, preceded by several years their own earliest essays in this vein, and those of Allan Ramsay (cat. A20).

Although *Countess Howe* represents a new departure for Gainsborough, based on his study of Van Dyck, the subject can be seen in many ways as a re-interpretation, in a major key, of his own early conversation pieces of the 1750's; for example his *Girl in a Park* (Mellon Collection), which depicts a girl seated beneath a pair of entwined trees, in a romantic river landscape complete with ruined buildings and sculpture.[21] A much more concrete point of departure, however, is found in two of Gainsborough's more ambitious, three-quarter length canvases of the later 1750's. The first is *Sarah, Lady Innes* (fig. 5), which prefigures the idea of a fashionably dressed sitter strolling in a landscape.[22] Even closer to *Countess Howe* is the untraced *Girl in a pink riding habit* of about 1759, which resembles the later portrait not only in the outdoor setting but in details such as the wide-brimmed hat, the hand on hip pose, the Van Dykian gloves, and even the colour of the costume itself! [23]

During the 1750's Reynolds, too, developed a series of atmospheric three-quarter length outdoor portraits, notably in *Mrs Bonfoy* (cat. A21), which, as we have seen, also anticipates *Countess Howe* in the choice of pose. The portrait was one of Reynolds's earliest compositions to be engraved, and it is reasonable to suppose that Gainsborough must have known, and could have absorbed, portraits such as this one, which precede in date his own early exercises in outdoor portraiture, and which share with *Countess Howe* an elegant refinement, filtered down from Van Dyck, which is lacking in the stiff, but delightful, naiveté of Gainsborough's own early three-quarter lengths like *Lady Innes*.

If the collections around Bath introduced Gainsborough to the portraits of Van Dyck, they also provided examples of the work of another artist who would deeply influence Gainsborough's style, this time in landscape. This was Claude Lorrain, whose paintings, together with those of other Roman 17th century landscapists like Gaspard Dughet, were ever popular with English 18th century collectors. Gainsborough's landscape background in *Countess Howe*, with its balancing on opposite sides of the composition of a single dominant tree against a more distant tree mass, and use of a range of mountains to close the composition in between, is arranged on broadly classical principles and owes something to Dughet, if not actually to Claude himself. The handling of the foliage of the foreground tree, moreover, with its patches of seemingly unattached, floating paint to describe the leaves, resembles the technique of Claude and Dughet in some of their early wash drawings.[24] However, similar dominant trees are also found in the work of Dutch artists like Jacob van Ruisdael, who was a major influence on the young Gainsborough, and Gainsborough may well have looked back here to the single birch tree which forms such an emphatic vertical in his own early landscapes like *Drinkstone Park* (São Paolo, Brazil), painted under the influence of Ruisdael, or, indeed, to his own early landscape drawings.[25]

Gainsborough and Reynolds

Gainsborough was in the vanguard of the development of English portraiture from the moment when, on the opening of the Society of Artists in 1760, it changed decisively and grand full-length portraiture became the order of the day. He provided, moreover, an important alternative to Reynolds, who, from 1759, embarked on his crusade to elevate the British portrait by marrying it to the classical style, and who would produce, in the early 1760's, in portraits like the *Duchess of Ancaster* (cat. A24) or *Lady Sarah Bunbury sacrificing to the Graces* (Art Institute of Chicago), some of the most severely neo-classical images of his career. Gainsborough, by contrast, could offer the public a different type of full-length portrait in which his sitters, wearing contemporary costume, and often rather more informally posed than in Reynolds's creations, were nevertheless invested with the authority and grandeur of the 'golden age' of Van Dyck.

The different approaches adopted by Gainsborough and Reynolds at this critical moment of their careers can, however, be too often stressed in literature on the artists. What is less often perceived is the strong similarity between certain of their works at this period, in the early 1760's, when they are often considered to be poles apart. Of no two paintings is this more true than Reynolds's *Mrs. Riddell* (cat. A23), almost certainly painted in 1763, and Gainsborough's *Countess Howe*, which probably belongs to the following year. In *Mrs. Riddell*, a portrait which was never intended to face the glare of public exhibition,[26] Reynolds gives us a preview of the subject of *Countess Howe* in this study of a fashionably dressed lady out walking in her park. He goes, in fact, even further than Gainsborough will do in his creation of an informal, outdoor portrait, for his sitter is seen walking into the centre of the canvas from one side, pausing as she does so with a perceptible, and touching hesitation, which is entirely in keeping with her evidently retiring personality. Reynolds has deliberately chosen to create a sense of off-balance, and indecision, which is in marked contrast to Gainsborough's supremely confident image, with all the assurance of Van Dyck behind it. This is not to say that Gainsborough was necessarily less perceptive about his sitter's character; the Countess may have been as imperious as Gainsborough portrays her, although it is fair to add that the rare glimpses we have of her in the biographical literature on her husband hardly bear this out.

The similarity between the two portraits even extends to the technique used in both; as Mannings has pointed out, in *Mrs. Riddell* 'the unusually thin, transparent handling of paint, especially in the background'[27] invites comparison with Gainsborough, and he suggests that the portrait looks forward to *Countess Howe*. This watercolour-like technique, however, was foreign to Reynolds's usual practice, and it is possible that it may reflect instead the passing influence of Gainsborough, to whom such a method came naturally. Indeed, one is left wondering how much the painting as a whole can be seen as a reaction to the new outdoor full-length portraits of Gainsborough, which began at about this time with *Lady Alston*. *Mrs. Riddell*, however, almost certainly pre-dates *Countess Howe* itself and although Reynolds's portrait was neither exhibited publicly, nor engraved, it is hard not to believe that Gainsborough was aware of his rival's development of a new and informal type of outdoor portrait before he came to paint *Countess Howe*. As if having proved that he could match Gainsborough on the ground of informality, Reynolds now retired to his olympian heights, and it was only many years later that he would attempt a portrait as informal as *Mrs. Riddell* or the lovely and comparable *Susanna Gale* in Melbourne (fig. 11).

Style

Countess Howe stands at that cross-roads in Gainsborough's career when the artist managed to combine truth to appearances with a powerful imagination. Behind, stand the pictures of the late Ipswich years, with their impressive bulk and solidity, but their still slightly awkward placing of the figure within the frame. Ahead, lies the delicious crumbling of form which separates later Bath works such as *Lady Sefton* (Walker Art Gallery, Liverpool) or *Dr. Ralph Schomberg* (National Gallery) from the portraits of the earlier half of the decade. For a few years in the early 1760's, however, Gainsborough seems to achieve in his portraits an almost crystalline sense of focus; every detail of the facial features, costume and landscape in *Countess Howe* is depicted with a clarity which will soon be lost in the poetic but unsubstantial forms of his late works. This quality in the portrait can perhaps best be understood by a comparison with a later work such as *Lady Brisco* of 1776 (fig. 7). Unlike these later creations, which Waterhouse unforgettably characterised as 'celestial beings, devoid of the grosser qualities of human personality, almost the loveliest garden statues come to life',[28] Countess Howe stands four-square on her buckled feet. Although the figure is now refined by the elegant contours of Van Dyck, it fills the frame as forcefully as do the portraits of the late Ipswich years. And if Gainsborough has learnt fully how to integrate his figure into the setting in terms of light, shade and the blurring of outline, there is none of that sense almost of the absorption of the figure into her setting which we find in *Lady Brisco*. Countess Howe's costume, although in places the brushwork is sketchy in the extreme, is nevertheless so precise in its description of each individual feature of the dress as to make the portrait a treasure-trove of information for costume historians, as Dr. Ribeiro shows in her essay on pp. 31–35. This quality is lost in the later portraits in a gossamer web of sheer paint. The same clarity is apparent in the landscape. Although the trees are generalised in type, as always in Gainsborough's work, they retain their sense of particular structure and growth; those in the late portraits are melting forms, suffused in light. Similarly, the plants which continue to fill the foreground space in the late works can no longer be identified as belonging to any particular species, whereas the thistle in *Countess Howe* surely has its origin in one of Gainsborough's sensitive and highly accurate plant studies from nature (see cat. A9).[29] Above all, Countess Howe has a force of personality and sense of character which is lacking in the otherwise supremely lovely late portraits of women. These are indeed 'garden statues', whereas Countess Howe is a living presence to be reckoned with.

As we have seen *Countess Howe* represents a decisive advance over *Lady Alston* both compositionally and in terms of the modelling of the face. Much closer in feeling to the Kenwood portrait is a group portrait of the *Byam Family*, (Marlborough College, fig. 8), in which Gainsborough now tackles the subject of a whole family out walking in a landscape. Both portraits probably belong to 1764, and show the new assurance with which Gainsborough can now deal with sitters in movement. The treatment of Mrs. Byam herself is almost identical to Countess Howe in the firmness and solidity of the modelling of both face and figure; the very full realisation of the forms of both husband and wife contrasts, in fact, rather oddly with the much more abstract handling of the stormy landscape behind them. A year or two after *Countess Howe*, Gainsborough would paint a portrait which is almost a reprise of his earlier portrait in terms of costume, setting and even pose, in the perhaps rather self-consciously romantic *Anne Spencer, Marchioness of Donegall*, in Detroit (fig. 9). However, it is perhaps

Fig. 7 (right) Thomas Gainsborough *Lady Brisco*, 1776. The Iveagh Bequest, Kenwood.

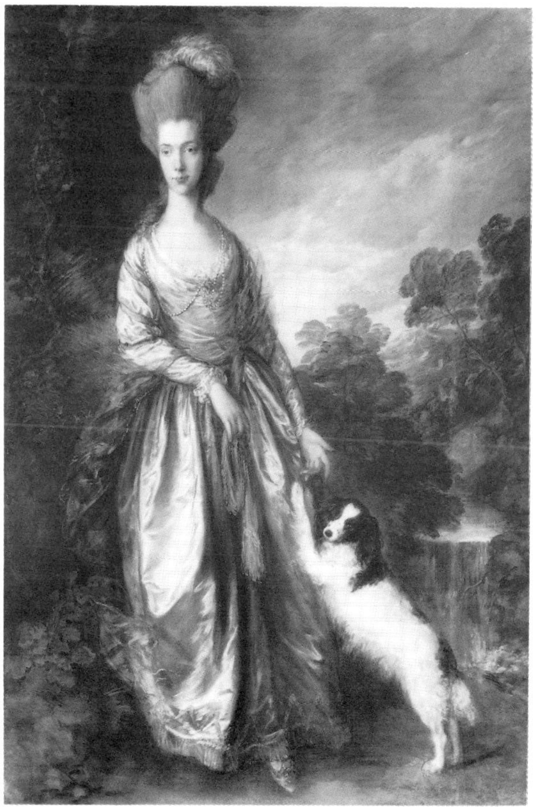

Fig. 8 (far right) Thomas Gainsborough *The Byam Family*. Marlborough College.

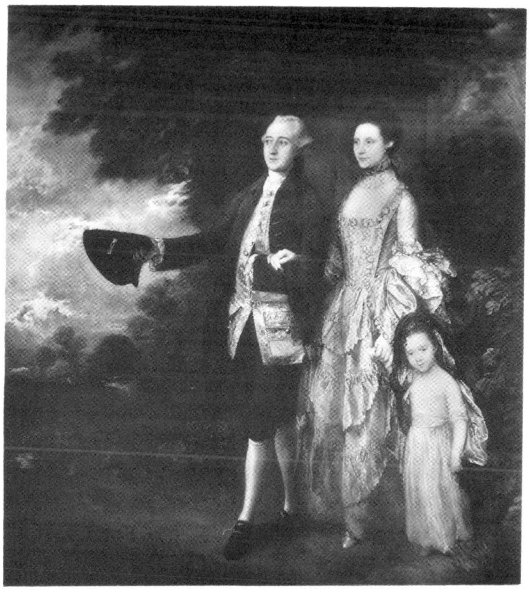

no accident that a painting which has one of the strongest affinities to *Countess Howe* is the portrait of a man, *Edward Craggs Nugent*, exhibited at the Society of Artists in 1765. Here the sitter adopts the same rather aggressive hand on hip gesture, and faces us with the same assured gaze, and yet incomparable elegance, which characterises Countess Howe herself.

Design and preliminary drawings

Although Gainsborough produced preliminary studies for some of his more complex compositions, for example *Mrs. Thicknesse* (British Museum), he generally preferred to work direct onto canvas, and *Countess Howe* provides us with a fascinating insight into how the artist developed his ideas and his design as he progressed; many of his changes of mind, or *pentimenti*, are clearly visible on close inspection, and these, together with other technical aspects of the painting, are discussed on pp. 37–43 by Viola Pemberton Pigott.

One aspect of Gainsborough's female sitters he did, however, study with particular care before beginning on a canvas: their costume. A large number of costume studies, usually in black chalk or pencil, survive from the early Bath years to illustrate how Gainsborough grappled with the problem he now encountered for the first time – that of painting the incredibly complex folds of contemporary costume in a full-length format. Three of these drawings are included in the exhibition (cats. A3–A5); of these, one (cat. A3) can almost certainly be identified, as Lindsay Stainton has pointed out, as being directly related to the portrait of *Countess Howe*.[30] However, the sitter in this costume study was evidently not the Countess herself, but a studio model employed while Gainsborough experimented with the fall and disposition of the dress.[31]

Gainsborough may also have made use of a preliminary drawing for the thistle in the bottom left-hand corner of his canvas. Although he is known to have incorporated individual motifs from his drawings into his landscape paintings, Hayes suggests that this practice is less likely to have occurred in his portrait compositions.[32] However, the superbly realised specimen found here surely has its origins, at least in memory, in Gainsborough's brilliant recording of plants from nature.

With the exception of these two instances, Gainsborough appears to have approached his canvas with almost no preparation. He established his design as he worked, and a close examination of the painting shows that the figure was originally positioned rather further to the left; a 'third' foot, seen clearly in an infra-red photograph (fig. 18), belongs to this earlier design. Gainsborough seems to have had particular difficulty with the area of lace below his sitter's right sleeve, perhaps because the hand itself was originally positioned slightly differently. The outline of the skirt was also the subject of at least two attempts, and, similarly, the line of the apron was once quite different. The very sketchy painting of the figure on the right-hand side also obscures major changes in the design; the sitter's hand, now gloved, was once bare, and she wore a companion black wristband to the one on her right arm. The tree, so dominant and majestic, was probably a late addition; it was once considerably leafier, and perhaps rather more naturalistic, than the present rather stylised affair. Apart from the sheer pleasure obtained by following an artist in the very process of creation, these *pentimenti* suggest the exceptional importance Gainsborough must have attached to this commission. This was certainly no routine production, but one where the artist has constantly striven to achieve perfection.

Richard, Earl Howe

Pose and sources: Van Dyck and the antique

As we have seen, the portrait of *Earl Howe* is very different from that of his wife. At first sight, the painting provides a classic example of what Ellis Waterhouse called 'that foolish cross-legged style, which was to haunt British portraiture'[33] for over fifty years from the time of its first appearance in the 1720's. The pose is, in origin, a classical one. Several of the most famous statues of antiquity adopted it, among them the *Marble Faun* and the *Faun in Rosso Antico*, both in the Musei Capitolini, Rome, and, the source which corresponds most closely to Gainsborough's and other portraits, the *Mercury* (cat. A27). In the early 18th century this sculpture, which had been moved to Florence in the mid-16th century, again began to attract the attention of scholars and artists after a period of comparative neglect.[34] With its upright format, it was judged by English 18th century cognoscenti to be particularly appropriate for use in English country house interiors, and numerous casts were produced in England from about 1725 onwards. From sculpture, and the walls of the English country house, the pose passed rapidly into portraiture. Perhaps its most commanding use by a British portraitist was by Thomas Hudson in his fine *Theodore Jacobsen* (1746) in the Foundling Hospital (fig. 10), but artists such as Allan Ramsay and Arthur Devis also used it extensively, and Gainsborough would have known the pose from its almost countless number of appearances in the work of the generation of artists slightly older than himself.

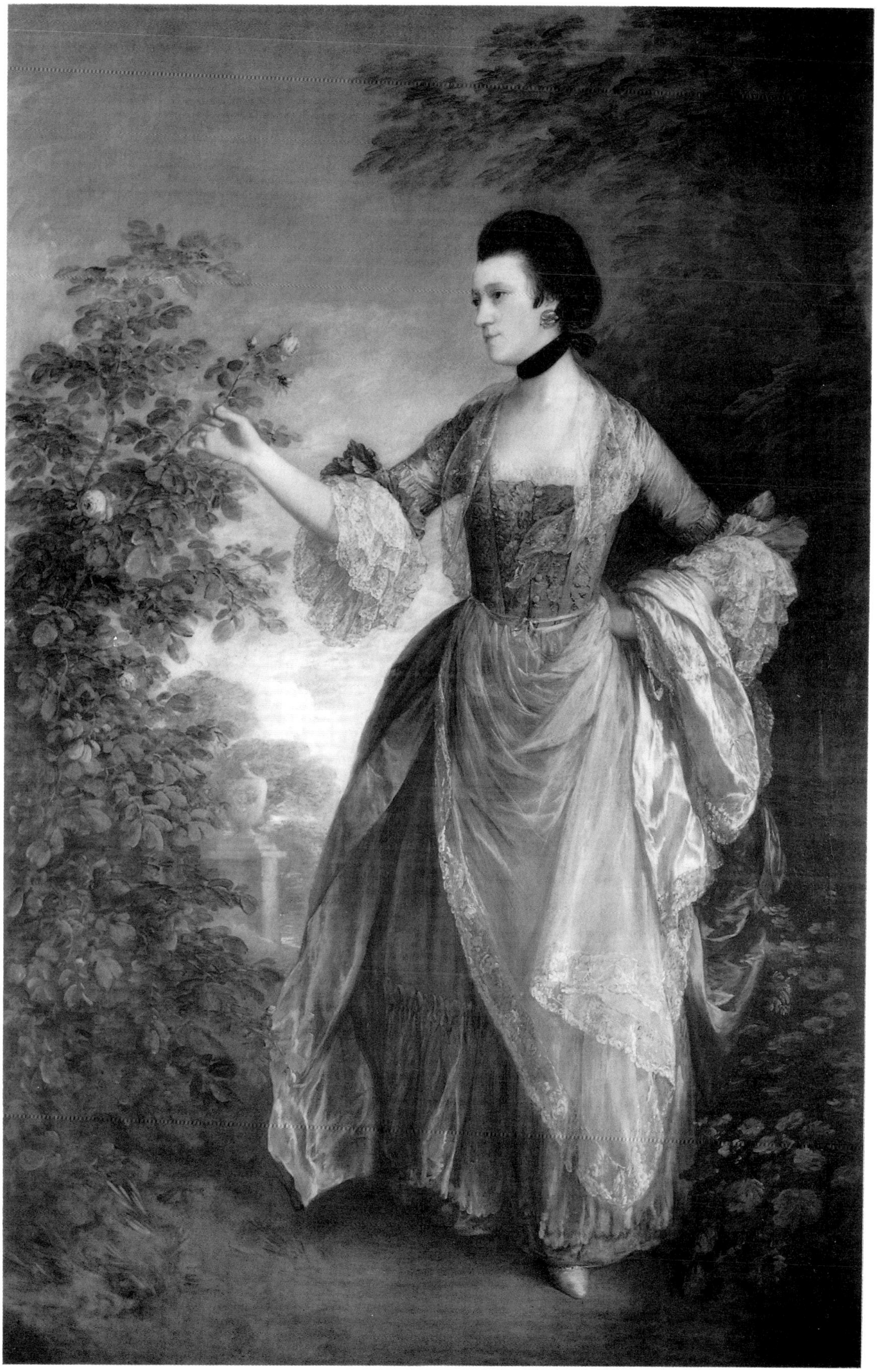

Fig. 9
Thomas Gainsborough
Anne Spencer, Marchioness of Donegall, mid 1760's.
Detroit Institute of Arts.

Obviously portraitists like Hudson, and Gainsborough himself – who became one of the worst offenders in this respect, using the pose indiscriminately for a whole series of portraits throughout his career of military men, aristocrats in Van Dyck dress or ceremonial robes, country squires and naval officers alike – would have been aware of its classical connotations.[35] They used it, however, simply as a handy compositional device – one which managed to combine elegance of deportment with a solution to the difficult problem of how to arrange the lower half of a male full-length portrait. It is noticeable that Gainsborough adopts the pose right from the beginning of his Bath period, when he first became faced with this dilemma; it appears in both *William Wollaston* of c. 1759 and *William Poyntz,* exhibited at the Society of Artists in 1762[36]. *Earl Howe,* which follows shortly afterwards in c. 1764, provides one of Gainsborough's most considered interpretations of the pose, which is accorded here a seriousness it never achieved in the hands of a painter like Arthur Devis. From the almost exact correspondence between his figure and an 18th century plaster cast of Mercury such as cat. A27, it even seems possible that Gainsborough may have studied one of these copies after the antique for himself, although it is certainly much more likely that he simply borrowed the pose from one of its many appearances on canvas. The head, although closely resembling other portraits of Howe, also has a touch of idealisation which is perhaps in keeping with its classical origins. By contrast, Thomas Hudson's portrait of *Theodore Jacobsen* is based rather more loosely on the antique.

If Lord Howe's pose derives, ultimately, from the antique, for the general conception and setting of his portrait Gainsborough turned once again to Van Dyck. The depiction of a man of action against an outcrop of rock, while a vista, often of a sea or land battle, opens up to one side, has its origins in Van Dyck portraits of men such as the *Earl of Strafford* or the *10th Earl of Northumberland* [37]. However, this successful formula was later taken up by Hudson, and then by his pupil, Reynolds, in a series of three-quarter length portraits of naval officers of the late 1740's, notably *Captain Hugh Bonfoy,* c. 1746, or his early portrait of *Augustus Keppel* in 1749. By the time Gainsborough came to make use of the setting in 1764, it had become almost *de rigueur* for a portrait of a naval officer.

Gainsborough and Reynolds: Commodore Howe and Commodore Keppel

We have seen in *Mrs. Riddell* and *Countess Howe* how close Reynolds and Gainsborough could come in certain portraits of the early 1760's. A comparison of *Earl Howe* with Reynolds's naval portraits of the 1750's and 1760's, however, only serves to point up the differences between them. Reynolds's famous 1752 portrait of *Commodore Augustus Keppel* (cat. A30), which effectively took London by storm on his return from Italy, also shows a young naval officer walking along the shore and Reynolds, too, has based his figure on a classical statue – this time of the *Apollo Belvedere.*[38] Here all resemblance between the two portraits ends. Reynolds had given us a forceful picture of action, his sitter plunging forward along the seashore, in a setting which is suggestive not only of an impending storm but of actual danger. By contrast, Gainsborough's static but elegant Commodore seems almost to be something of a dreamer, while the tranquil coastal inlet contrasts forcibly with Reynolds's hostile shore. Of the two portraits, Gainsborough's is the later by almost a decade, but this would hardly be apparent on first inspection. For whereas Reynolds has mastered in Italy the lessons of 'sfumato', so that his sitter blends almost imperceptibly into the turbulent setting, Gainsborough's portrait depends instead on pure elegance of line; Earl Howe, unlike his Countess, stands silhouetted clearly against the background in a portrait which seems to hark back to the clean-cut lines of the generation led by Thomas Hudson. If it is a truism to say that, of the two, Reynolds was the more accomplished painter of men, whereas Gainsborough, like Ramsay, was 'formed to paint women'[39], a naval portrait such as Reynolds's *Lord Bridport,* painted in 1764 and thus almost exactly contemporary with *Earl Howe,* reminds us how successfully Reynolds could charge his male portraits with an insistent energy and dynamism. Perhaps wisely, Gainsborough chose not to compete, preferring to concentrate instead in his male portraits on images of studied informality.

Other Bath male portraits

Earl Howe is among the more formal of the full-length portraits of men produced by Gainsborough during his early years in Bath. Other male portraits of this period show him experimenting with a much more relaxed type of image, as when he portrayed Thomas John Medlycott balanced on top of a stile, in a portrait shown at the Society of Artists in 1763[40]. The slightly earlier *William Poyntz* (Society of Artists, 1762) or *William Wollaston* (late 1750's), both make use, as we have seen, of the same cross-legged pose found in *Earl Howe,* but in the context of the portrait of a country squire where such a pose seems rather more natural and at ease. *Earl Howe* can perhaps be seen as representing a return to a more measured style, after the unaffectedness of these remarkable works which, as discussed above, did not meet with the entire approval of Gainsborough's clientele. The portraits which followed, such as *Edward Craggs Nugent* (Society of Artists, 1765), *Dr. Rice Charleton*

(1766)[41], or *Augustus Hervey* (1768) – an almost exact repetition of the Earl Howe format (cat. A29) – suggest that by now Gainsborough had the measure of what his clients preferred, although portraits like *George, Lord Vernon* (Society of Artists, 1767)[42] in which the sitter's dog leaps up at him in a gesture which almost threatens to overset the rhythm of the composition as a whole, show that he had by no means abandoned his unconventional approach.

Style and design

If *Earl Howe* differs from its pendant in terms both of conception and composition, it is also dissimilar in treatment. The brilliant blending of figure and background found in Gainsborough's portrait of Lady Howe is replaced here by a design which throws into relief the Earl's elegant silhouette against a rather empty landscape background. Whereas the landscape in *Countess Howe* is detailed almost exhaustively, in *Earl Howe* Gainsborough has relied on almost abstract passages of paint – a sumptuous mixuture of impastoed beiges, green and browns – to conjure up the rocks behind and to the left of his sitter. There is little or no detailing in the foreground. If, taken together, these perhaps suggest that the canvas may have been painted in haste, some confirmation of this may be provided by the fact that Gainsborough has not fully concealed the areas of 'laying-in' around his sitter's face and legs; the background texturing stops well short of them. Moreover, Gainsborough made few changes to his design as he worked. Although the line of the coat has been lengthened, and the hat was probably once worn arched over the brow rather than flat, as now, there is no evidence of any further *pentimenti*. The slight flatness and awkwardness in the painting of the sitter's left sleeve might suggest that Gainsborough retained his sitter's uniform in his studio when Lord Howe himself could not be present; certainly the drawing of this area is uncomfortably two-dimensional in form. There is, however, no doubting the exceptional quality of the head, or the bravura treatment of the gloves or sword; the latter assumes almost the clarity of a still-life.

In the end, the discrepancies between the two portraits of Lord and Lady Howe must remain a matter for conjecture. Whether they are the result of Lord Howe's professional commitments, which would probably have limited the length of his stay in Bath at any one time, or whether the two paintings were even painted some months apart, on separate visits to the city, will probably never be known.

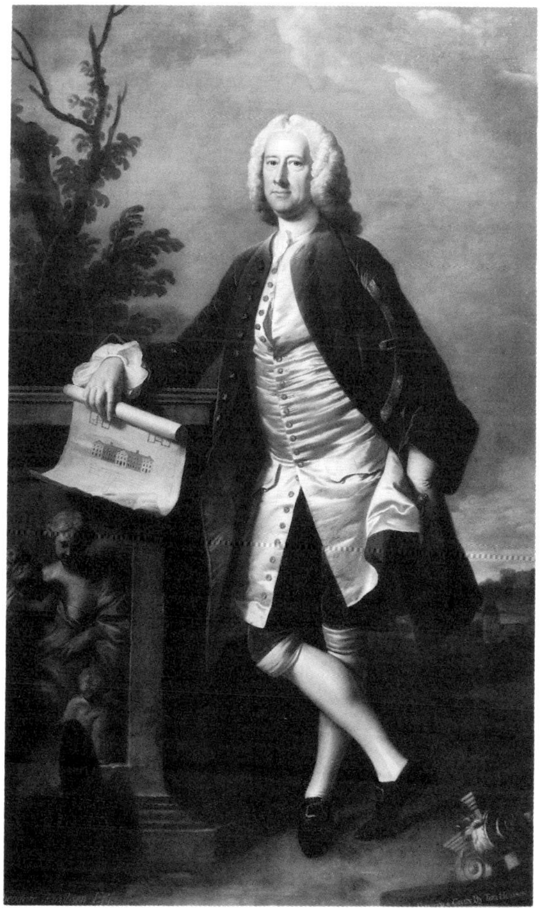

Fig. 10 (right) Thomas Hudson *Theodore Jacobsen,* 1746. The Thomas Coram Foundation for Children.

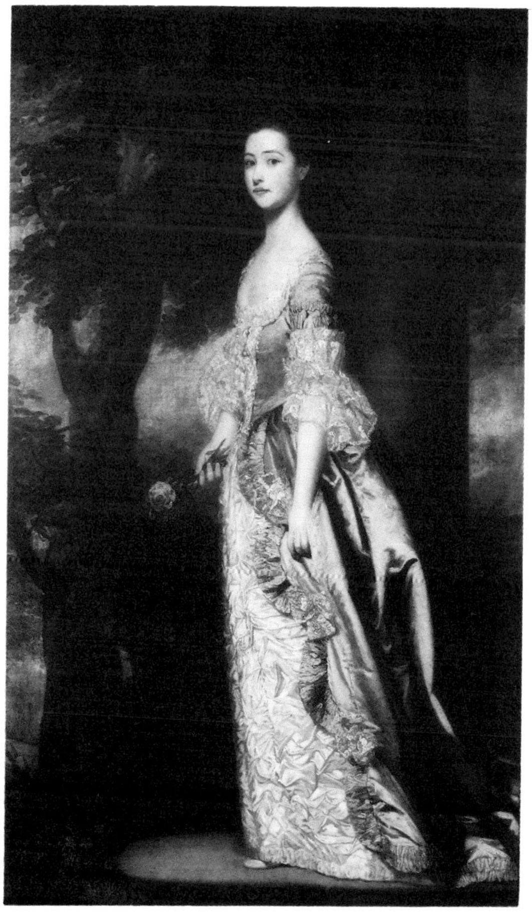

Fig. 11 (far right) Sir Joshua Reynolds *Susanna Gale,* 1764. National Gallery of Victoria, Melbourne.

Indeed, finally, it hardly matters. If this exhibition has tended to highlight their differences, rather than their similarities, it is only when the two portraits are seen together that they can be appreciated to the full. No one seeing them together can doubt that they are among the very finest achievements of Gainsborough's early Bath years, a period which saw the artist working in new directions, and at the very height of his powers.

1. The portrait(s) are listed in the posthumous sale of Devis's house in 1822 as 'Portraits of Commodore and Lady Howe' by 'Devis Sen' (British Library, *Sales Catalogues, 1818-22,* Book 29; D'Oench, 1980, no. 86). While one should place no reliance on the accuracy of titles used in early sale catalogues, the use of the prefix 'Commodore' for Earl Howe makes one wonder if the portrait(s) date from before Howe inherited the Viscountcy, which would place them firmly in early 1758. If these were wedding portraits, the Howes did not, apparently, take delivery of the portrait(s), which remained in the artist's studio.
2. Hayes, 1981, cat. 27. Waterhouse, 1958, p. 75, suggested that the portraits were 'probably from the middle 1760's'.
3. Communication from Dr. John Hayes, on file at Kenwood.
4. These visitor lists can be consulted on microfilm at the British Library, *18th Century English Provincial Newspapers, Series One, Bath Newspapers.* The Howes' 1763 visit is recorded in *Pope's Bath Chronicle and Weekly Gazette,* Vol. IV, no. 10, p. 40, for 1763: 'Bath, December 15. Arriv'd here The Duke and Duchess of Devonshire, Earl Cowper and Lady, Lord and Lady Arundel, Lady Huntingdon, Lord Howe and Lady . . . [etc.].' *Boddeley's Bath Journal,* Vol. XX, no. 51, p. 210, records their arrival as having taken place on 19th December. Countess Howe returned on September 27th 1764: 'Arriv'd here, Lord Chief Justice Pratt and Lady, Lady Frances Blood, Lady Howe . . . [etc.].' *(Pope's Bath Chronicle,* Vol. IV no. 51, p. 204). Her attendance at a ball on 25th October 1764 is recorded in Vol. V, no. 4, p. 16 for Thursday, November 1st, 1764. The Howes also visited Bath in 1760. *The Bath Advertiser* gives their arrival date as April 5th (Vol. V, no. 234), while *Boddeley's Bath Journal* records this as being on April 7th (Vol. XVII, no. 14, p. 5-6). *Boddeley's Bath Journal* also records their arrival on May 12th, 1760 (Vol. XVII, no. 19, p. 76). There is no record in any of the journals of the Howes having visited Bath in 1761 or 1762. Countess Howe also visited Bath in 1759, but in February, several months before Gainsborough's move to the city. I am grateful to William Monroe for researching this subject for me.
5. Woodall, 1963, p. 149.
6. The tree is, however, probably a late addition to the canvas.
7. *Countess Howe* was cleaned in 1976, whereas *Earl Howe* is covered by a fairly thick yellow varnish; this explains many of the differences in tonality between the two.
8. However, Rica Jones and Anna Southall of the Tate Gallery have kindly informed me that, in their research into 18th century painting technique, they have found other examples of pendant portraits not being prepared on the same canvases and grounds.
9. The early rate books for Grafton Street, then called Evans Row, are lost, and the earliest reference to the Howes living in the street is in 1771 (St. George's, Hanover Square, Poor and Highway Rates (Collectors Book), Dover Street, 11, iv, 1771, p. 17. The earliest reference to the number in Grafton Street at which the Howes lived is in *The Fashionable Court Guide or Town Visiting Directory,* 1792, ed. P. Boyle, when Lord Howe is listed at no. 3.
10. Hayes, 1970, p. 35 and note.
11. Woodall, p. 155. Hayes, 1970, p. 58 points out that Gainsborough also visited Corsham, Longford Castle and Stourhead during these years.
12. Waterhouse, 1953, p. 176.
13. *The Autobiography and Correspondence of Mary Granville, Mrs. Delany,* 1861, III, p. 605.
14. *The Farington Diary,* 10th November 1809; quoted in Hayes, 1970, p. 48.
15. A Devis portrait of *Thomas Starkie,* signed and dated 1749 (Harris Museum and Art Gallery, Preston) similarly makes use of a fence and deer to define an estate.
16. The relationship between the two artists is the subject of a long article by Deborah Cherry and Jennifer Harris: 'Eighteenth-century portraiture and the seventeenth-century past: Gainsborough and Van Dyck' in *Art History,* Vol. 5, no. 3, September 1982, pp. 286-309.
17. His copy of Van Dyck's *Lord John and Lord Bernard Stuart* (Art Museum, St. Louis) is a brilliant study, entirely in keeping with the prevailing spirit of the Stuart court.
18. Millar, 1982/3, nos. 60 and 61. Van Dyck's nature studies also profoundly influenced Gainsborough (cf cat. A9 and Millar no. 84).
19. Hudson, 1979, fig. 2 and no. 16.
20. Einberg, 1987, no. 116.
21. I am grateful to Rica Jones for drawing this comparison to my attention, and for discussions in which she emphasised the importance of Gainsborough's earlier conversation pieces in the development of *Countess Howe.*
22. Lady Innes holds a rose, and it is interesting to note that in the preliminary drawing for *Countess Howe* (cat. A3) a rose replaces the gloves held in the hand in the finished portrait; the motif serves to emphasise the affinity between the two compositions.
23. Hayes, 1975, cat. 36.
24. eg John Shearman and Anthony Blunt, *Poussin Drawings,* IV, pp. 33 ff.
25. eg Hayes, 1975, nos. 22, 24, 28.
26. D. Mannings in *Reynolds,* ed. Penny, 1986, no. 51.
27. Ibid.
28. Waterhouse, 1953, p. 178.
29. See note 18 above for the influence of Van Dyck on these studies.
30. Hayes & Stainton, 1983, no. 34.
31. As is pointed out in Hayes, 1970, p. 35.
32. Op cit, p. 27 and pp. 32-33.
33. Quoted in Einberg, 1987, cat. 158.
34. Haskell & Penny, 1981, p. 266.
35. See cat. A28 for other uses of this pose.
36. Waterhouse, 1958, nos. 734, 554.
37. Millar, nos. 23, 25.
38. D. Mannings in *Reynolds,* ed. Penny, 1986, cat. 19, points out that while the pose turned out like the Apollo Belvedere, this was 'probably almost accidental, though not of course entirely so'.
39. See also cat. A19.
40. Waterhouse, 1958, no. 477.
41. Op. cit., nos. 524, 136.
42. Op. cit., no. 693.

Aileen Ribeiro

Gainsborough's Countess Howe: the artist's use of dress

Perhaps no other portrait at Kenwood has captured the popular imagination as an expression of 18th century refinement, as much as Gainsborough's *Countess Howe*. Stepping through an early evening summer landscape in her stunning pink silk dress, Lady Howe embodies in her costume and pose a very English charm, restrained elegance and obvious good breeding, allied to a sense of personality without which a 'society' portrait would be little more than a fashion plate.

The portrait has that typical 18th century combination of artifice and naturalism so dear to the pre-Romantic imagination. While we can presume that Lady Howe's features are accurately portrayed (Gainsborough was supremely gifted at catching a likeness, which he described as 'the principal beauty and intention of a Portrait') her face, costume and pose are formed by fashion, although the intention is to appear natural and uncontrived, with Nature as a setting. Gainsborough's lyrical genius is to blend costume and landscape into a poetic whole; it is a triumphant affirmation of his expressed aim 'to make the Heart dance'.

This combination of chic and a kind of aristocratic aloofness Gainsborough learnt from Van Dyck, the first artist who flattered the English by offering them self-images of unsurpassed elegance. On the whole Gainsborough proved more successful than his great rival Reynolds in adapting Van Dyck to English taste, particularly with regard to women. With his readier acceptance of the importance of fashion in women's lives, Gainsborough always places his sitters firmly within the current fashion aesthetic. While, like Van Dyck, he occasionally modifies and sometimes invents fanciful costume, he never makes the mistake of turning English ladies into unlikely goddesses in what Reynolds calls the 'heroick style'.[1] Although Reynolds would later disavow the minutiae of high fashion as the 'trifling details of vulgar reality', some of his more sensitive portraits of the early 1760's, nearly contemporary with *Countess Howe,* show him displaying them with virtuoso skill. In his portrait of *Susanna Gale,* 1764 (fig.11) we see how fashion can bring out character as well as pinpoint status. A wealthy heiress, aged just fourteen, she is portrayed with great tenderness in what is perhaps her first formal dress, a rich pink satin gown worn over a petticoat (the contemporary name for a skirt) of ruched white silk; somewhat self-conscious in her finery, she stands in a pose taken by Reynolds from Van Dyck's *Marchesa Elena Grimaldi.*

The dominant features of the dress are a concentration on curvilinear forms, three-dimensional trimmings, and a delight in the tactile qualities of the textiles – all these are characteristics of the rococo influence on dress, the prevailing fashion in the middle decades of the 18th century. The presiding genius of this style is the *Marquise de Pompadour* whose taste for frills and flounces, serpentine curves, scallop shapes, and exquisite decoration, is the definitive fashion statement from the mid-1740s and

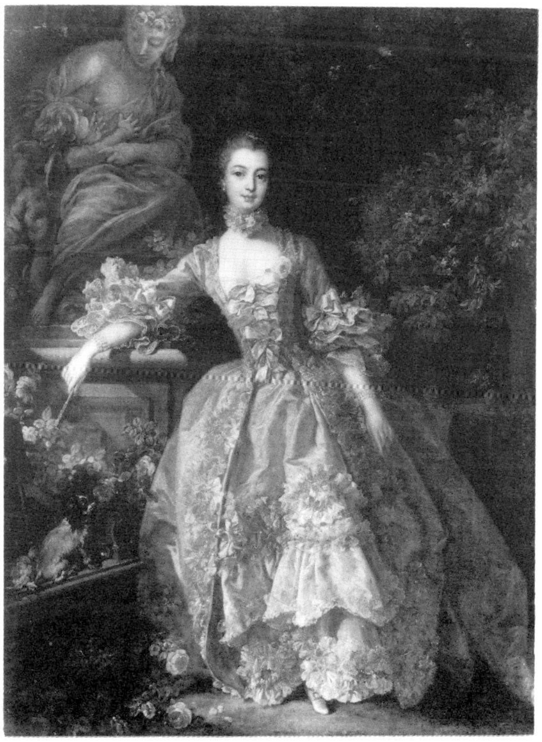

Fig. 12 (right) François Boucher *Madame de Pompadour,* 1759. The Wallace Collection.

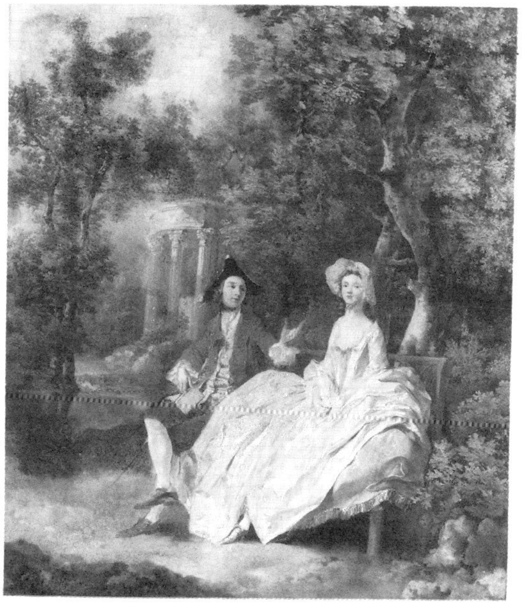

Fig. 13 (far right) Thomas Gainsborough *The artist and his wife, c. 1746-7.* Musée du Louvre.

throughout the 1750s. As interpreted by Boucher in 1759 (fig. 12), Madame de Pompadour's quintessentially rococo dress, a pale peachy-pink silk, is a riot of trimming, of ribbons and frothy blonde (silk) lace. The *tout ensemble* is a triumph of artifice, from powdered hair to white satin shoe; even the setting looks like a stage for the sort of rococo pastoral performed in the marquise's private theatre, the Théâtre des Petits Cabinets.

Belatedly adopted in the less hot-house and more prosaic climate of England, the rococo assumed a more restrained form; the curves prevailed, but the dress trimmings were less flamboyant. Instead of the three-dimensional flounces and furbelows, women experimented with all-over ruching of silks as in Gainsborough's *Lady Alston* (fig. 4) of the mid 1760's. Here the bodice and skirt are of ruched sea-green silk, and the fashionable soft width of the silhouette from the waist downwards is created by bundling up the white satin of the gown. Lady Alston's gown is a *sacque* or *robe à la française,* i.e. distinguished by its back drapery which falls from the shoulders to the hem. The same style of gown can be seen in Gainsborough's *Ann Ford, later Mrs Philip Thicknesse* of 1760 (fig. 3) worn here with a matching petticoat, both trimmed with serpentine lines of pleated ribbon which echo the striking pose of the sitter.

Appropriately for a less formal occasion, Lady Howe's dress is less dominated by its trimmings and is less rococo in feeling. It is possible from a distance to see the pleated flounce close to the hem – a muted version of the more opulently frilled skirt worn by Ann Ford. You have to get very close to notice the lightly painted-in decoration down the edge of Lady Howe's open gown, from bodice to hem. This applied trimming, usually of the same fabric as the gown, was called a *robing;* it was gathered into puffs or pleats (as here), occasionally edged with narrow braid, and sewn in undulating curves from neck to hem.

Such decoration is totally subordinate to the effect of the pink silk, a rose-coloured taffeta called a lustring (or lutestring), a lightweight summer silk especially popular for less formal dress[2]. The deliberately changeable quality of this silk is reflected in Gainsborough's portrait; one must always be aware of the artist's selectivity in painting textiles (and costume) but here he is noticeably skilful in depicting the varying effects of light on the silk, and its different effect when taut (as at the bodice) and floating (as in the skirt).

Such lustrings were meant to float and billow round the wearer, to flatter with becoming pastel shades, of which pink was the most popular. Gainsborough paints a similar silk in the double portrait known as the *Artist and his Wife* of c. 1747 (fig. 13). Margaret Gainsborough, seated in the rather ungainly pose created by the wearing of the large square hoops of the 1740s, (the line caused by the whalebone can be seen under the fringed blue silk of the petticoat) wears a plain English dress called a *nightgown.* This was an informal style, a gown with a tight-fitting bodice, (as opposed to the French *robe à la française),* little ornamentation, and usually worn with an apron. It was fashionable for the less formal occasions of the social round in the mid-18th century, such as walking in the Park, and paying informal calls.

This is probably what Lady Howe wears in her portrait. The nightgown was a popular style of dress at the highest level of society by the 1760s. Lady Mary Coke stated that it was favoured by Queen Charlotte, and foreign visitors like P. J. Grosley, intrigued by the English lady with her 'short gown, long white apron and hat', approved of such 'an agreeable negligence'.[3] English ladies were distinguished from their sisters on the continent in their preference for being painted in informal rather than formal dress.

The day of a lady of fashion was firmly regulated by changes in dress. In the morning there were various kinds of *déshabillé* and informal costume or *undress;* in the evening (or from late afternoon when a lady was formally dressed) there was *full dress,* usually (in the 1760s) a *sacque,* magnificently trimmed and worn with a full parure of jewels. The gap between was filled by *half-dress,* a simply-trimmed gown, of which the most popular was the nightgown. This conformed to the prevailing fashion for relative simplicity, and yet it could be decorated with accessories in the most exquisite taste. In the portrait of Lady Howe, these include her fine straw Leghorn hat trimmed with satin ribbons, which she wears over a small lace or net cap which keeps the hair in place. Grosley, while declaring – as did many foreigners – that Englishwomen had little dress sense, made an exception for the way in which they wore hats, with a particular grace which added vivacity to the face. Such a hat, while becoming, was mainly functional, to keep the sun off the face. There is not, however, the slightest touch of the practical about the fine lace-edged cobweb apron (either brocaded silk gauze, or the highest quality embroidered muslin) which Lady Howe hitches up with her right hand in an elegant gesture deriving from Van Dyck,[4] and which also serves to show off her glorious lace sleeve ruffles, or *engageantes.*[5]

Further touches which would remind the educated viewer of the link with Van Dyck's world, are the plain kid gloves (one held in the other gloved hand), and the black silk bracelet, a style first appearing in the early 17th century, and which helped to emphasize the whiteness of the skin.[6]

Also flattering, particularly to a delicate English skin, were pearls. Those worn by Countess Howe – seed pearls for the large round earrings, and five strands of real pearls for the necklace tied at the back with ribbon which matches that on the hat – look startlingly modern. Pearls were especially suitable for day-time *toilettes* where the flashy hard brilliance of diamonds and other precious stones would have been inappropriate. In addition, pearls were the favoured choice of Van Dyck's elegant ladies; this hallowed association made them *de rigueur* with both artist and sitter.

Lady Howe's softly gleaming pearls echo the pearliness of her complexion, maybe literally so, as pearl powder was used to give the lightly glazed translucent look so admired in high fashion in the mid-18th century. 'The Face is the chief Seat of Beauty', stated a contemporary cosmetic treatise,[7] and a world of artifice was used, paradoxically, to make the face appear 'natural' by which was meant a white skin, touched with pink on the cheeks, and rosy lips. Lady Howe's face looks natural to us at first sight, but the skin is somewhat chalky (various unguents based on white lead, mercury, or – far less dangerously – on lemons and almonds, blanched the skin), and the hair is lightly powdered. Probably Englishwomen used cosmetics at this period in moderation, but in any case the conventions of the time demanded that the face appear in portraiture, at least, fairly natural; in France, on the other hand, the fashionable artificial complexion, rouge and all, could be depicted without the accusations of immorality which would have been the case in England.

According to Rouquet *(The Present State of the Arts in England,* 1755) the ideal Englishwoman: 'must have a fine white skin, a light complexion, a face rather oval than round, a nose somewhat longish but of a fine turn and like the antiques, her eyes large and not so sparkling as melting; her mouth graceful without a smile, but rather of a pouting turn, which gives it at once both grace and dignity, . . . her shape tall and erect, her neck long and easy, her shoulders square and flat. . . '[8]

The finest clothes and the richest jewellery were of no avail if the 'shape' – what we would call the figure – did not conform to the contemporary notion of perfection; by the 1760s the heavy, dignified, rather full 'baroque' figure of early in the century had given way to a slender, lighter and infinitely more graceful line.

Clothes, however, were no easier to manage. Even in informal dress such as Lady Howe is wearing, it was an art – and one that had to be taught – to hold the body correctly when still and in movement, to live with boned corsets, elaborately fastened clothes, yardages of expensive silk, fragile and gossamer accessories that could easily tear, and high-heeled shoes which imposed their own deportment. The correct deportment was an important part of every upper-class girl's education, and it was usually taught by the dancing master. Dancing and deportment complemented each other; the former produced good posture and elegant gestures, essential to the 18th century notion of good manners, and the latter was necessary to perform the stately formal dances in vogue in high society. Like so much in the 18th century, dancing was imbued with reason and harmony, and a search for 'the natural graces'. Gallini's *Treatise on the Art of Dancing* (1762) declared that the chief aim in dancing was 'to bring forth the natural graces, and not to smother them with appearances of study and art'; dancing, if taught properly, helped to promote a 'graceful address' and 'delicacy and suppleness' to the figure.[9] Gainsborough's portrait of Lady Howe is apt testimony to the art of graceful deportment; it is almost as though she has been captured on canvas, poised to take the next step in a formal dance, frozen music in an Arcadian landscape.

Grace, elegance and gentility were key words to the cultivated English mind of the mid-eighteenth century. Modesty and subtlety in dress were also to be admired. 'The body and limbs should all be cover'd, and little more than certain hints be given of them thro' the cloathing' was Hogarth's view in his *Analysis of Beauty* (1753). The décolletage of 18th century dress was all the more alluring if it was veiled, as with Lady Howe, by a gossamer-fine fichu which only serves to accentuate the white bosom beneath. In the same way that a slight touch of sexuality in the display of feminine charms had to be merely hinted at – the eighteenth century had a complex code linking morality and dress – so costume itself had to be a finely judged mixture of allowable 'feminine' frivolity and simplicity. Hogarth admired the pleasure of variety he saw in women's dress but urged the virtues of simplicity; he disliked 'tawdriness', by which he probably meant a superfluity of frills and flounces and over-elaborate trimmings.[10]

Contemporary fashion magazines (which appeared spasmodically in the middle years of the 18th century – they were not published on a regular basis until the 1770s) attacked the propensity of

Englishwomen to follow French styles slavishly: 'They have loaded themselves with ornaments of all sorts; besides jewels and embroidery, ribbands, lace, furbelows and pinking have been lavishly spread over all parts of their dress . . . silks of all colours are made up with a profusion carried to great excess, and at present it requires as much silk to robe two ladies as to hang a balloon'.[11] The rococo styles favoured by the French (and by English ladies too, in the 1750s and 1760s, from the evidence of surviving fashion plates) were not always thought suitable for the relatively informal atmosphere of much English portraiture of the period.

The question which one always has to ask of eighteenth-century artists is, to what extent are we seeing reality with regard to the costume? In later life, for example, Gainsborough was – especially in the 1770s – infected with prevailing artistic notions of the Grand Style. This could take the form of a totally invented costume like the vaguely oriental-cum-historical outfit worn by Lady Dartmouth in 1771 (fig. 14, on loan to Gainsborough's House in Sudbury), which the artist admits to be 'a fictitious bundle of trumpery of the foolish Painter's own inventing. . . '.[12] Or it could take the form of a compromise mixture of the fashionable and the fanciful – what Leslie and Taylor describe as 'a certain generalising management of their actual dresses'(see note 1) as in Gainsborough's rather fey *Lady Brisco* (fig. 7); this costume (an unlikely mingling of two different types of silk entwined with gold ribbons and gauzy drapery [13]) is at least linked to the current fashionable line, and although the face is somewhat characterless (this is often an unfortunate by-product of fanciful dress in this decade) there is a successful harmony between the 'romantic' costume and the landscape.

With Gainsborough's Lady Howe we are as close to reality in the costume as it is ever possible to be, given that we are seeing her via the artist's personal and individual vision. Not only does her costume convey notions of status, good breeding and perfect taste (ideas immediately perceived by 18th century eyes), but to *our* eyes it is one of the most delightful examples of mid-eighteenth century dress, that period which produced perhaps the most exquisite modes of all time. To adapt a comment made by the *Grand Magazine* (1760) on the love of the English lady for walking in the Park, Countess Howe 'walks there to be taken notice of, and to entertain our eyes'.[14]

1. See C. R. Leslie and T. Taylor, *The Life and Times of Sir Joshua Reynolds*, London, 1865, I, p.249: 'Gainsborough painted his ladies with a certain generalising management of their actual dresses, invariably reducing the circumference of petticoats, and getting rid of buckram generally, but never mythologising his sitters'.
2. Lustring was according to Johnson's Dictionary (1755) 'a shining silk, commonly pronounced lutestring'.
   It was a taffeta which, under tension, was smeared with a gum which was then dried to give the material a glossy sheen. See P. Thornton, *Baroque and Rococo Silks*, 1965, p.27. It was especially popular for summer wear; Lord Chesterfield in his *Letters* notes in 1765 that Charles Townshend called the government a 'Lutestring Ministry, fit only for the summer'.
3. P. J. Grosley, *A Tour to London; or New Observations on England, and Its Inhabitants*, trans. T. Nugent, London, 1772, I, p.253.
   The nightgown with its tight-fitting bodice and relative simplicity of style (although there were a number of different versions) became the fashionable *robe à l'anglaise* of the 1770s and 1780s.
4. The gesture of slightly hitching up the skirt, or pinching the folds at the side, goes back at least to Van Dyck. It was given a new lease of life via the drawings made by (or attributed to) Joseph van Aken, after Kneller's *Countess of Ranelagh*, 1690 (Hampton Court Palace) which thus entered into the repertoire of, among others, Hudson and Ramsay. Less well known is the fashionable link with the Orient. Turkish ladies (and European ladies painted *à la Turque* see, for example, J. B. Vanmour's *Lady Mary Wortley Montagu and her son*, National Portrait Gallery, London) sometimes wore a caftan hitched up slightly to one side and tucked into a belt. Lady Mary Wortley Monagu set the trend for sartorial *Turquerie;* see her portrait attributed to J. Richardson, c. 1725 (The Earl of Harrowby). A similar pose – one hand on the hip, the fingers facing outwards, and the other hand clutching the folds of the skirt – can be seen, for example, in Reynold's *Lady Cottrell-Dormer*, 1764 (Rousham). On the vogue for Turquerie in dress, see A. Ribeiro 'Turquerie: Turkish dress and English Fashion in the eighteenth century', in *The Connoisseur,* May, 1979.
5. It is always difficult to be precise about textiles. It has been suggested that these ruffles are Brussels bobbin lace but they are filmy enough to be of blonde (silk lace) or of silk gauze edged with real lace. It is possible, although less likely, that they could be very fine embroidered muslin.
   The gesture of placing hand on hip shows off the elegant fall of the ruffles, as well as the quality of their fabric. The male equivalent was to put the hand through the middle buttons of the waistcoat, a gesture which lingered on into the early 19th century when lace ruffles were rarely seen except at court.
6. Such bracelets were usually worn in pairs; in Lady Howe's case, one bracelet is hidden beneath her glove (see p.39). Similar black bands can be seen in Gainsborough's *Lady Alston* (fig. 4) with a matching necklace. *Mrs Thicknesse* (fig. 3) has bracelets and choker of black bugle (glass) beads.
7. *Abdeker: or The Art of preserving Beauty* by A. Le Camus, London, 1754.
   This work, a treatise on the properties of perfect beauty, includes a number of recipes for cosmetics to improve and enhance the complexion. For a discussion of the female face in life and art, see A. Ribeiro, *The Female Face in the Tate's British Collection 1569-1876,* The Tate Gallery, London, 1987.

8. M. Rouquet, *The Present State of the Arts in England,* London, 1755, p.46.
See also *Grosley* (op. cit., I, p.255): 'A good shape is the most striking article of English beauty'.

9. G. A. Gallini, *A Treatise on the Art of Dancing,* London, 1762, pp. 146 and 76.
Contemporary comment in letters (Lord Chesterfield's are the best known example) and in novels testify to the importance of the dancing master's art as an aid to good deportment. In Fielding's novel *Amelia* (1751) we read that 'persons whose feet have never been under the hands of the professors of that art (i.e. dancing) are apt to discover this want in their education in every motion, nay even when they stand or sit still'. See also books of etiquette, such as F. Nivelon's *The Rudiments of Genteel Behavior,* 1737. When Gallini comments that in dancing 'the study of nature is especially to be recommended ', this is not the 'simple unaffected nature that we see, but nature sitting for her portrait' (Hazlitt on Gainsborough's fancy pictures); that is, it is not the wild, untrammelled nature of our post-Romantic imagination, but an 18th century nature regulated to the conventions of society and the prevailing taste, a Capability Brown version of Nature.

10. W. Hogarth, *The Analysis of Beauty,* 1753, ed. & intr. J. Burke, Oxford, 1955, p.34 and (above) p.53.

11. The *Grand Magazine,* Oct. 1760, p.501.

12. Gainsborough's letter to the Earl of Dartmouth, 1771, quoted in Woodall, 1961, p.53. This letter is now owned by Gainsborough's House, Sudbury, Suffolk. Gainsborough's second portrait of Lady Dartmouth shows her in a loose cross-over gown, close in style to a fashionable morning déshabillé.

13. Here Gainsborough's assumption of the closest he gets to a 'Grand Style', contradicts his comment (apropos of Reynolds's Fourth Discourse, 1771) that such a style needed simplicity, and 'that silks and satins, Pearls and trifling ornaments would be as hurtful to simplicity as flourishes in a Psalm Tune... ' (Woodall, op. cit., p.97). All the ingredients he describes are present in Lady Brisco's costume.

14. *Grand Magazine,* op. cit., p.502.

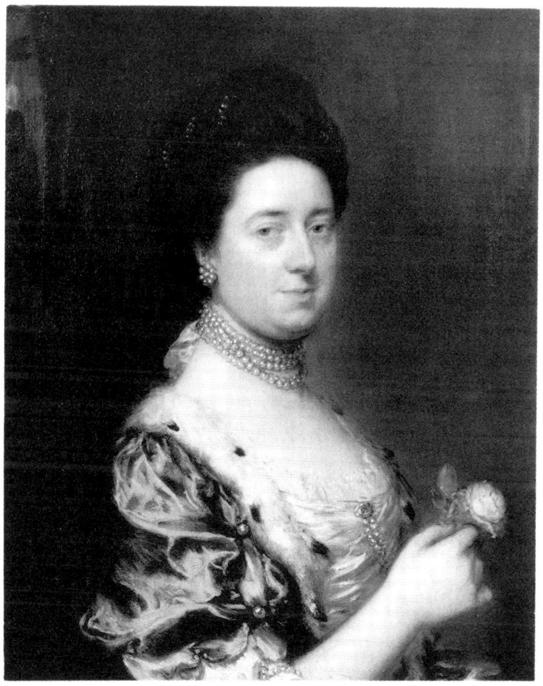

Fig. 14 Thomas Gainsborough *Lady Dartmouth,* 1771. Private collection on loan to Gainsborough's House, Sudbury.

Aileen Ribeiro

Gainsborough's Earl Howe: a note on naval dress

Lord Howe is depicted in the undress or everyday uniform of a Commodore (a senior captain) in the navy. He wears a double-breasted coat of blue faced with white, and ornamented with gold lace (the word also had the meaning of braid in the 18th century), a white waistcoat also trimmed with gold, and knee-breeches.

The uniform follows fashionable lines. The coat has the generous cut of the mid-18th century, with stiffened side-pleats, and the cuff has a vertical scallopped opening, a style taken from informal dress of the time, but soon known as a cuff *à la marinière*. His hat is the customary fashionable black three-cornered style, trimmed with gold and worn with a silk cockade. His wig has the single sloping side curl of the fashion of the late 1750s/early 1760s; it is tied at the back with a black silk ribbon, one end of which is allowed to fall over the shoulder. A similar touch of casual elegance can be seen in the handling of the fine kid gloves. His white stockings and black shoes with buckles (gold, gilt or pinchbeck) are fashionable as well as being part of his uniform.

Although we have a number of portraits of naval officers in the mid-18th century, there is some confusion both about the early uniforms themselves and their appearance in painting; there is very little contemporary documentation, and no set of patterns (i.e. surviving uniforms) from 1748, the date when they were introduced.[1] Before that date, naval officers could wear what they liked, although one authority has noted that by the early 18th century 'a creeping uniformity of dress in some ships' was apparent; in some cases, army uniforms were adapted.[2] Even when, in 1748, uniform was introduced, it was some years before every officer (especially those serving abroad) would wear it, and some men, according to personal taste, preferred to mix fashionable dress with uniform.[3]

Early naval uniform, as far as we know it, was basically a blue coat (decorated, according to rank, with cuffs and facings of white, and gold lace), white waistcoat, and blue breeches; white breeches were introduced in 1774. Naturally, it followed the lines of the fashionable suit; thus, during the late 18th century the coat became tighter in cut, sloping away at the sides, and by the 1790s it had become (as in high fashion) a tail coat.[4] To begin with, uniform was established for Flag-Officers (Admirals, Vice-Admirals, Rear-Admirals), Commodores, Captains, Commanders, Lieutenants and Midshipmen. As the century progressed and the concept of uniform took greater hold, the regulations became more detailed and extended to a wider range of naval personnel.

Historians of naval uniform[5] outline the different types of full dress and undress introduced during the course of the 18th century, and list the minutiae of such details as braid, buttons and epaulettes, indications of status in an increasingly uniform-obsessed world.[6]

1. The National Maritime Museum at Greenwich has three 1748 uniforms; they are a full dress coat and an undress coat (frock) of a Lieutenant, and the all-purposes uniform coat of a Midshipman.
2. P. G. W. Annis, *The First British Naval Uniform*, in *Costume*, 1969, p.21.
3. Reynolds's portrait of the *Hon. Augustus Keppel*, 1754 in the National Maritime Museum (see Cat. A30) shows him in the correct style of undress uniform as a Commodore, but the colours – predominantly grey, with just a touch of blue on the coat – are wrong. This may have been Keppel's own version of uniform (a subject which interested him) or it may be that Reynolds, in depicting an event said to have taken place in 1747 (when the sitter was shipwrecked off the coast of Brittany), i.e. before the introduction of uniform, decided to paint a costume which toned in with the stormy scene and which at the same time had a distinctive element of naval dress about it.
4. For example, note the difference between the loose-fitting coat worn, as a naval captain (in general purposes uniform, full dress having been abolished in 1767) by the Earl of Bristol, 1768 (see Cat. A29) and the skimpier, cut-away coat worn in Henry Singleton's portrait of Lord Howe, in undress uniform as an Admiral in the National Portrait Gallery (engraved 1799) (see Cat. A32).
5. The following are useful: C. King, 'The Evolution of British Naval Uniform', in *The Connoisseur*, vol. CIII, 1939. D. Jarrett, *British Naval Dress*, 1960.
W. E. May, *The Dress of Naval Officers*, National Maritime Museum, Greenwich, HMSO, 1966.
6. In 1787, for example, comprehensive changes were introduced into naval uniforms; these included the restoration of full dress, and a complex system of indicating rank via gold braid, cuff stripes, etc. – see Mather Brown's *Earl Howe at the Battle of the First of June 1794* (see Cat. C20) in his full-dress uniform as an admiral.
In about 1795 epaulettes were introduced, admirals being allowed two; they can be seen in Copley's portrait of Lord Howe (Howe collection).

Viola Pemberton-Pigott

The development of the portrait of Countess Howe

The impression of spontaneity and movement that Gainsborough has created in his portrait of *Countess Howe*, of a breezy summer day whipping forward her skirts as she walks towards us, was not achieved with the ease that the free and vivid brushwork might suggest. The pendant portrait of *Earl Howe*, painted in a standard and much practised pose, seems to have presented few problems; whereas the challenge of filling the large canvas with perhaps only his third commission for a life-size female sitter, and the opportunity to indulge himself in the joy of paint and colour in capturing the scintillating pink silk and the gossamer translucence of the muslin and lace, have inspired Gainsborough to new heights of brillliance.

Each of the two full-length portraits of beautiful women that pre-dates *Countess Howe* is a *tour de force* in bravura handling of paint. Gainsborough has revelled in the play of light and texture of the white satin dress of *Mrs Thicknesse* (fig. 3) and in the rippling effect of the blue ruched skirt of *Lady Alston* (fig. 4)[1], but just as the poses of these two portraits are directly inspired by Van Dyck, so too the treatment of the folds of material and his manner of painting the dresses are also deeply indebted to his observations of Van Dyck, and there is an almost over-worked and laboured quality to his paint. It is during the re-working of the dress of Lady Howe that Gainsborough suddenly attains a new command of his materials. His brushwork becomes lighter and freer and excitingly impressionistic and he creates, with a new economy of paint, an image of texture and colour that is both beautiful to look at and reveals the very substance and character of the fabrics.

The sense of movement running through the picture was intended from the outset: the strong diagonal lines of the muslin apron sweeping across the skirt were sketched boldly onto the canvas in the first lay-out and the Countess was shown striding across the landscape, with her feet originally spaced considerably wider apart. Gainsborough, however, has changed, modified and developed his ideas, working out his composition direct onto the canvas, one layer of paint on top of another. The painting is filled with *pentimenti* and signs of re-working; these *pentimenti* are now mostly visible to the naked eye, because, with the passage of time, the upper layers of paint have become thinner and more translucent and allow the earlier paint layers to show through. With the additional help of X-radiography (fig. 15)[2] and infra-red photography (figs. 17–19)[3], some of the stages of Gainsborough's re-working can be unravelled.

The formation of the design

Ozias Humphry, describing Gainsborough's painting technique in the early 1760's, records his method of working in very subdued light, either by candlelight or a 'kind of darkened Twilight' so that 'having previously determined and marked with Chalk upon what part of the Canvasses the faces were to be painted they were so placed upon the Eisel [for this purpose the canvas was not yet attached to its stretcher, but remained loose, secured by small cords] as to be close to the Subject he was painting, which gave him an Opportunity (as he commonly painted standing) of comparing the Dimensions and Effect of the Copy, with the original both near and at a distance; and by this method (with incessant study and exertion) he acquired the power of giving the Masses, and general Forms of his models with the utmost exactness. Having thus settled the Ground Work of his Portraits, he let in (of necessity) more light, for the finishing of them; but his correct preparation was of the last Importance, and enabled him to secure the proportions of his Features as well as the general Contours of Objects with uncommon Truth.'[4]

This method becomes clearly recognisable when looking at the X-rays of the Earl and his Countess (figs. 15, 16), where the 'Masses and general Forms' of the figures are emphasised. After the extensive re-working of the painting of *Countess Howe*, the final effect of light and airiness tends to camouflage these broad beginnings, whereas in the dark dramatic 'Masses' of *Lady Alston* and the strong 'Forms' of *Miss Ford*, this technique has been worked up and developed to a conclusion. The first stage of *Countess Howe* seems to have been far closer to the pyramidal composition of *Lady Alston* (fig. 4), and perhaps also of Van Dyck's *Countess of Peterborough* (cat. All). The X-ray of *Countess Howe* (fig. 15, compare col. p1.1) shows that the figure was initially turned squarer to the viewer and her form, broader and more static, was anchored to the ground by an outline which extended at the elbows into fuller and longer cuffs and then fell straight into the wide heavy folds of the skirt; the outer fold of the overskirt on the left dipped to a deep point, almost level with the toe of the nearby foot, making a straight base to the pyramid, as in *Lady Alston*.

The sequence of painting the portrait follows that related by Ozias Humphry. Gainsborough would first map out the figure onto the prepared canvas; he would then 'dead colour' the general forms, in this instance in a grey underpaint over the red ground; he would emphasize the intended highlights and perhaps introduce some colour into his sketch. The next stage would be to complete the face and head from *ad vivum* sittings, something he was most particular about. He writes of another portrait: 'I

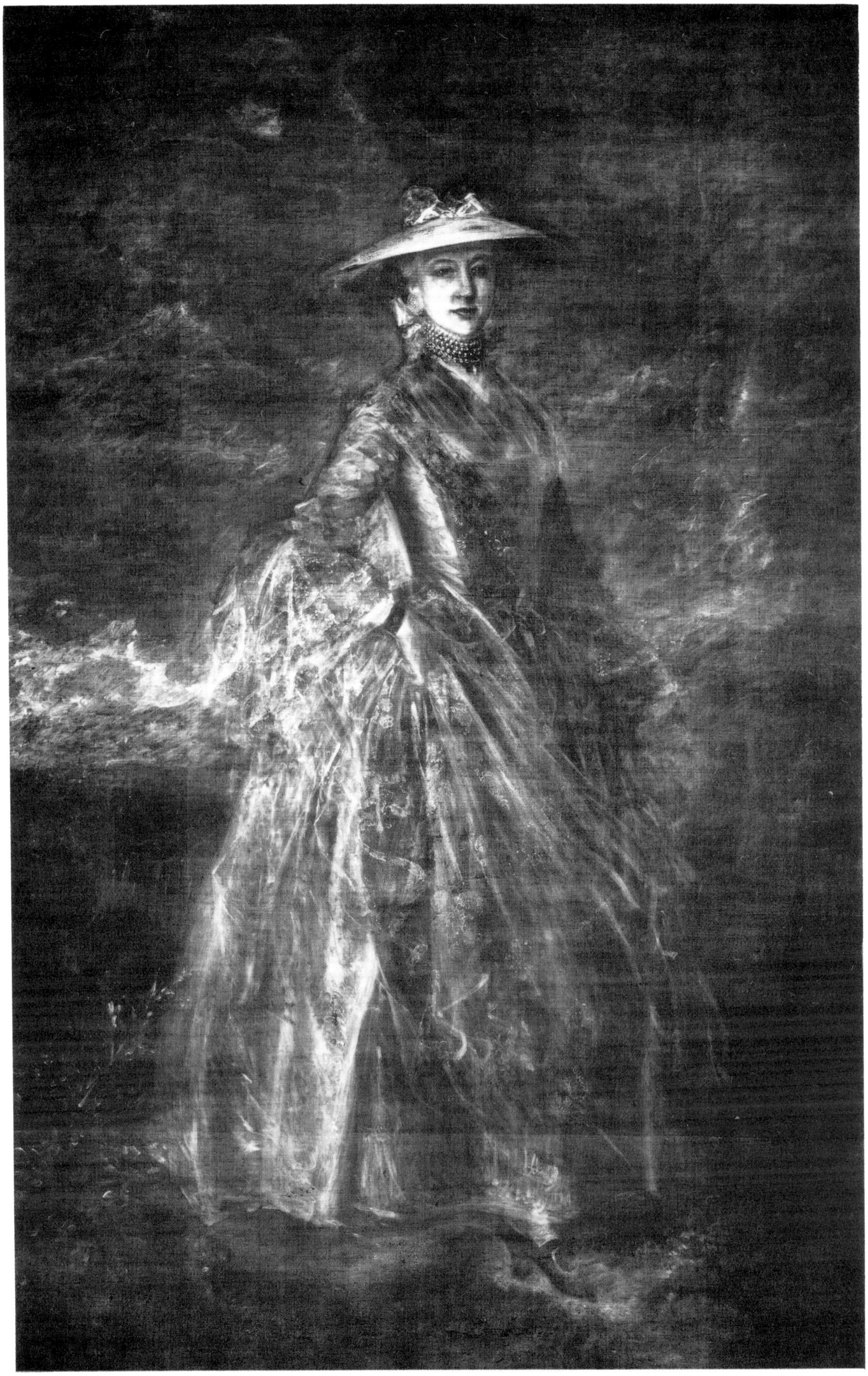

Fig. 15
X-ray
photograph of
Countess Howe.

cannot (without taking away the likeness) touch it unless from the Life.' And again: 'I am vastly out in my notion of the thing if the Face does not immediately look like'[5]. This is the stage that is most easily defined in the X-ray (fig. 15), which clearly shows the wider outline of the skirt, the deeper hemline and the muslin apron brushed across. The painting would by now have reached a point not unlike the unfinished sketch of *The Artist's Daughters Chasing a Butterfly* (fig. 20), painted about 1757, also on the same red ground. Here, too, movement is the essence of the picture; this is conveyed not just by the outstretched arm of the little girl and the scampering feet but, perhaps most strongly, by the few broad strokes of the brush that is all he needed to suggest the child's apron tossed backwards by the sudden surge towards the butterfly.

Gainsborough then worked to complete the figure and background landscape, either from sketches (cat. A3) or by using his lay figures as a model. He reduced the bulk of the skirt by narrowing the left-hand outline and lifting the bottom of the overskirt; he introduced touches of movement to the straight folds of the skirt and a serpentine swing to the hemline; he painted the sleeves on both sides with fuller pink cuffs and longer lace ruffles which hung deep down over the skirt; and he completed the muslin apron with its lace edging, looped up to her hip, with the lower corner flicked back: (much of this can be picked out in the infra-red photograph, fig. 17). With the portrait nearing completion, the landscape and sky were then painted up to the figure.

It was at this advanced stage of completion that Gainsborough began the radical re-working of the composition that transformed his painting into a masterpiece. Although he barely changed the face and head (no more than a slight adjustment was made to the size nd shape of the hat to reduce and straighten the curve of the brim on both sides), from the shoulders downwards hardly anything was left untouched. The line of the body was narrowed into the waist in a diagonal swing. The pink silk cuffs and lace ruffles of both sleeves have been completely repainted, lifting them into the waistline and effectively lightening the weight. On the left, the mountainous landscape has been extended into the figure to break the earlier rigid outline (the wider form of the first pink cuff and the longer folds of lace are still discernible); and on the right the previous fuller shape is now hidden under a strong green patch of trees. A new foot appeared to the right of the original, reducing the Countess's step to a measure more compatible to the style of her shoes (the three feet are nicely visible in the infra-red detail (fig. 18)). The kid glove on the right was painted over another matching black wrist-band, suggesting that the hand might originally have been bare and carrying both gloves; certainly the infra-red photograph shows a fuller form sketched between the fingers and curving out to the side. There is no sign of an earlier hand on the left to correspond with the lower lace ruffle, but there is a space visible immediately below the existing hand, which remained uncovered by the first painting of the skirt and apron; this position could have been intended initially for a hand relating to the longer ruffle.

It is the final solution to the treatment of the skirt and apron that encapsulates the feeling of movement which Gainsborough has striven from the outset to achieve. Over the original heavy folds of the skirt he superimposes the swirling red brushstrokes and sparkling white highlights that lift up the skirt in a rustle of wind. He repeats the movement in the twisting corner of the muslin apron – the earlier design below also shows the corner blown over, but lower, clinging to the skirt, and not tossed forwards as the sharp highlights now suggest. As a last touch, the windswept line is echoed once again in the flick of the pink skirt on the right, blown out across the tree trunk. The feeling of movement is generated by the repeated diagonal lines, driving the figure across the landscape, and is enhanced in a diagonal play of light that sweeps through the picture and out down the path at the bottom. Perhaps the most subtle of all the changes that Gainsborough made was to paint out a heavy mass of foliage that originally festooned the trunk of the birch tree: the leaves crowded into the arm of Lady Howe and impeded her progress. By reducing them to few wispy sprays, the landscape has been opened up to give a sense of air and space around the advancing figure.

By constrast, the portrait of *Earl Howe* appears to have been painted with hardly a second thought. The X-ray (fig. 16) shows straight-foward progress, with only slight adjustments to the tricorn hat, which has been lowered across his forehead, and to the outline of the arms, and possible alterations to the positions of the legs.

Canvas, ground and palette

It is curious that neither the canvas nor the ground in this pair of portraits is identical, suggesting that they were not prepared for work at the same time. The *Countess* is painted on a fine, plain weave canvas with a pinky red ground, whereas the *Earl* is on a fine twill weave canvas with a more orangey red ground. The sizes of the two paintings are unusual, taller, at 94 and 95 ins., than Gainsborough's

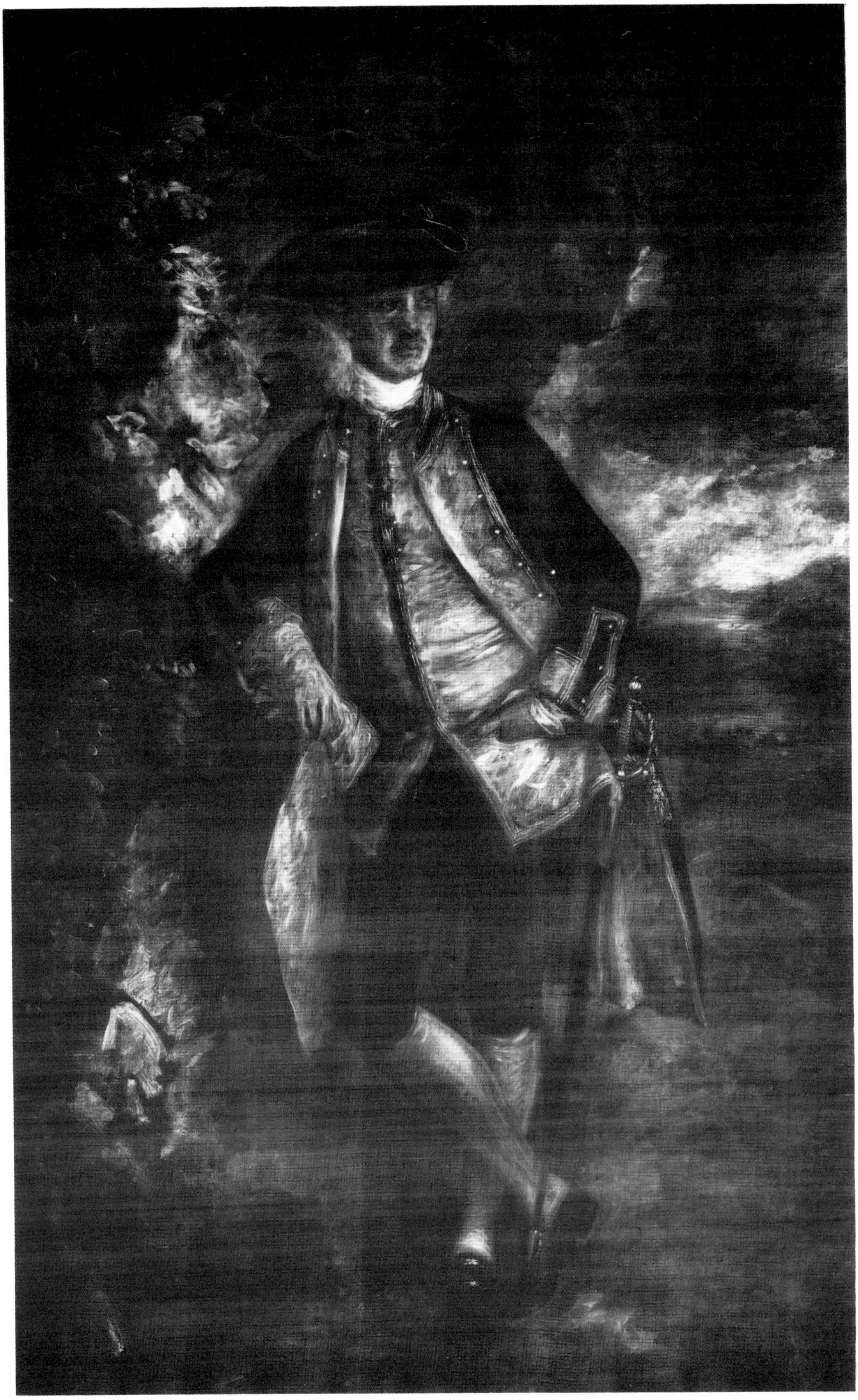

Fig. 16
X-ray
photograph of
Earl Howe.

standard full-length height of around 90–92 ins.; other exceptions are the very large canvases of the *Byam Family* (98×94 ins., fig. 8) and *General Honywood* (124½×115½ ins.), which were probably both painted shortly after the Howes; no other portrait exceeds this standard height until the occasional portrait from about 1778 onwards until his death. The width of his full-lengths remains constant at about 60 ins., which must have been the average loom width.

Gainsborough is rare among British artists of the mid-eighteenth century in his use of a warm red ground or priming which he seems to adopt about the time of his move to Suffolk and continues to use throughout his Bath period, perhaps influenced by his study of Italian paintings or by the red grounds used by Watteau, whose paintings were becoming increasingly popular in England, and whose influence on Gainsborough is recognized. Reynolds made a brief excursion onto a red underpaint in his portrait of *Commodore Augustus Keppel*, (cat. A30), painted immediately after his return from Italy in 1752, but thereafter he used the conventional grey or beige grounds, generally recommended in the painting manuals of the day. Gainsborough is also unusual in the extent to which he makes use of his ground colour, incorporating it as half tones in both his landscapes and portraits, and often leaving considerable areas barely covered.

The earliest paintings from Gainsborough's London period are generally painted on a beige ground, sometimes covered by a warm wash, or more often on a cool grey ground in the manner of the Dutch landscape painters that he admired and copied, for example '*Gainsborough's Forest*' of 1748, on a steely grey ground, and *Mr and Mrs Andrews* of about 1748–9 (both National Gallery), where the beigey-grey ground has been left exposed in the middle of Mrs. Andrews's lap, probably for a dead pheasant that was never painted. By the early 1750's Gainsborough has switched to the warm red ground that can be seen in *John Plampin* of 1753–4 (National Gallery), or the slightly paler red ground to be seen in both unfinished sketches of his two daughters (National Gallery; see fig. 20), thought to be from about 1757 and 1759. This is the colour that we find under almost all his Bath period pictures, including the *Earl* and *Countess Howe*, though towards the end of the 1760's he reverts to a pale grey or white ground for the occasional landscape, as in *Going to Market* (The Iveagh Bequest, Kenwood).

From the time of his return to London in 1773 until the end of his life, Gainsborough's grounds are invariably either pale grey or beige, sometimes with a warm pinkish wash, which is very evident in *Lady Brisco* of 1776 (fig. 7: Kenwood), or cool grey as in *Greyhounds coursing a Fox*, 1784–5 (Kenwood). It is possible that, once he had moved back to London, he would have had access to suppliers of ready-prepared canvases and therefore adapted his painting to the conventional pale ground, but that during his years in Ipswich and Bath he may have been priming his own canvases and could choose his colour to suit his purpose.[6]

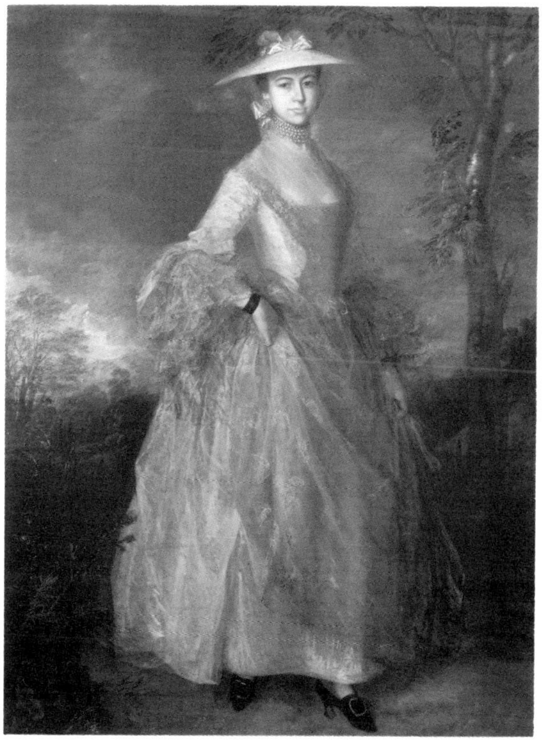

Fig. 17 (right) Infra-red photograph of *Countess Howe*.

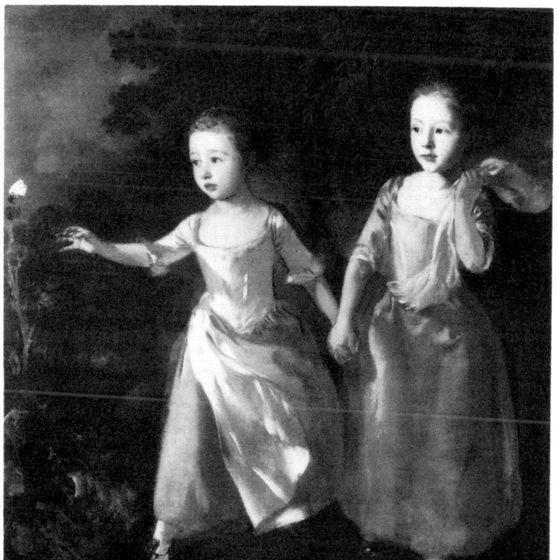

Fig. 20 (far right) Thomas Gainsborough *The painter's daughters chasing a butterfly*, 1756. The Trustees of the National Gallery, London.

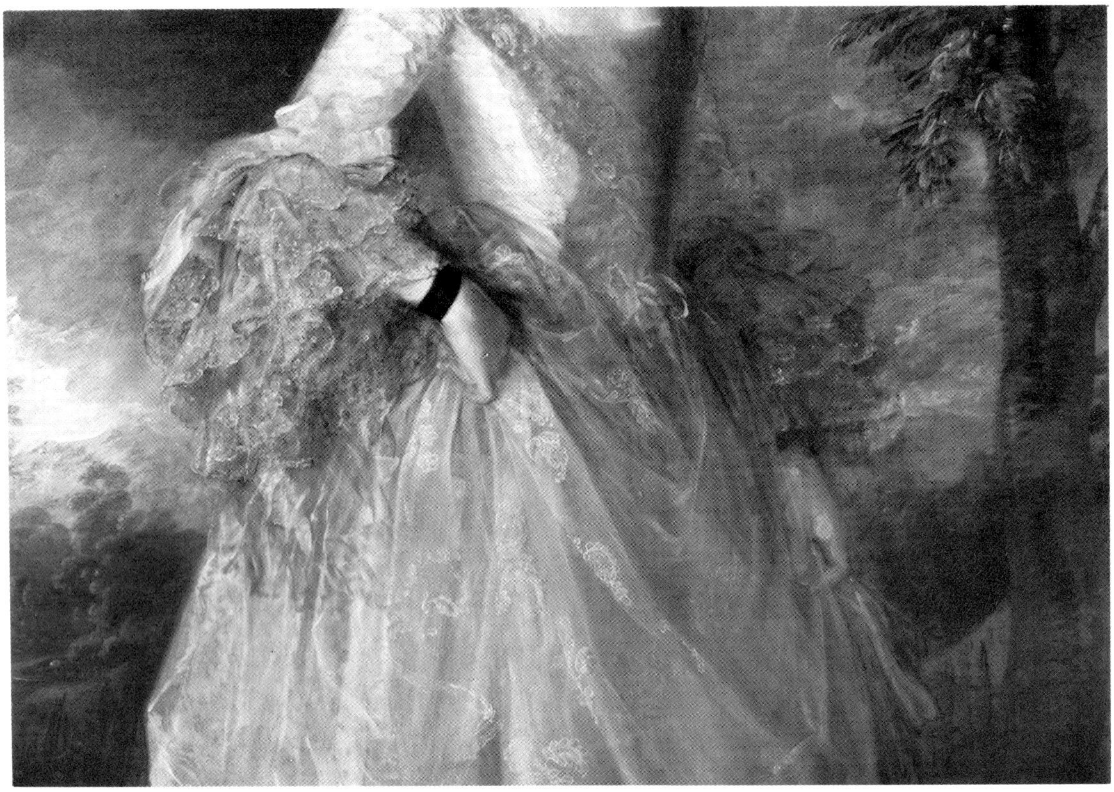

Fig. 19
Infra-red detail of *Countess Howe,* showing the early outline of the lace ruffles and the black wrist band.

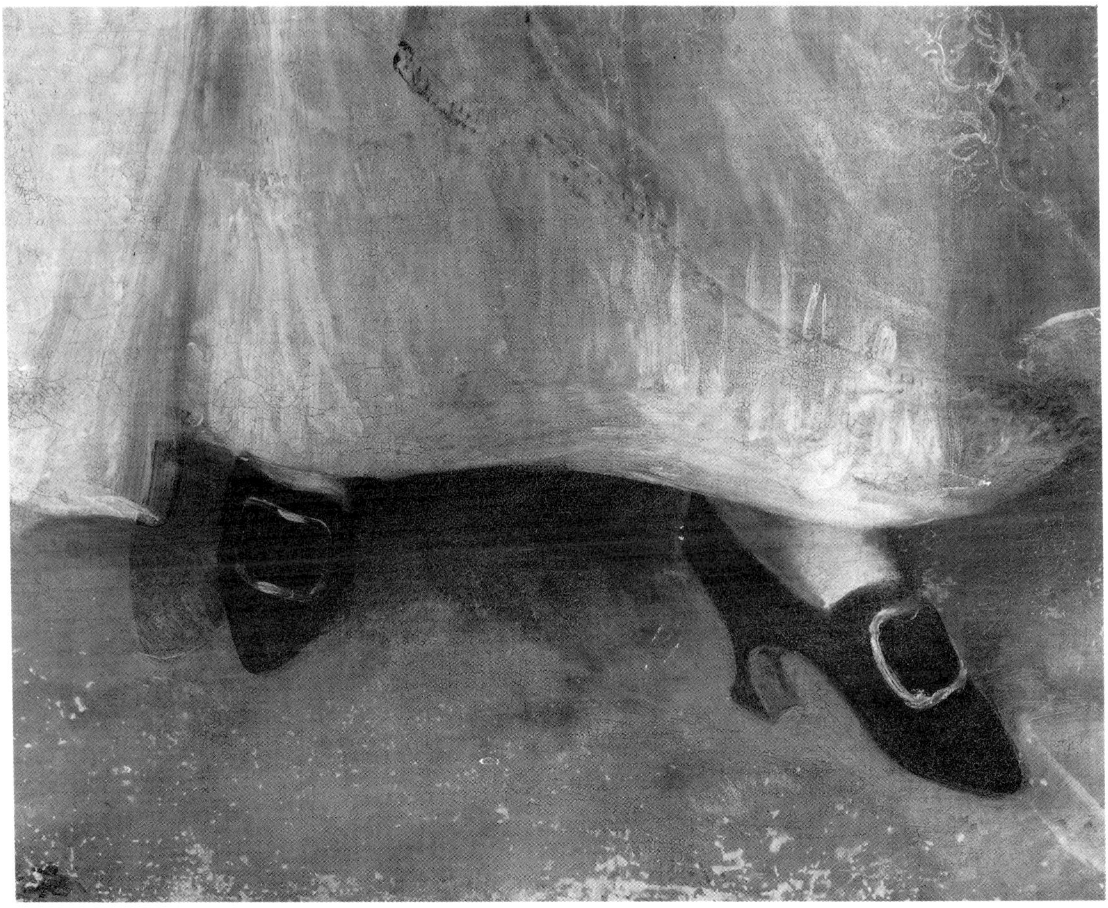

Fig. 18
Infra-red detail of *Countess Howe,* showing the re-positioning of the feet.

Remarks in his letters and in other sources testify to Gainsborough's concern for the quality of the materials that he used in his oil paintings, watercolours and drawings. His technique is very sound and many of his paintings have survived in an excellent condition. This is largely due to his habit of greatly thinning down his oil paints and applying them almost as colour washes, so that the problems of excessive drying craquelure do not occur as often as in the works of some of his contemporaries. This technique also enabled him to vary the texture of his paint and to achieve an exquisite subtlety of modelling and gradation of tone in his sitters' faces, as in *Countess Howe*, and in such passages as the almost tangible lightness of her apron.

Gainsborough's palette for *Countess Howe* is both conventional for the period and restrained. The red ground has been analysed by the National Gallery's Scientific Department[7] as a mixture of lead white, chalk and a natural earth pigment, red iron oxide or red ochre; this analysis has been confirmed by comparison with several other similar grounds from his Ipswich and Bath periods. The blue of the sky is Prussian blue (invented in 1704 and in general use in England from the 1740's); this is used in combination with a grey of lead white and charcoal black, and, when brushed sparingly over the red ground, they create the effect of depth and atmosphere of the sky, an Italian technique of the seventeenth and eighteenth centuries. The pink paint of the dress is a red lake, almost certainly a carmine, or cochineal lake, and is particularly well preserved. The pigments used in the landscape are the standard organic and mineral pigments, with ochres and umbers predominating; the intense green of the foliage on the right edge has a glaze of pure green earth. There is evidence of some slight fading of the colours from the stronger tones of the paint preserved under the rebate of the frame around the edges.

The painting has been relined several times in the past and heavy ironing and possible over-heating during relining has caused some damage to the paint. The impasto has been flattened and some abrasion and 'scouring' of the paint across the chest and skirt has occurred. However, despite all that time and 'restorers' have inflicted on the painting, the portrait of *Countess Howe* remains one of the masterpieces of English painting.

1. There are signs that Gainsborough has extensively re-worked the blue skirt of *Lady Alston*. A very prominent craquelure has developed, revealing a rose red paint underneath. This suggests that either Gainsborough was attempting to achieve a 'shot' effect to the silk by underpainting in an opposite colour, or, more probably, that his original intention was to dress Lady Alston in red.
2. X-radiography: X-rays are a powerful electro-magnetic radiation that can pass through objects to varying degrees and be recorded as a photograph. The ability of a material to retard the passage of X-radiation is dependent upon its atomic mass, the thickness of the object and upon the power of the beam. Pigments of low atomic weight such as organic pigments will barely retard the passage and appear dark in X-ray photography; those of higher atomic weight such as copper containing blues and earth pigments will retard penetration to a slightly greater degree, and those of high atomic weight such as lead and mercury containing pigments (lead white and vermilion) are able almost to prevent penetration and will result in a very pale image on the X-ray film. Thus an X-radiograph will show as pale the areas of paint containing the heavy metal elements, in varying degrees depending upon the thickness of the paint, and can be used to demonstrate *pentimenti* and the characteristics of the brushwork. It is only by looking at the painting that one can see which layer or type of paint lies above other layers.
3. Infra-red: Infra-red radiation can pass through paint layers to some extent. It will be absorbed by some pigments such as carbon blacks and copper containing blues and greens, and reflected by other pigments such as chalk and lead white. The image recorded is the reflected IR radiation, and will thus show a black paint, e.g. underdrawing, as dark on top of a white paint, but only if the layers of paint above do not impede the passage of the IR rays. Thus it is possible to see the earlier painting of the shoe and the bracelet in the infra-red photograph of *Coutness Howe*.
   I am indebted to Amelia Jackson for supplying these explanations.
4. Ozias Humphry, Vol. I, *Correspondence*, Royal Academy. Quoted by Hayes, 1980.
5. Woodall, 1963, pp. 49, 51 (To the Earl of Dartmouth, April 8th, 1771 and April 13th, 1771).
6. There are of course exceptions to this simplification of Gainsborough's priming colours – he is too various an artist to be restricted to a formula, e.g. *The Charterhouse*, 1748, (Thomas Coram Foundation) on a warm orange ground or the unfinished painting of *Landscape with Gypsies*, 1753–4 (Tate Gallery), on a pale beige ground.
7. I am very grateful to Dr Ashok Roy (Scientific Department, National Gallery) for so kindly undertaking the analysis of these paint samples.

The Catalogue

The Catalogue is divided into three sections. *Section A* includes comparative material on Gainsborough's portrait of *Mary, Countess Howe* (nos. 1-24) and on *Richard, Earl Howe* (nos. 25-30). Works by Gainsborough himself precede those by other artists. Also included in this section are other portraits of the Howe family and associated items (nos. A31-40). *Section B* is on the costume worn by Countess Howe and includes surviving examples of 18th century dress and accessories related to the portrait (nos. 1-7), and trade cards illustrating the items worn (nos. 8-13). The trade cards are catalogued in groups (e.g. Haberdashers, Mercers, etc.) rather than individually. *Section C* is on Lord Howe and the Navy: it is divided chronologically into the major campaigns and engagements of Howe's career; *Quiberon Bay*, 1759 (nos. 1-2), the *American War of Independence*, 1775-81 (nos. 3-8), *The Relief of Gibraltar*, 1782 (nos. 9-11) and the events of 1793-1794 (nos. 12-37). Oil paintings, drawings and prints precede memorabilia, books and documents in Sections A and C. Inevitably there is some overlap between the three sections; for example, John Singleton Copley and Henry Singleton's portraits of Earl Howe (A31-32) are included in the section on Howe family portraits, and not under Gibraltar and 1794.

Catalogue entries in sections A and C are by Anne French, with the exception of those paragraphs in Section A relating to the sitters' costume, which are by Aileen Ribeiro. Section B is by Aileen Ribeiro with the exception of B7, which is by Anne French.

Provenance, previous exhibitions and literature are recorded in detail for the two Gainsborough portraits of *Earl and Countess Howe*. For other entries readers are referred to the standard work(s) of reference cited in the *Bibliographical Note* on pp. 94-5 (often, but not always, this will be the most recent publication on the subject) for further information. Bibliographical information is not included for prints; full information on portrait prints can be found in F. M. O'Donaghue, *Engraved British Portraits,* 1908, etc., and John Chaloner Smith, *British Mezzotint Portraits,* 4 vols. 1883. Naval prints are recorded more briefly in Harry Parker, *Naval Battles,* London, 1911. References are given in abbreviated form where the work is listed in the Bibliographical Note.

Measurements are given in inches and centimetres, height before width for paintings, drawings, and prints. For the section on costume measurements vary depending on the item of dress being described. Measurements for individual trade cards are not included.

Section A

THOMAS GAINSBOROUGH, 1727-1799

A1 *Mary, Countess Howe* (*Col. pl. 3*)

Canvas, (95¾ × 60¾) (243·2 × 154·3), stretcher size

Prov: Possibly painted, together with its pendant (cat. A25), for the Howes' house in London at no. 3 Grafton Street. Bequeathed by the sitter in her will (PRO, Prob 11/1346) to her youngest daughter Louisa, Marchioness of Sligo; by descent in the Sligo family to George John, 3rd Marquess (1820-96), who sold the portrait c.1880 to Richard William Penn, 3rd Earl Howe (1822-1900); Thomas Agnew & Sons; Edward Cecil Guinness, later 1st Earl of Iveagh, 1888.

Exh: Thomas Agnew & Sons, 1908 (21); Manchester, 1928 (57); Royal Academy, 1928, (224) and British Portraits, 1956-57 (226); Gainsborough, *Grand Palais, Paris, 6 Feb-26 April 1981 (27).*

Lit: Sir Walter Armstrong, Gainsborough, *1904, p. 270; E. K. Waterhouse, 1948-50, p. 60, and 1958, pp. 21, 75, no. 387 and repr. John Hayes* Journal of the Royal Society of Arts, *1965; The Iveagh Bequest, Kenwood,* Catalogue of Paintings, *1972, pp. 13-14; Hayes, 1975, pp. 38, 211-2, 215, pl. 61 and frontispiece; David Piper,* The Genius of British Painting, *1975, p. 171; Waterhouse, 1981, p. 136; Cherry and Harris, 1982, pp. 287-309.*

The Iveagh Bequest, Kenwood.

Gainsborough's *Mary, Countess Howe* in The Iveagh Bequest is generally regarded as one of his portrait masterpieces. As the principal subject of this exhibition, the portrait is discussed in detail on pp. 19-30, 31-35 and 37-43 of the Introduction, and the information contained there is summarised briefly here. As is suggested on pp. 19-20, there is good reason to believe that the portrait was painted in c.1763-4. A primary indication of this is John Hayes's discovery of a payment from Lord Howe in Gainsborough's bank account for 21 July 1763: 'By Lord Howe £32.11'. This may represent some form of part and advance payment, as a perusal of the visitor lists in Bath local newspapers suggests that the Howes were only in Bath in 1763 from 15th December onwards. Presumably they had arrived for Christmas and the New Year (we know that they spent several later Christmases in Bath)[1], but what we know for certain is that Lady Howe was again in Bath in September and October 1764. This seems a likely time for at least some of the many sittings Gainsborough demanded of his clients to have taken place. However, it is worth recording that the Howes also visited Bath in April and May 1760, and this must remain an alternative date for their portraits. Another reason for placing *Countess Howe* in 1764 is that, unlike most of Gainsborough's great full-lengths, it was not exhibited at the Society of Artists. This would be highly surprising in any other year, but Gainsborough did not send any works to the Society in 1764. The style of the painting also fits well with a dating around this time; it can be compared closely with *The Byam Family*, (fig. 8) which probably also dates to around 1764. Although in the past Blunt[2] proposed an earlier date of around 1760 for *Countess Howe,* the sophistication which marks it out from portraits like *Mrs. Thicknesse* (fig. 3), surely indicates that it belongs to somewhat later in the decade. If so, this would appear to rule out the much canvassed possibility that the two Howe portraits were intended as a celebration of their marriage in 1758; as is argued on p. 19 they probably commemorate, instead, the Howes' arrival on the national stage, after the years 1758-62, which saw their inheritance of both wealth and titles, Lord Howe's early victories at sea, and the birth of their eldest child, Sophia. Where the portraits hung after their completion remains a mystery; probably they were delivered to the Howes' London home in Grafton Street (see p. 20 and note 9, p. 30).

As is discussed on pp. 21-23, *Countess Howe* is an exercise in the manner of Van Dyck, whose work Gainsborough now saw at nearby houses such as Wilton, which he is known to have visited in 1764. From Van Dyck comes the sheer grandeur of scale, vision and conception which marks the portrait out from its earlier 18th-century predecessors, and the setting of a whole-length composition in the open air.

Gainsborough also inherited Van Dyck's vision of the aristocratic portrait; in contrast to the penetrating insight into psychology which an artist like Rembrandt brought to the study of his sitters, Gainsborough, like Van Dyck, prefers to adopt a sense of distance and reserve. As in earlier aristocratic portraiture of the Elizabethan era, it is the costume which, instead, attracts much of the attention. Yet Gainsborough's examination of it, like Van Dyck's, is always more than skin deep; textiles come alive in their hands as in the work of few other artists, and Gainsborough's portrait develops in a highly sophisticated way the sense of movement which in Van Dyck is always implied rather than actual: Countess Howe steps forward confidently in a way new to English portraiture. Gainsborough also makes use of specific traits inherited from Van Dyck, notably the pendant gloves (see cat. A12), and the hand on hip gesture with the skirt gathered up beneath her hand. His inclusion of a foreground plant derives from Van Dyck's use of this motif in his full-length male portraits, while the influence of Van Dyck's sensitive nature drawings can be seen in the lively specimen of a thistle found here.

Countess Howe is dressed in a 'nightgown' of rose pink silk. This type of costume was preferred by English ladies to the more formal dresses worn on the continent, and the dress is entirely suitable attire for walking in a park, as the Countess does here. The gossamer-fine apron, usually worn with informal dresses such as the 'nightgown', adds a touch of decoration to a dress that lacks French rococo frills and trimmings, and which depends instead on the infinite variety created by the shimmering silk lustring. Other accessories include the 'Leghorn' straw bonnet with small lace cap underneath; a lace fichu pinned across the bosom; the magnificent treble sleeve ruffles or *engageantes;* the black silk bracelet (originally one of pair; see fig. 19), which was worn to emphasise the whiteness of the skin; and the plain kid gloves. The Countess wears seed pearl earrings, but a real pearl necklace, tied at the back with silk ribbon. Probably these were something of a studio prop since so many canvases of the Bath period show the same or very similar pearl necklaces and earrings. The rather chalky quality of the skin is not to be associated with the artist's technique but is, instead, due to the use of cosmetics; the Countess's brown hair, worn swept off the face in the style of the time, is lightly powdered.

Although the setting of full-length portraits in the open air had been practised by Van Dyck, and can be found occasionally in portraits of the early 18th century by Richardson, Hudson and others (see p. 23), the year 1759 marks a watershed in English portraiture. In this year, just before the opening of the new Society of Artists in 1760, Reynolds and Allan Ramsay painted their first full-length portraits of women standing in a landscape (p. 23). *Countess Howe* represents what is perhaps Gainsborough's second experiment in this vein, after his earlier and rather formal *Lady Alston* (fig. 4). In *Countess Howe* he has given us a much more convincing portrayal of a fashionably dressed lady taking a stroll in her own landscape park. The subject was anticipated by Reynolds in his sensitive and unconventional portrait of *Mrs. Riddell,* of 1763 (cat. A23), in which he goes beyond even Gainsborough in the direction of unaffected naturalism (p. 24). Gainsborough's painting, however, is the first English portrait to define the effects of weather and climate; no other artist before Constable would capture so brilliantly the sensation of a summer's breeze, or the slightly threatening summer evening sky. If Gainsborough's portrait looks forward to the new exhibition pictures of the later 1760's, it also harks back to his own earlier Ipswich three-quarter length portraits like *Lady Innes* (fig. 5) or the *Girl in a Pink Riding Habit,* both of which make use of fairly advanced outdoor settings. Gainsborough, however, must have learned, too, from Reynolds's romantic three-quarter length outdoor portraits of the 1750's like *Mrs. Bonfoy* (cat. A21), which even shares the same hand on hip pose. His portrait belongs to that specific moment in the mid-1760's when Gainsborough's art was still rooted firmly in reality, and when he balanced out the claims of the flesh against the more abstract imperatives of his canvas. *Countess Howe's* charismatic presence is fully felt, unlike the rather anaemic *Lady Brisco* of 1776 (fig. 7), in which his sitter melts almost indistinguishingly into the background.

It is extraordinary to realise that, with the exception of a costume drawing (cat. A3), which enabled him to study the arrangement of his sitter's dress, Gainsborough embarked on his portrait with almost no preparation. His design was, quite literally, developed on the canvas as he worked, and pp. 37-39 trace its evolution from the earliest stages through to the final and radical reworking which turned the painting into the masterpiece it is today.

Lady Howe was also painted by Arthur Devis in or after 1758, in a portrait of 'Commodore and Lady Howe' which may have been a single conversation piece, or two small-scale portraits. It is suggested on p. 19 above that the portrait may have been commissioned at the time of the Howes' marriage, but apparently they did not take delivery of their portrait, which was in the posthumous sale of the artist's house in 1822. Lady Howe was also painted by Francis Cotes in a portrait now at Westport House, County Mayo; this is probably not the portrait of 'Mrs. Howe, later Mrs. Barnard' listed in Edward Mead Johnston's monograph on Cotes as no. 55. The painting is said to date from around 1758 so this, too, may have been a wedding portrait.[3]

1 Information on file in Bath City Archives (Mural Tablet to Howe, erected in 1931).
2 *Catalogue of Paintings,* The Iveagh Bequest, Kenwood, revised ed., 1972, p. 14.
3 Information kindly supplied by Viscount Altamont.

A2 *Henrietta, Countess Grosvenor*, 1767

Canvas, cut down to 39½×34½ (100.3×87.6)

Prov: By descent.

Exh: Gainsborough, *Tate Gallery, London, 1980 (99).*

Lit: Waterhouse, 1953, cat. 332; Hayes, 1975, note 65, plate 64.

His Grace the Duke of Westminster D.L.

Countess Grosvenor is surely among the most supremely beautiful and powerful of all Gainsborough's portraits. As it exists today, the painting is only a fragment; it was once a full-length of the same scale and grandeur as *Countess Howe,* and as such it was exhibited at the Society of Artists in 1767. Painted approximately three years later than *Countess Howe,* it is very close in conception to the

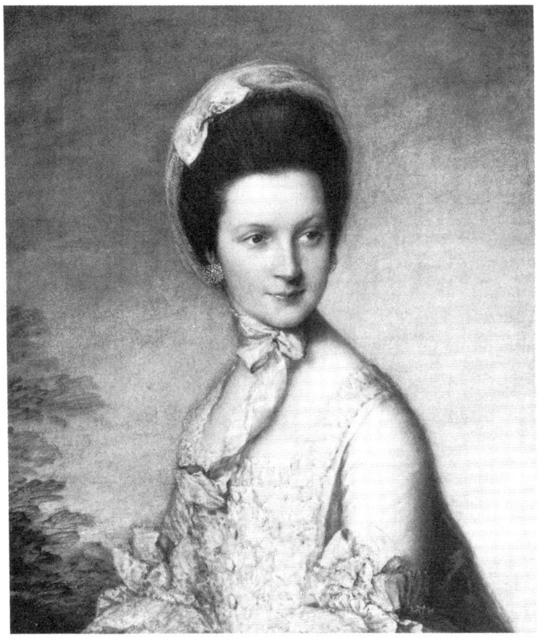

earlier portrait; evidently the sitter originally stood in a landscape, as the foliage in the background to the left of her shows.

Here, too, Gainsborough pays detailed attention to his sitter's costume. Lady Grosvenor wears a *sacque* dress with a buttoned front bodice decorated, as are the sleeves above the ruffles at the elbow, with ruched ribbon. The hair is quite high and smooth, an effect which was sometimes created by being combed over a roll or pad, and pomaded to keep it in place. Lady Grosvenor wears a net hood, rather turban-like in shape – scarves and turban headdresses were especially popular in the 1760's – which echoes the fashionable plain, rounded hairstyle of the period. An alternative to the back-fastening necklace worn by Lady Howe is a length of silk ribbon tied, as here, in a bow under the chin. Lady Grosvenor's earrings, although more sketchily painted, are of the same type as Countess Howe's. Indeed, one suspects that these were something of a studio 'prop', since a whole series of portraits of women of this period (for example, *Lady Mostyn,* Institute of History and Art, Albany, New York; *Elizabeth Cochrane,* Sotheby's 15.3.1967 (91); or the *Portrait of a Woman,* Manchester City Art Galleries, also include them, usually in conjunction with a choker of pearls.

Although the handling of paint in *Countess Grosvenor* is rather more textured and more loosely brushed than in *Countess Howe,* lending a slightly more impressionistic appearance to the costume, the faces in the two portraits are remarkably close in technique. Both are superb examples of the almost porcelain-like quality of the flesh, which is in such marked contrast to late Bath works like *Lady Innes* (fig.5), where the brushwork is noticeably rougher and is drawn diagonally across the face in a series of parallel lines. However, whereas in *Countess Howe* the expression remains rather distant and remote, Lady Grosvenor is much more approachable, captured by Gainsborough as she turns her head to look, either at the spectator or at some object which has aroused her attention below her and to her left. Her glance is interested, perhaps even slightly humourous. This degree of expressiveness is something new in Gainsborough's portraiture and, as John Hayes comments, is probably owing to the influence of

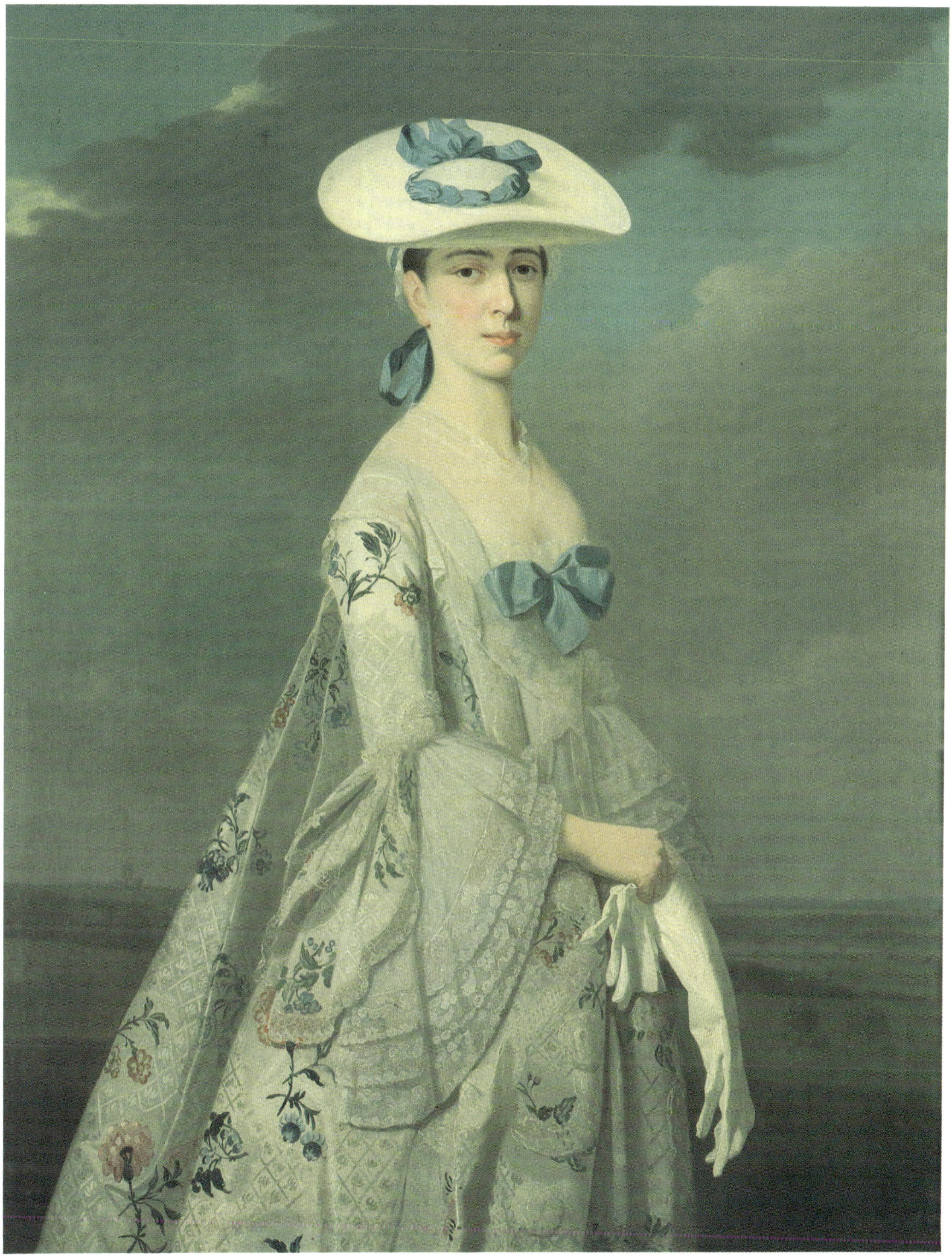

Colour plate 1. Attributed to Henry Pickering, *'Eleanor Frances Dixie'* (cat. A15).

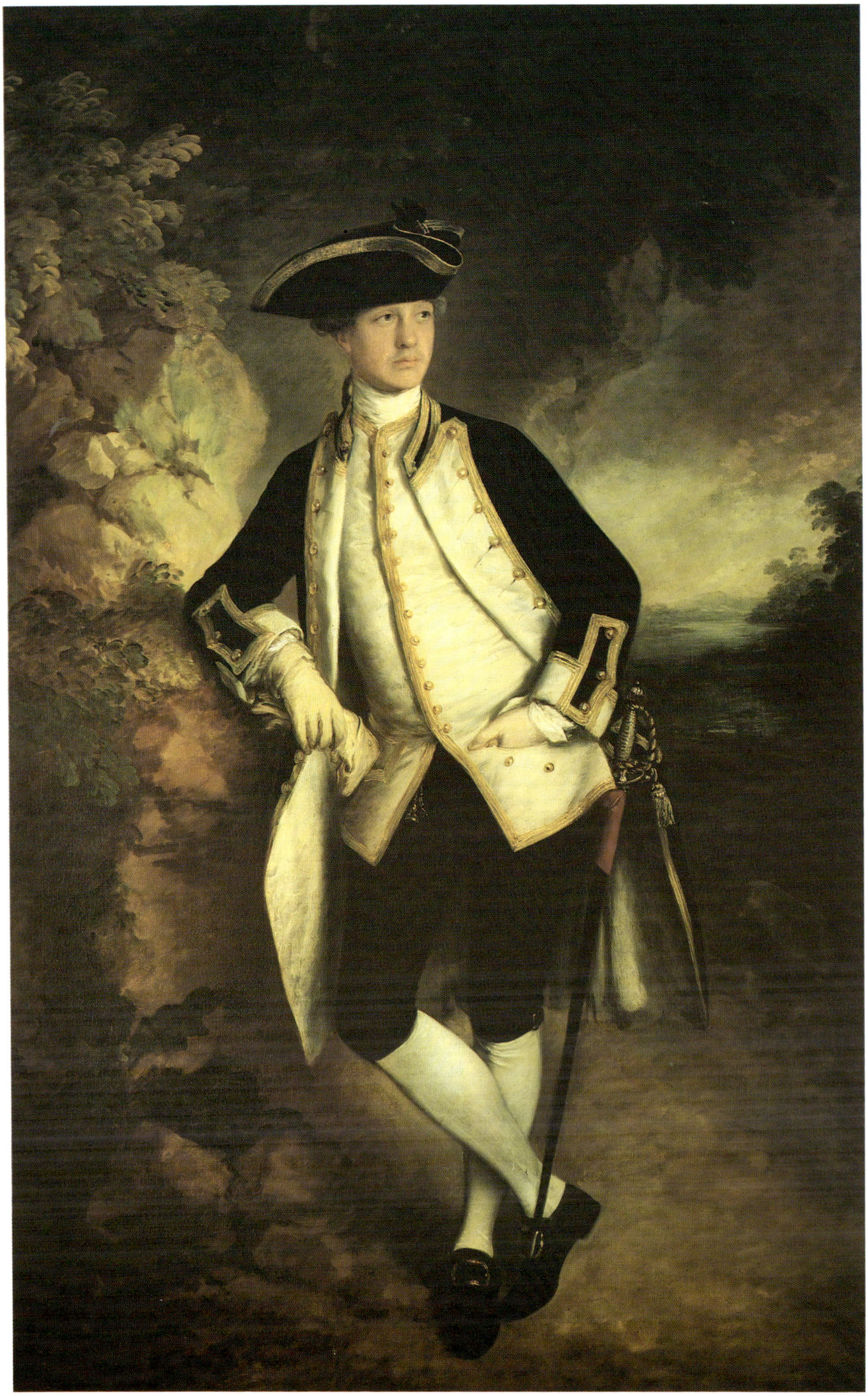

Colour plate 2. Thomas Gainsborough *Richard, Earl Howe* (cat. A25).

Colour plate 3. Thomas Gainsborough *Mary, Countess Howe* (cat. A1).

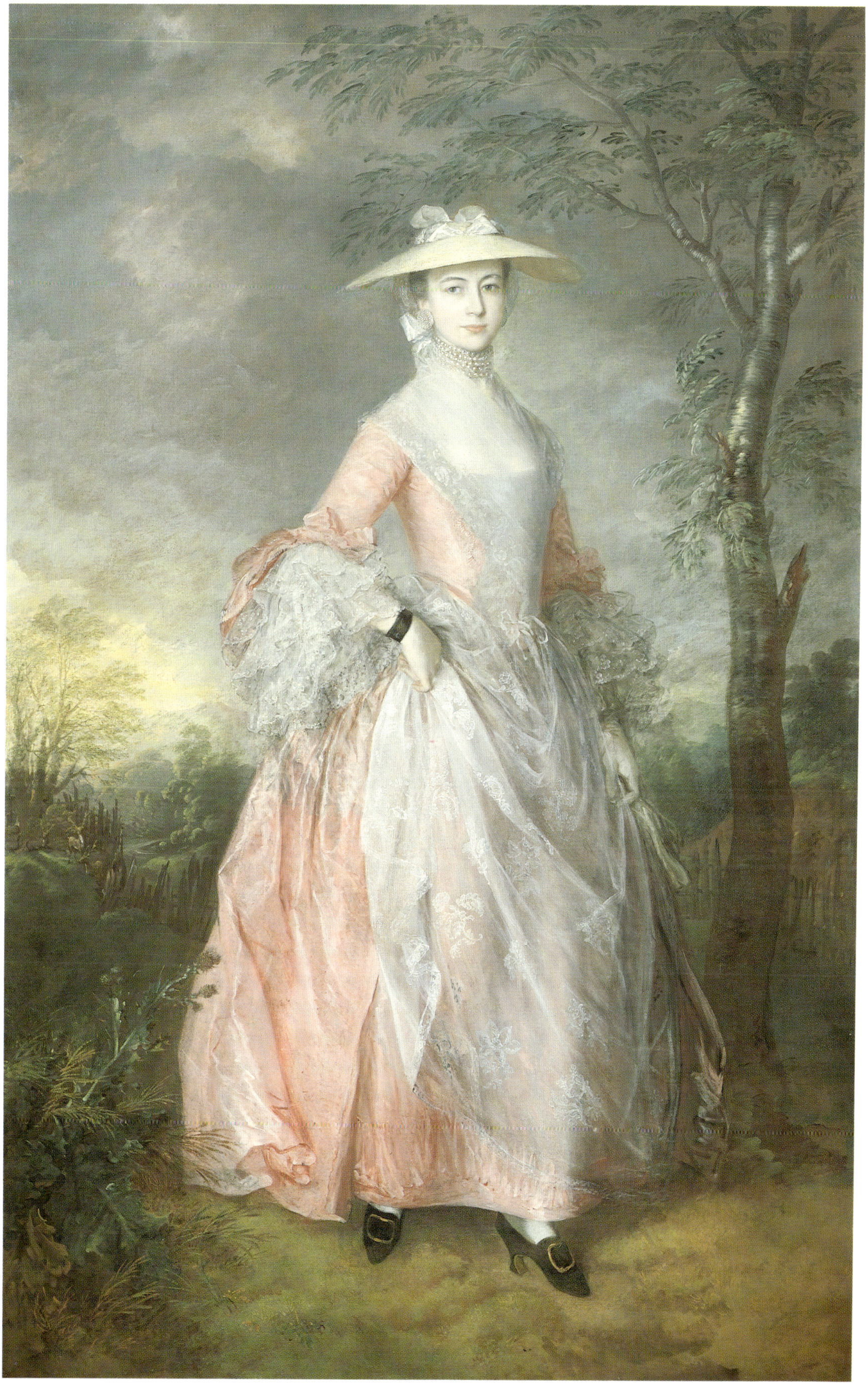

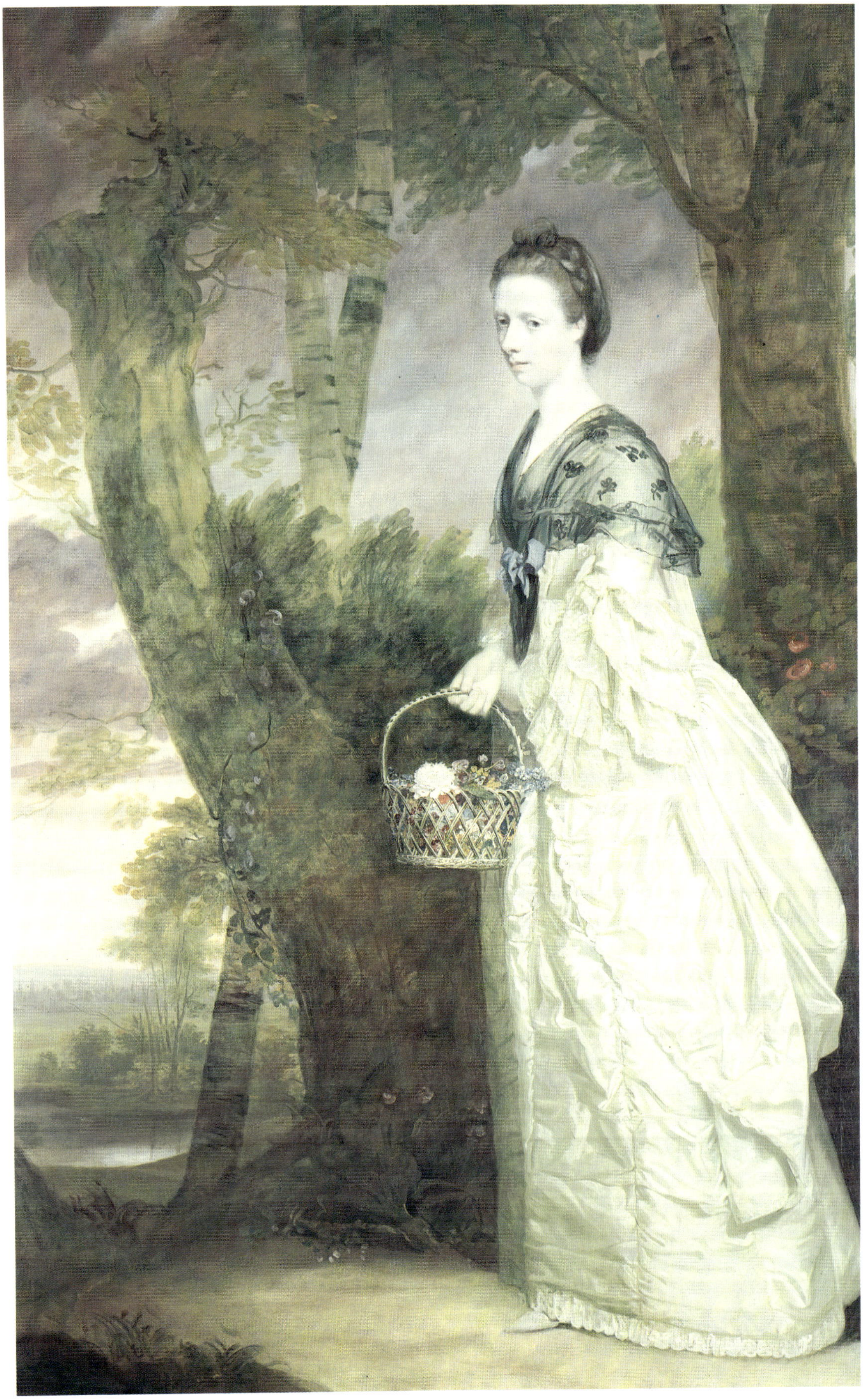

Colour plate 4.
Sir Joshua Reynolds
Mrs Thomas Riddell
(cat. A23).

Rubens, whose work began to exercise a profound impact on Gainsborough's landscape style at this same period.

A3 ***A woman with a rose, c.1763-5***

Black chalk and stump, heightened with white, on greenish-buff paper, 18 15/16×13 (46.6×33.0)

Prov: *With Tiffin, from whom purchased 1855.*

Exh: Gainsborough and Reynolds in the British Museum, *1978 (41). Hayes and Stainton, 1983 (34).*

Lit: *Hayes, 1970(29) and pp.35, 43.*

The Trustees of the British Museum, 1855-7-15-70

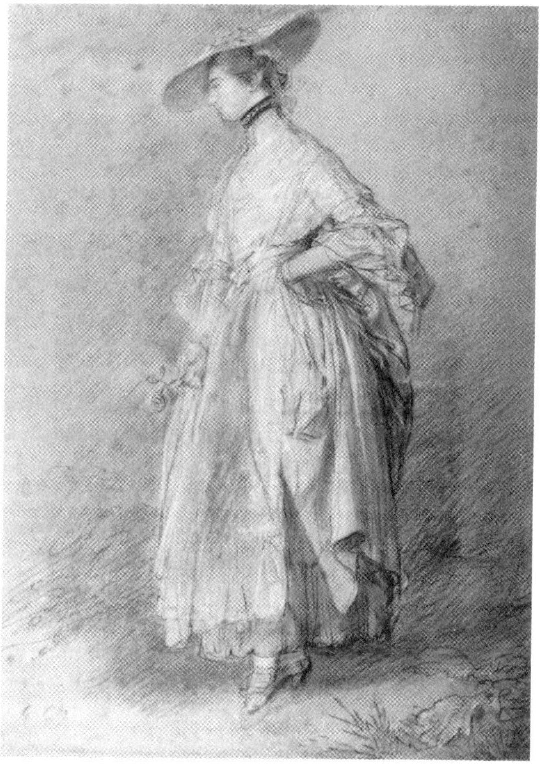

This costume study in the British Museum, as Lindsay Stainton has pointed out[1], is probably to be associated with the Kenwood portrait of *Countess Howe*. It seems likely that Gainsborough was here attempting an early profile rendering of the figure, which he would later convert into the more square-on pose of the finished portrait. The hand on hip pose, gathering up the drapery below, is, however, already in place, as are details of the costume such as the Leghorn bonnet (seen here in profile) with cap underneath, the fall of the embroidered apron, the rather shortened hem-line of the dress above the buckled feet, and even the tying of the apron strings at the waist. The highly sketchy rendering of the side of the body turned away from the spectator is repeated in the finished canvas; given the many alterations in that area to the sitter's left hand and gloves, it is possible that the portrait was also intended originally to show Countess Howe holding a rose. Like Countess Howe, the figure here is portrayed out walking; Gainsborough gives an early indication of the landscape setting in the burdock(?) leaves in the right hand corner.

The drawing is one of a group of full-length costume studies of women executed by Gainsborough, usually in black chalk, during his early years in Bath[2] (see also cats. A4, A5). As he embarked on his full-length portraits of these years, he evidently felt the need to study closely the fall and disposition of his sitters' dress, and the drawings are properly to be understood as costume studies, rather than as compositional sketches; as Hayes remarks, they show little interest in structure or anatomy[3]. The drawings have a close affinity with the full-length costume studies of women drawn in the 1740's by Gravelot, when Gainsborough was working in his studio, although Gainsborough has transformed these carefully accurate depictions into highly atmospheric studies entirely his own. There has been much discussion as to the extent to which Gainsborough, like Gravelot, made use in these drawings of articulated dolls. He is certainly known to have used such figures, and two of them were included in the sale of his studio effects after his death.[4] However, Lindsay Stainton has suggested that many of the chalk drawings of this period were probably done instead from the life; as she points out, although the faces are often sketched in summarily, they are lively and convincing. The present highly sensitive study certainly has all the appearance of having been drawn from life; the sitter is not, of course, *Countess Howe* herself, to whom the features and expression bear no resemblance, but, presumably, a model employed by Gainsborough in the studio.

The sitter's costume – an informal nightgown – is not unlike that worn by Lady Howe, but simpler. The dress is without robings, and the artist has only indicated, with the sketchiest of lines, the fichu and lace ruffles. Some aspects of the dress, however, have more elaboration: these include the pattern (either embroidered or woven) on the apron, the shallow crowned, ribbon-trimmed Leghorn hat, and the necklace of beads on black silk. As dress fabrics become plainer from the mid-18th century, the bundling up of increased yardages of thinner and lighter silks became a fashionable feature; such gestures as we see here and indeed in the portrait of Lady Howe herself, produced an attractive effect of soft, bunched-up drapery.

Gainsborough returned to the presentation of costume studies in a landscape setting towards the end of his life in five brilliant drawings, possibly executed in connection with the *Richmond Water Walk*. Here the boldly sweeping lines of black chalk, highlighted in broad areas of white, can be contrasted with the controlled precision of the present drawing which, on stylistic grounds, can surely be dated to the early years of the 1760's, the period of the *Countess Howe* portrait.

1 Stainton, op cit.
2 These include: *A woman holding a shawl* and *A woman seated beside a plinth* (Pierpont Morgan Library); the *Study for a portrait of an unidentified lady with two children* (Ehemals Staatliche Museum, Berlin-Dahlem); the *Woman holding a fan* (British Museum); and two studies of *A woman seated in a landscape* (Frick collection). Several of these can also be compared generally, in terms of pose or costume, with *Countess Howe*.
3 Hayes, 1970, p.35. Compositional studies of the period do survive, for example the one for *Mrs. Thicknesse* in the British Museum.
4 W.T. Whitley, *Thomas Gainsborough*, 1915, p.351.

A4 ***Study of a woman seen from behind***

Black chalk and stump and white chalk on greyish-brown paper, 19 3/16×11 15/16 (48.8×30.4)

Prov: *As in Hayes.*

Exh: *Hayes & Stainton, 1983 (35).*

Lit: *Hayes, 1970, pp 101, 103 and 118 (30). Brown, 1982 (673)*

The Visitors of the Ashmolean Museum, Oxford.

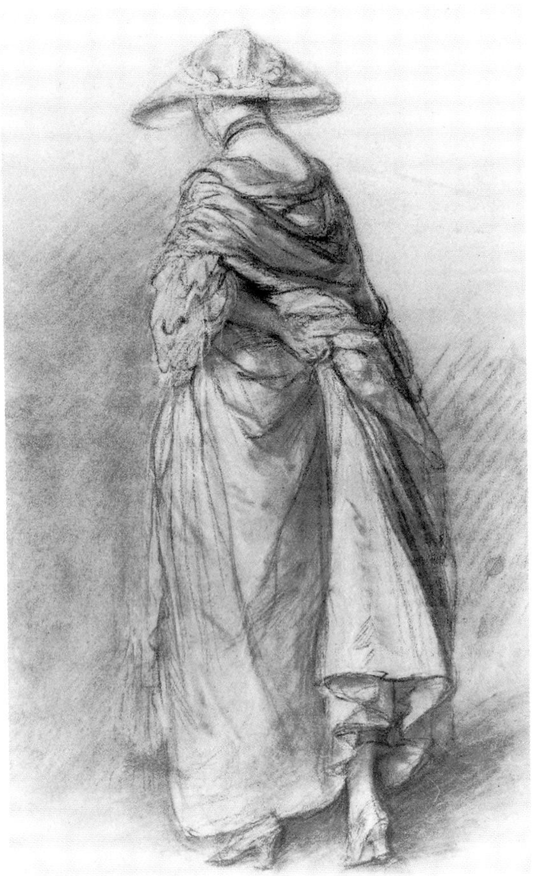

This study of a woman walking, drawn from behind, is closely related to the *Woman with a Rose* in the British Museum (cat. A3), in which the sitter also hitches up her gown with her arm akimbo. Although there is no direct relationship here with the Kenwood portrait of *Countess Howe,* the drawing can be seen, imaginatively, as providing us with a back view of the Countess as she strolls along. Now that he was faced for the first time with the design of standing, full-length portraits of women in his early years in Bath, Gainsborough was evidently preoccupied, as Hayes comments, with the question of how the 'folds and flounces of ladies' dresses' would fall when in movement.[1] Costume studies such as these, which show the female figure from several different angles, were his way of learning to overcome the problem before embarking on a full-length canvas.

Eighteenth century dress was meant to be as attractive when viewed from behind as it was from the front. The emphasis on back drapery (whether flowing from the shoulders as in the graceful *sacque* gown, or the various forms of kilting the skirt up in swags *à la polonaise*), is evidence of the appeal of the woman in retreat. A typical gesture at this period is to lift up the side or back drapery of the gown; this had the further advantage of showing off a fine pair of ankles and elegant high-heeled shoes; those shown here are of exactly the same type as in *Countess Howe*. Like the model in the British Museum drawing, this fashionably dressed sitter wears a gown of English design, but this time with a silk hooded mantle appropriate for out-of-doors. The folds of her apron can just be glimpsed on the left. The rather large mushroom shaped hat is of a very different design from Lady Howe's bonnet. It is in the Chinese taste satirised by Oliver Goldsmith in his *The Citizen of the World* (1762); the dreadful Mrs. Tibbs at Vauxhall Gardens appears in 'flimsy silk. . . and a hat as big as an umbrello'.

From its rather broader use of chalk, the Ashmolean drawing can probably be dated to a few years later than the British Museum study, aroung 1765-70. It is particularly close in handling to the chalk study of *Mary Gainsborough,* also in the British Museum, and there is general agreement that this drawing, too, was done from life, and not from an articulated doll.

1 Hayes, 1980, p.35.

A5 *Study of a woman seated*

Black chalk and stump and white chalk, on blue paper, 12⅜×9⁹⁄₁₆ (31.4×23.7)

Prov: As listed in Hayes, then Sotheby's, 30.6.1986 (103); bt. Baskett & Day; private collection.

Exh: Hayes & Stainton, 1983 (43).

Lit: Hayes, 1970 (32).

The J. Paul Getty Museum, Malibu (photograph exhibited)

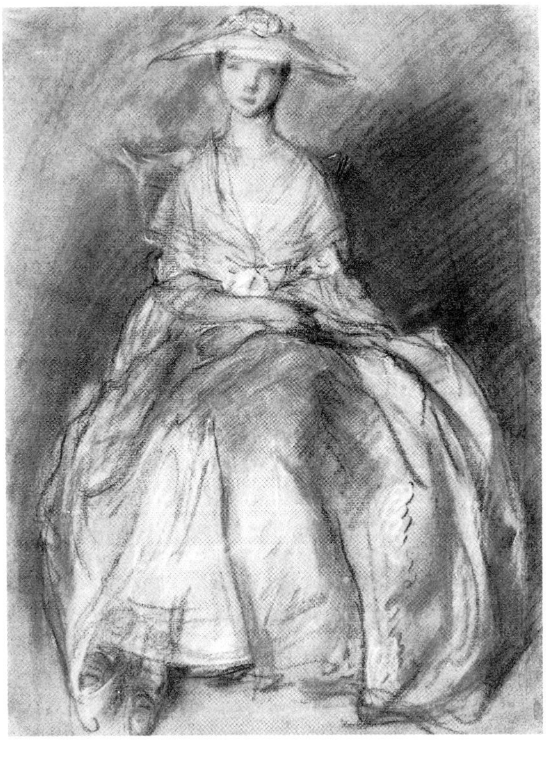

The woman in this chalk drawing of the 1760's wears her Leghorn straw bonnet flat on her head, at almost exactly the same angle as *Countess Howe,* although, if anything, pulled slightly further down over the face. Perhaps it is this which lends to the composition the same 'bergere' quality as the Kenwood portrait; the affinity between the two has often been remarked on. The dress, which is voluminous in cut, looks as if it may have been made for a hoop petticoat. It consists of a gown with modest ribboned robings down the side, and a plain skirt; a shoulder mantle hides the construction and decoration of the bodice.

One can perhaps detect here, as Lindsay Stainton suggests, the use of a lay model; the face is rather formless, the feet are placed at an impossible angle to the body, and the fall of the dress over the knees is unconvincing.[1] The frontal pose is unusual for Gainsborough, and the drawing is not connected to any known portrait.[2] The drawing again forms one of the group of costume studies of women executed by Gainsborough during the 1760's (see also cats. A3, A4). However, with its rather soft use of chalk, it can probably be dated to the second half of the decade, although Aileen Ribeiro points out that the costume is typical of the earlier 1760's.

1 Hayes and Stainton, loc.cit.
2 As Hayes points out, citing, however, one portrait of the mid 1760's in which it occurs (Waterhouse, 1958, no. 341).

A6 *Hilly wooded landscape with oxen, cottage and distant mountain*

Grey and brown washes, over pencil, 11¼×15 (28.6×38.1)

Prov: Anon. sale, Sotheby's, 15.4.1953 (18); bt. Colnaghi, from whom purchased 1953.

Lit: Hayes, 1970, (268); Brown, 1982 (676).

The Visitors of the Ashmolean Museum, Oxford.

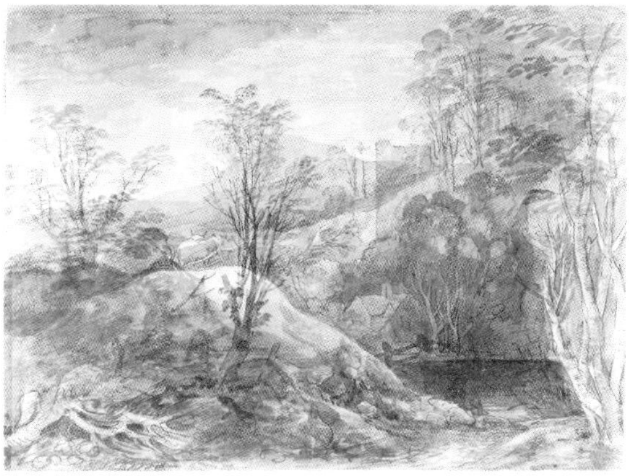

To understand the formation of Gainsborough's landscape background in *Countess Howe*, and in other portraits of the 1760's, one must turn to his landscape drawings of the same period. Not only are the 'ingredients' or vocabulary basically the same; Gainsborough's handling of foliage in *Countess Howe* also closely resembles his wash drawing technique.

On his arrival in Bath, Gainsborough turned his back on the wooded, low-lying scenery, enlivened by cottages, church towers, rivers and ponds, which formed the vocabulary of his Suffolk landscapes. Instead he began to depict more 'picturesque' mountainous scenery, inspired by Wyck and Hampton rocks nearby, and by the Cheddar Gorge. The rococo rhythm of the 1750's frequently remained, but Gainsborough now saw for the first time the 17th century classical landscape paintings of Claude Lorrain, Gaspard Dughet and their contemporaries, whose work became accessible to him in country houses nearby. The present drawing is arranged on broadly classical principles: a dominant tree group to one side, offset by a smaller, more picturesque grouping of trees in the middle distance, while a mountain closes the view through the centre. This is exactly the arrangement found in *Countess Howe*, if one makes allowance for the placing of the figure itself. Indeed, the affinity between drawing and painting goes beyond this, extending even to details such as the shape of the tree groups on the left, their relationship to the mountains beyond, and the way in which the tree on the right forms a strong vertical accent up the full height of the composition, with the top-most branches arching over to the left. If the composition is classical in feeling – with the exception of the contemporary staffage – so, too, is the handling; the large, detailed patches of wash used to conjure up the leaves of the foreground tree certainly owe much to the drawings of Claude, Dughet and Nicolas Poussin.[1] This technique is repeated almost exactly in oils in *Countess Howe*.

The Ashmolean drawing, which has been dated by Hayes to the early 1760's, is a compositional sketch for a projected landscape painting, and there is no direct relationship between the drawing and Gainsborough's portrait. However, there can surely be little doubt that Gainsborough had precisely this type of drawing in mind when he came to paint the landscape background in *Countess Howe*. Although in his portraits he worked almost directly onto the canvas, the assurance with which he was able to approach his portrait backgrounds must have owed a great deal to his frequent experimentation with motifs and compositional arrangements in his landscape drawings.

1 e.g., John Sharman and Anthony Blunt, *Poussin Drawings, IV*, pls. G3, G15, G38.

A7 *A wooded landscape with a peasant boy asleep in a cart*

Watercolour and bodycolour over pencil on brown paper, 11×14¹⁵⁄₁₆(27.9×37.9)

Prov: Mrs W.F.R. Welde; presented to the Museum, 1934.

Exh: Hayes & Stainton, 1983 (30).

Lit: Hayes, 1970 (266); Brown, 1982 (675).

The Visitors of the Ashmolean Museum, Oxford.

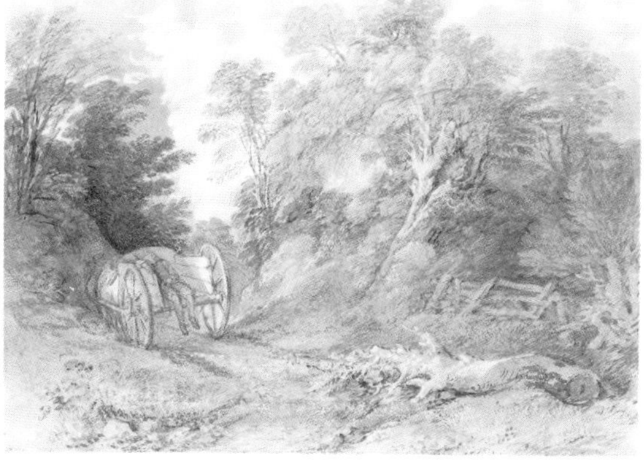

Although the compositional arrangement in this drawing by Gainsborough, which has also been dated to the early 1760's, is entirely different to *Countess Howe*, the handling of the foliage is again markedly similar. The tree on the right hand bank suspended over the track, or the foliage above the cart to the left, both have exactly the same feathery delicacy of touch which characterises the smaller tree group in Gainsborough's portrait. The luminous quality of the foliage at the horizon, silhouetted against the fleecy clouds, is also directly comparable with Gainsborough's more pronounced use of this device in *Countess Howe*. Although the foliage, as always in Gainsborough's work, remains generalised in form, it is noticeable that it retains the sturdy sense of individual structure and growth which typifies the drawings of the mid-1760's, and which is found also in *Countess Howe*.

Like cat. A.6, but in a different way, this drawing again shows the influence of Italian landscape painting. Gainsborough's extensive use of white bodycolour, which began during his early years in Bath, must derive from the gouaches of artists like Marco Ricci, or G.B. Busiri.[1] These had found their way in large numbers into English country house collections, and Gainsborough would now have seen them for the first time.

Other drawings of the early 1760's which can be compared either in composition or in technique with the landscape background in *Countess Howe* are: *Three Horses and a Drover on a Country Road* (Christie's 20.11.1984); *Wooded Landscape with Gypsy Encampment* (Hayes 276); *Wooded Landscape with Herdsmen and Cattle* (Hayes 273); and another *Landscape* in the Ashmolean Museum (Hayes 265).

1 Stainton, cat. 28.

A8 *A boy with a donkey, c.1762-4*

Canvas, 11⅛×12¼ (28×31)

Prov: As in Hayes.

Lit: Hayes, 1982, cat 78.

Private collection (on loan to Kenwood)

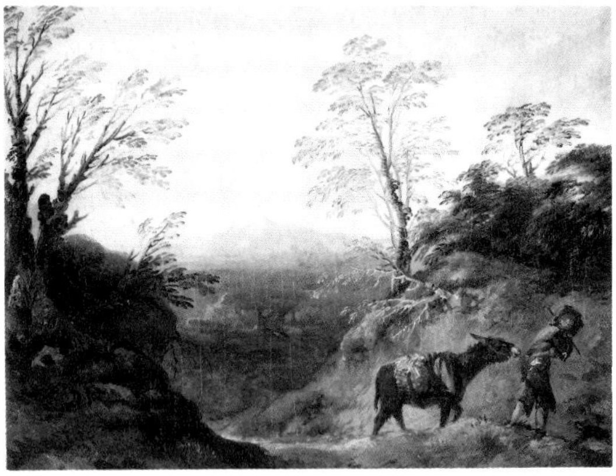

Gainsborough's delightful small oil sketch of *A boy with a donkey* belongs to almost exactly the same period as *Countess Howe*. Despite the differences in scale between the two works, it provides a good example of the way in which Gainsborough's portrait backgrounds and landscape paintings correspond so closely in the early years of the 1760's.

The sketch is clearly an exercise in the manner of Claude Lorrain, although transformed into an 18th century idiom by Gainsborough's strong sense of linear rhythm. From Claude derive the contrasting tree masses, the airy distant view, and way in which the landscape is permeated with light. Only the boy with the donkey lends a contemporary touch to the composition; Gainsborough had a strong aversion to the use of classical staffage, considering that figures should be used to 'create a little business for the eye', not to contain a history. *A boy with a donkey* resembles *Countess Howe* not only in its use of picturesque scenery, and in the classical structuring of the composition, but also in the handling; the treatment of the foliage, with small separate strokes of the brush used to conjure up the leaves, is paralleled in the much larger tree in the Kenwood portrait. Other landscapes of this period which come particularly close to *Countess Howe* are two *Wooded Landscapes,* in the Philadelphia Museum of Art (1762–3), and in the collection of the Earl of Crawford and Balcarres (c.1759–60, Hayes, 1982, nos. 78 and 74). See also Gainsborough's landscape drawings of the early 1760's (cats. A6, A7).

A9 *Study of a thistle and a bank*

Pencil, 5⅜×6⅛ (13.7×15.6)

Prov: From the sketchbook purchased by Richard Payne Knight at the Gainsborough sale, Christie's, 11th May 1799 (85); bequeathed 1824.

Lit: Hayes, 1970, cat. 135 and pl. 30.

The Trustees of the British Museum, 0.0.2-1

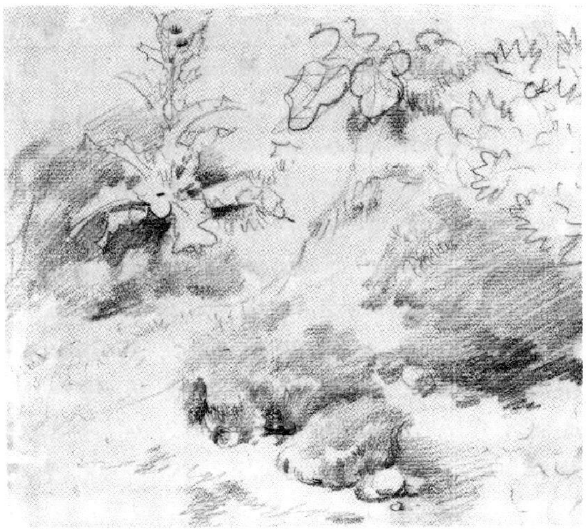

This study of a thistle was probably sketched by Gainsborough in the early to mid-1750's, while he was still living in Suffolk. Although it is considerably earlier in date than *Countess Howe*, and is not directly related to it, this is the only sketch of this type of plant by Gainsborough to have survived. It is therefore included in the exhibition to illustrate the way in which Gainsborough's detailed studies from nature enabled him to give life to the plant forms in his finished paintings.

Gainsborough frequently sketched from nature during his Suffolk years. The majority of his studies, in pencil or chalk, are of trees, but a number of highly sensitive plant studies survive from this period, notably the lovely *Burdock Leaves* in the British Museum. In these, as Millar has observed[1], Gainsborough was influenced by Van Dyck, whose brilliant *ad vivum* plant studies share the same strong feeling for natural growth. Hayes has shown that, contrary to what is often suggested, Gainsborough continued to sketch from nature when he moved to Bath. Indeed, Ozias Humphry, writing in 1763, the year before *Countess Howe* was painted, mentions accompanying Gainsborough on his afternoon rides on horseback to visit the 'circumjacent scenery', and of the sketches and finished drawings which resulted from these expeditions.[2]

Although for Gainsborough sketching was very much an activity in itself, and not simply a quest for motifs to include in his paintings, Hayes points out that he did retain some of his more careful studies by him in the studio, to incorporate into his oil landscapes. This is true, for example, of the study of burdock leaves. Although this practice does not appear to have carried over into his portraits, it seems likely that Gainsborough's carefully precise recording of the thistle in *Countess Howe* has its origins, at least in memory, in a drawing from nature – either a quick record sketch like the one exhibited here, or a more finished drawing similar in type to the burdock leaves or the *Study of Mallows* (Hayes, cat. 177).

If Gainsborough was profoundly influenced by Van Dyck's sketches from nature, he was also indebted to him for the inclusion of plant forms in the foregrounds of his full-length portraits (see p 23). The thistle which just brushes Countess Howe's skirt derives, in compositional terms, from the spreading plants which occupy the foregrounds of Van Dyck's full-length male portraits of his later English period, for example *Lord George Stuart, Seigneur d'Aubigny*, in which Van Dyck even provides a precedent for the thistle shown here.

Gainsborough's early Bath years are characterised by a clarity of form which informs every detail of his paintings (see p 24). This is apparent in his depiction of the thistle in *Countess Howe*, which is very different from the more generalised plant forms which inhabit his later portraits.

1 Millar, 1982/3, p.115.
2 Hayes, pp.28–29.

After THOMAS GAINSBOROUGH

A10 ***Landscape***

Soft ground etching by J. Laporte, 1803
7½×10½ (19.2×26.7), image size.

Witt Print Collection, Courtauld Institute of Art

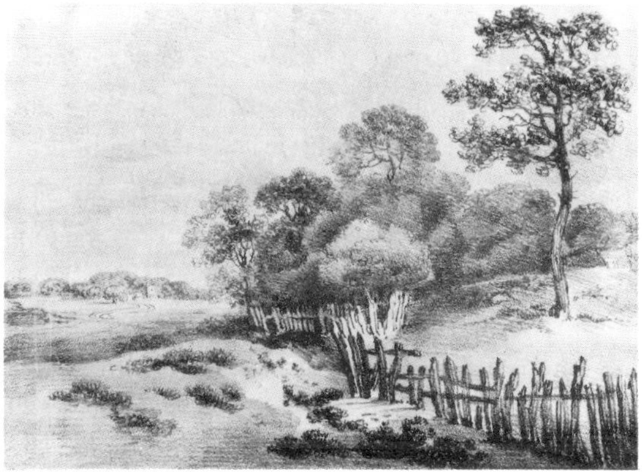

This etching by Laporte is included in the exhibition as an example of the same type of fence shown behind the sitter in *Countess Howe*. In the portrait, this is used to demarcate the boundary of the man-made park in which Lady Howe stands; inside are the herd of deer and clumps of planted trees, while more mountainous scenery can be glimpsed beyond.

Fences were a popular motif with Gainsborough, who, from his Suffolk period onwards, frequently included them in his paintings and drawings. His *Study of an Old Hurdle* of the mid to late 1750's, (Courtauld Institute of Art, Witt collection, no. 3884), suggests where the appeal lay – in the highly picturesque qualities suggested both by the rather ragged shapes, and by the hint of decay.

SIR ANTHONY VAN DYCK

A11 ***Elizabeth Howard, Countess of Peterborough***

Canvas, 91×49¼ (231.1×125.1); includes additions of 4 (10.2) at top and of 2 (5.1) at bottom

Prov: By descent at Drayton.

Exh: Van Dyck in England, *National Portrait Gallery, London, 1982/3 (34).*

Lit: As above.

L. G. Stopford Sackville

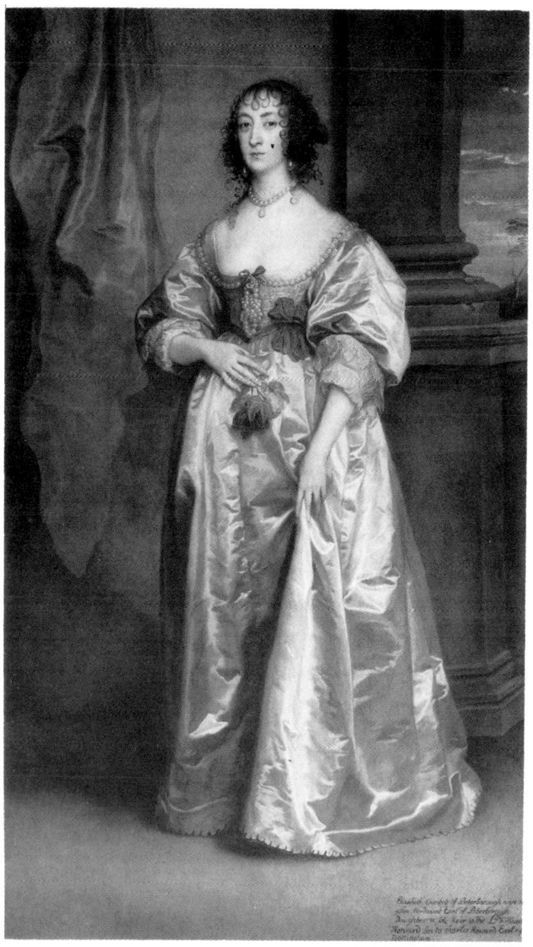

Countess Howe, as John Hayes has remarked,[1] represents Gainsborough's personal transmutation of the qualities of Van Dyck, who could offer a whole repertory of poses and settings for Gainsborough, as he embarked on his full-length portraits of the 1760's. It was undoubtedly Van Dyck's presentation of a female sitter, whole length, against a back-drop of a terrace, or even in the open air (as in *Anne, Countess of Clanbrassil* in the Frick collection) which led Gainsborough to suddenly 'come of age', and produce from 1760-64 his first three great full-length portraits of women, *Mrs. Thicknesse, Lady Alston* and *Countess Howe*. These represent a remarkable change in scale from his earlier work. The *Countess of Peterborough* was painted around 1636-9 towards the end of Van Dyck's life, when, during his second stay in England from 1632, he had evolved the perfect formula for his presentation of the Caroline court. As one might expect, it is these portraits of his second English period with which *Countess Howe* has most in common; these were the paintings which Gainsborough now saw on the walls of English country house collections near Bath, and it is worth noting that there was a version of this portrait at nearby Wilton, which Gainsborough is known to have visited in 1764.

In *Countess Howe* Gainsborough adopts the same type of frontal pose which Van Dyck has used in his portrait of Lady Peterborough. However, his study of Van Dyck went far beyond compositional arrangements. He even looked at details such as the way in which Lady Peterborough's hand, lifting the folds of her dress, creates, as Millar has commented, a subtle sense of movement[2]. In *Countess Howe* Gainsborough takes this a stage further by showing her actually gathering up her apron; in Van Dyck such movement remains implied. It may be only coincidence that the hooded eyes, arched eyebrows and long noses found in Van Dyck portraits such as this one come so close to the features in *Countess Howe,* despite the fact that Lady Peterborough's hair-style, with the curls falling in tendrils over the forehead and cheeks, would have been antithetical to the mid-18th century, when it was *de rigueur* to sweep the hair completely off the face. However, it is surely likely that it was the study of Van Dyck's smooth flesh tones which led Gainsborough, from the beginning of his Bath period, to abandon the rougher, textured brushstrokes of his Ipswich paintings (fig. 5). Lady Peterborough, a renowned beauty, was also a formidable woman of Republican sympathies. Gainsborough, too, has shown in *Countess Howe* how equal he was to the challenge of painting a woman of similarly forceful character.

Like Van Dyck himself, but unlike the 18th century imitators of 'Van Dyck' dress (cat. A13), Gainsborough portrays his sitters in the height of contemporary fashion. Few other artists have painted glossy satins, floating silks, cascades of lace and strings of pearls with such conviction, so that the different materials shimmer and crease in their hands. The muted colours, too, are a response to Van Dyck; Mrs. Thicknesse, like Lady Peterborough, is dressed in white, while Countess Howe's rose pink silk, a popular fabric of the day (see also cat. A19) is relished for its pastel qualities.

Lady Peterborough's dress is fashionable both in fabric and cut: a lustrous white satin with a low lace-edged neckline, and the softly ballooning sleeves of the 1630's edged with what is probably fine Flemish bobbin lace. The hem of the dress is scallopped, a detail which incorporated the fashionable notion of the 'antique' as well as being part of the vogue for the decorative cutting (pinking) of silk; this can also be seen in 18th century women's costumes like *Countess Howe.* The pearls, favoured also by Gainsborough, serve to flatter the complexion both of face and bosom. A large pearl chain is draped over Lady Peterborough's shoulders, with a great twisted bunch of pearls at the centre front of her bodice, topped with a diamond fastened with a ribbon bow. This delightful touch appears in a number of portraits by Van Dyck.[3]

1 Gainsborough, 1980, p.106.
2 Millar, loc.cit.
3 For example, the portrait of *Henrietta Maria* in the National Portrait Gallery, after Van Dyck.

After SIR ANTHONY VAN DYCK, 1599-1641

A12 *Lady Anne Carr, Countess of Bedford*

Line engraving in reverse by P. Lombart, 12½×9⅜ (31.7×23.8)

The Trustees of the British Museum, 1868-8-22-842

The original of this engraving is Van Dyck's portrait of the *Countess of Bedford* at Petworth; with its cerulean blue drapery, this is one of the most magical of the artist's works.[1] The composition includes a classic Van Dyck conceit, later copied by Gainsborough; the plain kid glove, held in the sitter's hand and almost slipping off the end of her fingers. The arrangement allowed Van Dyck to contrast the wrinkled surface of the kid with the paler, smoother, flesh tones, and this was evidently a challenge he enjoyed. In *Countess Howe,* Gainsborough similarly paid great attention to his sitter's left hand and gloves, finally arriving at a solution whereby the Countess allows the sketchily painted right glove to dangle loosely from her gloved left hand. It is tempting to

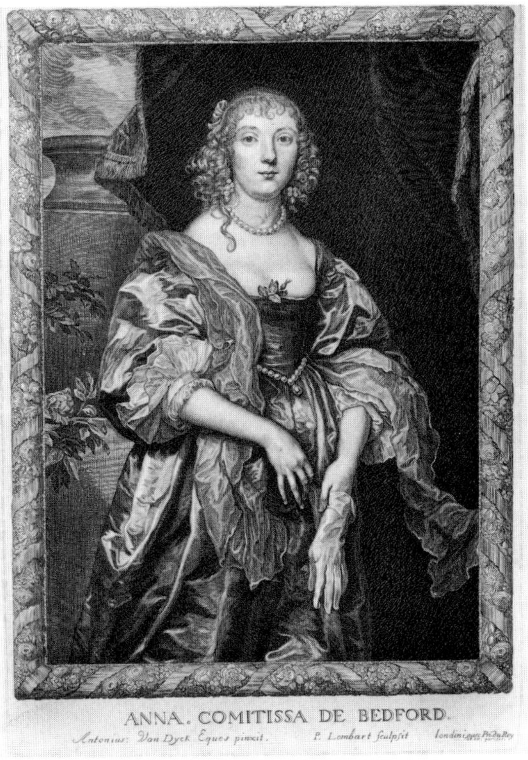

see in this touch of pure Van Dyck a deliberate reference to the source of the portrait as a whole.

A Van Dyck portrait such as the *Countess of Bedford* would have held further, and less obvious, lessons for Gainsborough. As Millar has commented, this is a picture in which the 'subtle sense of movement is enhanced by the flutter of the scarf. . . the stirring of the curtain and the trembling of the rose-bush.[2] Gainsborough's ability to capture such effects, essential if an outdoor portrait is to convey a convincing sense of reality, is above all what sets him apart from the earlier generation of portraitists led by Thomas Hudson.

The Countess of Bedford's dress is of satin, the fashionable silk of the 1630's, with the wide squashy sleeves of that decade. It is an example of the concept of 'generalising' the costume which Van Dyck promoted during the 1630's, partly owing to pressures of work, and partly to a preference for relatively simple styles of dress. For example, the very low décolletage, which is somewhat risqué even for a sophisticated court lady, is created by his omission of the neck frill of the shift. According to William Sanderson, Van Dyck was the first painter 'that e're put Ladies dresse into a careless Romance'.[3] A touch of the romantic or pastoral appears here in the short scalloped sleeve, which is vaguely 'medieval' or quasi-Roman in origin, while a touch of fashionable *déshabillé* – Herrick's 'delight in disorder' – is provided by the floating light gauze mantle. Pearls were *de rigueur* for fashionable beauties. The pearl necklace would probably have belonged to the sitter, but the artist has possibly gilded the lily with regard to the uneven bunches of pearls as earrings, and the pearl girdle; we read in the Verney Correspondence that the Countess of Sussex noted that Van Dyck had given her, in her portrait, more pearls than she possessed.

1 As Millar points out, *Van Dyck in England,* 1982/3, p. 83.
2 Ibid.
3 *Graphice,* 1658.

After SIR PETER PAUL RUBENS

A13 *Rubens's wife*

Mezzotint by James McArdell, after 1746, 13⅜×9⅞ (34.0×25.1)

The Trustees of the British Museum, 1902-10-11-3263

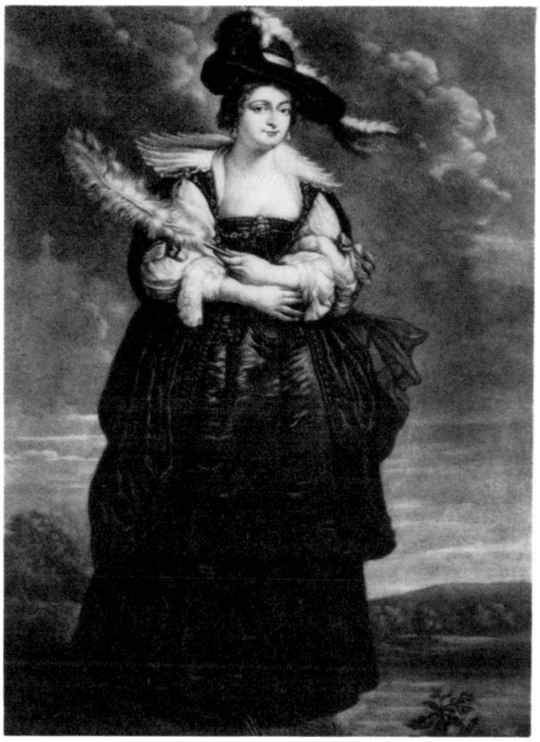

The Rubens portrait (now in the Gulbenkian Museum, Lisbon), from which this mezzotint was taken, had a seminal influence on British portraiture from the moment, in about 1730, when it entered the collection of Sir Robert Walpole. Although today it is thought to represent Rubens's sister-in-law, Susanna Fourment, in the 18th century the portrait went under the title of 'Rubens's wife', and was often ascribed to Van Dyck.[1] In this guise it became the ancestor of the almost countless English portraits of the 1720's onwards which portray sitters, similarly posed, in 'Van Dyke' dress. This fanciful costume was reserved only for that most popular form of all 18th century diversions, the masquerade[2] – and for portrait painting. As early as 1723 Vertue noted that some artists were painting 'the habits of the Time of Van dyke and Rubens',[3] but the popularity of the costume was at its height during the 1740's, due mainly to the work of the drapery painter Joseph van Aken; studies attributed to him in the National Gallery of Scotland show various interpretations of this dress and pose, which consequently appear in the work of artists such as Thomas Hudson and Allan Ramsay. The costume shown in such portraits could be either real fancy dress, as, for example, in Thomas Hudson's *Mary Panton, Duchess of Ancaster* (1757), or simply be part of the English mania for appearing in historical costume in portraiture, which was encouraged – or promoted – by a considerable number of artists.

McArdell's engraving shows a gown with looped-up overskirt, open sleeves tied with ribbon over the full, white shift sleeves, and a slightly raised lace-edged collar. The hat is fastened up to one side and decorated with ostrich feathers; the sitter carries an ostrich feather fan. A large jewel is pinned at the centre front of her bodice, from which a jewelled chain is draped over one shoulder and down the other side of the breast; the touch of asymmetry (as with the hat pinned to one side) is an essential part of baroque costume. It is worth noting that the original painting by Rubens shows fashionable costume of the early 1630's with pastoral elements (the feathered hat, the kilted-up skirt, and the gauzy ribboned sleeves). This may partly explain its appeal to the 18th century.

Gainsborough had certainly looked closely at Van Dyck in the original, as *Countess Howe* clearly shows. However, he must also have been aware of this famous Rubens image, either in McArdell's well-known print or in one of the many copies from the original made by English artists of the generation slightly older than himself. Unlike some of the later Gainsborough portraits inspired by Van Dyck (for example *Mrs Graham* in the National Gallery of Scotland) *Countess Howe* does not, of course, make use of 'Van Dyck' dress. Nevertheless, this print after Rubens might have helped Gainsborough, as he began to develop his new full-length portraits, in one very important respect. Unlike comparable portraits by Van Dyck, 'Rubens's Wife' stands silhouetted full-length against a background of sky, trees, plants and distant hills, unfettered by any man-made structures such as the terraces from which Van Dyck only rarely broke away. The freedom which this offered to the portraitist was surely not lost on Gainsborough when he came to devise his own standing out-door portraits of women in the 1760's.

1 'A celebrated Picture of Rubens's wife', by Van Dyck, *Aedes Walpolianae*, 1747, p. 61.
2 See C. Fox and A. Ribeiro, *Masquerade*, Museum of London, 1983 and A. Ribeiro, *The Dress worn at Masquerades in England 1730–1790, and its Relation to Fancy Dress in Portraiture*, 1984.
3 Vertue, III, p. 15.

After THOMAS HUDSON, 1701-1779

A14 *Miss Mary Carew*

Line engraving by James Lovelace, 1744, 13⅞×11 (35.2×27.9)

Lit: Miles, 1979 (10).

The Trustees of the British Museum, 1860-8-8-1405

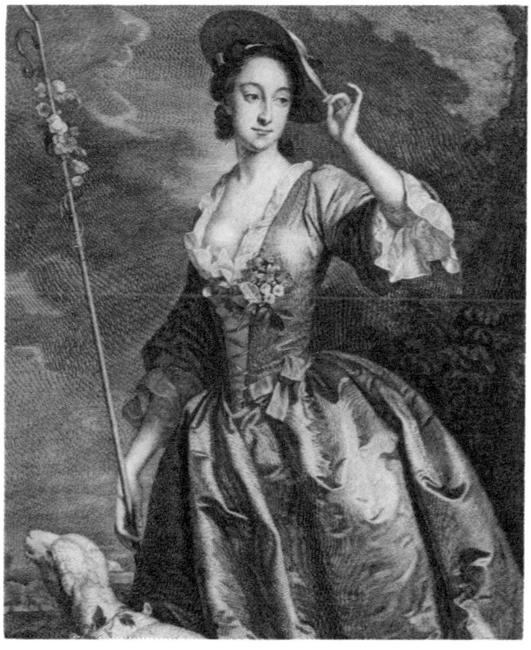

The pastoral theme was a popular one in English art and literature from at least the early 17th century onwards. It became almost a commonplace in English portraiture to portray ladies as shepherdesses – a flattering allusion to their youth and beauty and often, also, to their impending marriage. Thomas Hudson's portrait of Mary Carew was painted around 1741. A standard portrayal of the theme, complete with lambs and shepherdess's crook (properly an houlette), it conforms to a pattern laid down by Van Dyck, and then popularised by Lely, Wissing, James Maubert and many others. Although Miss Carew's dress contains pastoral elements, notably the flowers and the straw hat, it is basically in the style of the 1740's, with firmly boned, straight bodice and wide hoops. The lacing down the front of the bodice, and the ribbon at the waist, however, echo the styles of the 1630's; the costume is thus a happy marriage of the historical with the Arcadian. The hat, comparable to the one worn by Countess Howe, is both fashionable and suitable for a shepherdess.

The Arcadian theme was an obvious – some would say hackneyed – theme for 18th century masquerades in the pleasure gardens of London.[1] Harriet Byron, the heroine of Samuel Richardson's novel *Sir Charles Grandison* (1753–4) goes to a masquerade in the dress of an 'Arcadian princess'; rather like Miss Carew's, and somewhat to her disapproval ('they wore not hoops in Arcadia'), this was based on fashionable costume with the hooped petticoat of the mid-18th century.

Hudson's pastoral portrait – one of only two he is known to have painted – undoubtedly influenced his pupil, Reynolds, in portraits of the early to mid-1760's like *Anne Dashwood* and Kenwood's own *Lady Mary Leslie*. Its influence, or that of portraits like it, on Gainsborough, is less clear-cut, but in creating a new type of image of a sitter in an outdoor setting, as in *Countess Howe*, Gainsborough must surely have been aware of this long-standing tradition in British art.

1 See A. Ribeiro, 'Fashionable Rural Masquerades', *Antique Collector*, September 1983, which also reproduces this engraving.

Attributed to HENRY PICKERING, act. 1740–c.1771

A15 *'Eleanor Frances Dixie'*, *(Col. pl. 1)*

Canvas, 48×39 (121.9×99)

Prov: Henry Jacoby.

Lit: Aileen Ribeiro, A Visual History of Costume. The Eighteenth Century, *1983.*

Nottingham Castle Museum and Art Gallery

Henry Pickering belongs to the generation of portraitists, like Thomas Hudson, who rose to prominence in the 1740's. Although the clean-cut ouhe figure against the background, the rather flat contours, and the somewhat impassive face, are all still characteristic of that decade, the painting looks foward to *Countess Howe* in a number of respects, particularly in the costume.

The portrait has the almost photographic attention to detail, so helpful to costume historians, which often marks the provincial artist; although based in London in the 1740's, Pickering seems to have worked during the 1750's in Yorkshire, Lancashire, C,an-cut ouheshire and North Wales. Compared to the plain silk of Lady Howe's gown, the beauty of which lies in the colour and the play of light on the taffeta, Eleanor Dixie's dress appeals to the eye through the rendering of the exquisite patterned silk, probably a Spitalfields brocade. Within a lattice-work design there are flowers woven with the detail of a fine botanical drawing (a characteristic of Spitalfields silk designers of the mid-18th century), and the silvery silk is further enhanced on the petticoat with what appears to be blonde lace.

The dress is a *sacque* with increasingly regimented back drapery; the loose folds of earlier versions of this kind of dress have given way to formal pleats. In the 1750's the line of the bodice is long, and – as we read in Henry Fielding's novel *Amelia* (1751) – 'no woman can be genteel who is not entirely flat in front'. Like Lady Howe, Miss Dixie wears a be-ribboned Leghorn hat over a white under-cap; the forward tilt is characteristic of the mid to late 1750's. While in the Gainsborough portrait the gloves are almost lost behind the folds of the dress, here they play a prominent part as the sitter is caught in the act of putting them on. In Pickering's portrait, as in Gainsborough's, the motif must derive ultimately from Van Dyck, and it is interesting to note that the artist treats the gloves with a rich, and uncharacteristic, buttery impasto.

If the striking similarity in the costume, notably the hat and gloves, links the two paintings visually, Pickering's portrait also anticipates Gainsborough in the outdoor setting – which here consists of an unpretentious view of English agricultural scenery – and in the way in which he has turned his figure half towards us; both artists evidently found difficulty in rendering the perspective of the side of the sitter turned away from the spectator, and Gainsborough's canvas shows a number of second thoughts in this area.

Something of a question mark hangs over the sitter's identity. She has long been thought to be Eleanor Frances Dixie (1746–1823), daughter of Sir Wolstan Dixie (4th Bt.) of Bosworth House, and his second wife, Theodosia. However, the costume can be dated to the years around 1750–55, and the silks to 1746–53, so it would be reasonable to date the picture to around 1750–53, when Eleanor Dixie would have been still a child. It seems more likely that the sitter is instead an elder sister or alternatively Eleanor Dixie's mother, Theodosia (d. 1751), or her successor, the 3rd Lady Dixie, who married Sir Wolstan in 1753.[1]

1 We are grateful to Neil Walker of the Castle Museum for this information.

ARTHUR DEVIS, c1711-1787

A16 Alicia and Jane Clarke

Canvas, 36×28 (91.4×71.1)

Signed: Art^r Devis fe

Prov: by descent in the Clarke family to private collector; sale, Sotheby's July 6th, 1977 (12), bt. Thomas Agnew & Son; Richard Thune, Connecticut; private collection.

Exh: D'Oench, 1980 (35). Polite Society by Arthur Devis, *Harris Museum & Art Gallery, Preston, 1983 (45).*

Private collection

Arthur Devis painted this portrait of the two daughters of Richard Clarke of Walford Court, Ross-on-Wye, in c.1757-60, just a few years before Gainsborough embarked on *Countess Howe*. His painting, one of the masterpieces of his later style, is the quintessence of the English conversation piece, with its portrayal of 'small figures from the life in their habits and dress of the Times, well dispos'd gracefull and naturall'.[1] By contrast, Gainsborough's portrait is an essay in the grand manner of Van Dyck. Despite the fact that they belong to very different traditions in English portraiture, the two portraits

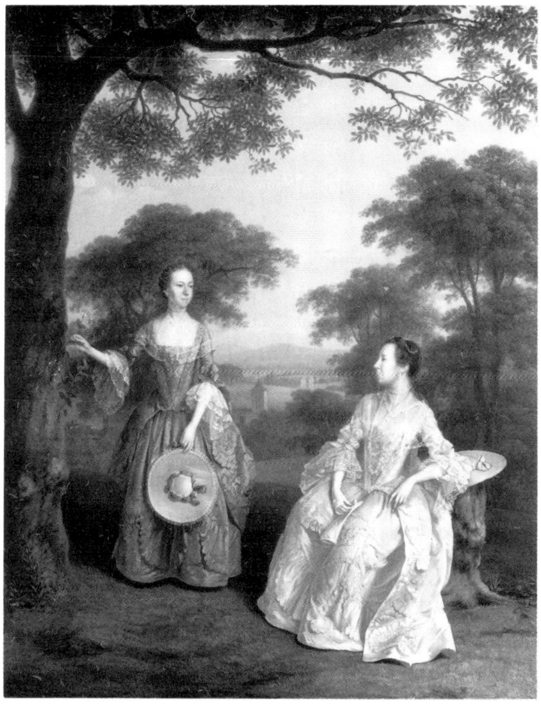

have, however, a number of features in common.

Devis's two sitters are conceived on a larger scale in relation to their setting than is usual in his work, and achieve, as a result, a small-scale monumentality which is perhaps a response to the new generation of portraitists led by Reynolds and Gainsborough. Devis had never been affected more than fleetingly by the English rococo, and the Clarke sisters have none of the quirky angularity and engaging informality which make conversation pieces like Gainsborough's own *Mr. and Mrs. Andrews* so delightful. Instead, they share with *Countess Howe* an emphasis on elegance and grace of deportment, preserving, as does Gainsborough's sitter, a certain distance from the spectator and, indeed, from each other. The broadly classical arrangement of the figures, who are presented nearly face on and rather formally, is repeated in the landscape setting, which makes use of a simple criss-cross pattern of verticals and horizontals in its balancing of tree masses and firm horizon line. A feature common to both portraits is the way in which the strong vertical accent of the foreground tree is used to echo the pose of the standing figure.

To turn to *Countess Howe* after looking at a portrait such as this, which makes use of many of the same ingredients in the setting of figures within a landscape, is to understand the breath-taking sophistication which Gainsborough brings to his task; the difference between the two paintings is essentially that between poetry and prose. It is worth remembering that Gainsborough had himself been a practitioner of the conversation piece earlier in his career, and it may be that paintings of this kind, which combine fashionably dressed sitters with a naturalistic setting, played some part in the formulation of *Countess Howe*, despite the fact that Gainsborough evidently saw it first and foremost as an essay in the manner of Van Dyck (see also p23). Whatever the case, *Countess Howe* emerges on canvas fully fledged, a brilliant combination of Van Dyckian splendour with a naturalism that had been for so long the preserve of the conversation piece, but that now began to appear in large-scale portraiture as well. The challenge of the new generation of portraitists would eventually prove too much for Devis, and his practice declined in the 1760's and 1770's.

Like Gainsborough, Devis was a faithful reflector of contemporary fashion, although he often seems to have difficulty in making his ladies, in their fashionable French-influenced finery, look anything but self-conscious as they pose in their pretty ruffled silks in the English countryside. Both sisters wear the same type of dress (probably a *sacque*), one in blue and one in pink, with straw hats like Lady Howe's trimmed with matching ribbons. For much of the 18th century (at least until the last quarter) there were not many varieties of dress in the fashionable female wardrobe. Uniformity was a desired ideal, although differences in decoration could add variety to a few basic styles (it is important to avoid falling into the trap of assuming that a studio model is being used when one sees a similar dress worn by more than one sitter). Here, both dresses are formal open robes, with pinned-in stomacher front; they have the long bodice of the 1750's, meeting at a point, and then opening out to reveal a flounced skirt. Both are decorated in the rococo style with curving ribbon robings on the gown, and large scallopped furbelows on the skirt. Although the dresses are virtually identical in style, there are slight differences in the way they are worn and in their accessories. Alicia Clarke, on the left, has looped up the skirt of her gown, and the sisters' fine fichus (probably of silk) are slightly different in pattern. Both ladies wear the ubiquitous pearls, but Jane Clarke has a touch of individuality about her costume, in the choice of mittens made of cream-coloured silk or fine kid.

1 Vertue, III, p. 81.

PAUL SANDBY, 1730–1809

A17 *A Lady Standing, c.1755*

Pencil, 4⅞×2⅞ (12.3×7.4)

Lit: A.P, Oppé, The Drawings of Thomas and Paul Sandby at Windsor, *1947, p. 71 (293).*

Lent by Gracious Permission of Her Majesty The Queen

This tiny but highly finished drawing of a lady out walking, dressed in the height of contemporary fashion, is probably a study for the principal figure in Paul Sandby's *View of the North Side of Virginia Water*, one of a series of prints of the pleasure gardens in Windsor Great Park which he produced in 1754. As a study which was intended to enliven a topographical engraving, it is poles removed from Gainsborough's conscious emulation of Van Dyck's grand manner in portraiture in *Countess Howe*. However, Sandby, like Hollar before him, was a fashion artist manqué and the costume depicted here has a number of features in common with that worn by Countess Howe.

The costume consists of an open robe, tight-fitting in the English style, like Countess Howe's, the crisp silk matches that of the petticoat. The skirt is allowed to trail on the ground, a fashionable fad of the mid-to-late 1750's which may derive from the abandonment of hoops, causing a surplus of material to form a train at the back and sides; the fashion was condemned as wasteful and unhygienic by many commentators such as Oliver Goldsmith, but its appeal lay in the element of conspicuous consumption which is such a crucial feature of fashion. The edge of the skirt of the gown is trimmed similarly to Countess Howe's with curving, pleated ribbon, which also forms a horizontal band across the hem of the petticoat. The artist has meticulously depicted the large flounce on the petticoat, and the way it comes

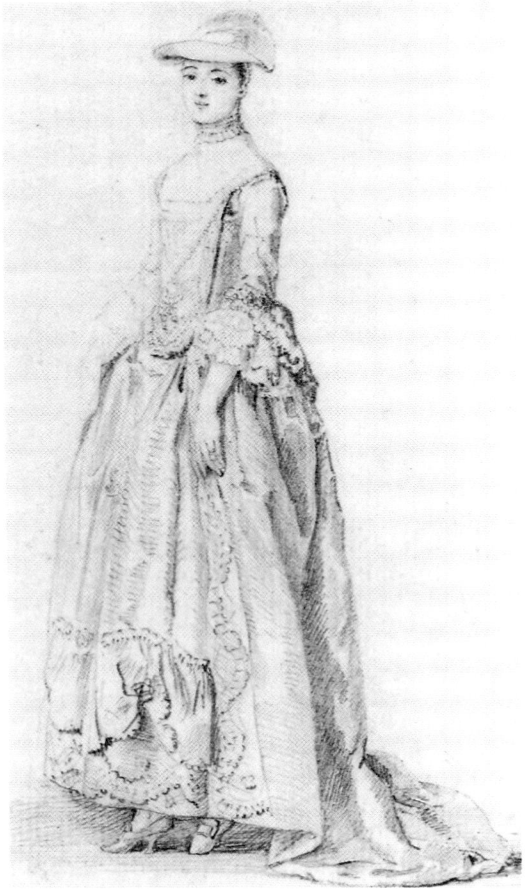

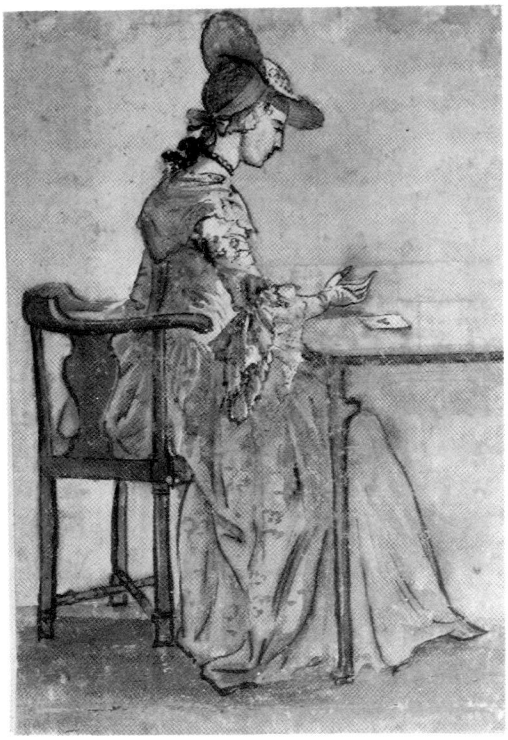

to an end as it meets the robings of the gown; such flounces only decorated the front of the petticoat where they would be visible. The drawing also demonstrates a different way of wearing the fashionable straw hat worn by Countess Howe; here it is turned up in the front and at the back in a style popular in the 1750's.

Sandby is better known as a topographical draughtsman. However, the delightful group of informal figure studies in the Royal Collection which he produced in the 1750's, many of them humourous in tone, place him in the forefront of English rococo portrait drawing, as practised by Gravelot, Mercier and Gainsborough, and reveal his ambition to succeed as a figure and portrait draughtsman. His study of *Two ladies walking a high wind* is an enchanting English equivalent to the delights and refinements of Watteau.[1]

1 Oppé, p. 13.

A18 *Lady Betty Harcourt, c. 1760*

Pen and ink and colour, 7½ × 5¼ (19·1×13·4)

Prov: Christie's, 24.3.1959.

Photograph exhibited

In this informal study by Paul Sandby, Lady Betty Harcourt wears a costume very close in style and feeling to Lady Howe's. Sandby's drawing has the added advantage that we can see what Countess Howe's costume would have looked like from the back. Thus, as the sitter turns slightly away from us, we can see the shape of the fitted English nightgown with its flat, sewn-down pleats at the back of the bodice, and the tiny pleats at the waist, which create the fashionable side fullness and bounce then in vogue. We can also get some idea of how Lady Howe's hat fastens at the back by means of ribbon tied at the nape of the neck over the small net or lace cap. The pearl necklace is fastened, like Lady Howe's, with a ribbon bow behind. With a gown of this kind it was usual to wear an apron, as Lady Betty does here. Her fichu and sleeve ruffles could be either of lace or embroidered muslin, although silk was also popular; a surviving bill in the Bodleian Library dated 14th February 1759 shows that Lady Betty purchased from the fashionable haberdasher, Spilsbury, in Covent Garden (cat. B9), gauze ruffles trimmed with blonde lace. It is pleasant to imagine Lady Howe making a similar purchase of her own magnificent treble ruffles.

ALLAN RAMSAY, 1713–1784

A19 *Lady Mary Scott*

Canvas, 40×30 (101.6×76.2)

Prov: By descent in the family of the sitter's brother, the 7th Earl of Northampton.

Exh: Paintings and Drawings by Allan Ramsay, *Royal Academy, 1964 (46).*

The Marquess of Northampton

Lady Mary Scott belongs to the series of enchanting and informal portraits of women which Ramsay painted in the years following his return to London from a second visit to Italy in 1757. Born in 1713, Ramsay was the leading portraitist in London from 1738 until the arrival of Reynolds, fresh from his own Italian visit in 1753, challenged his supremacy. Ramsay's response was to turn his back on the grand effects of Reynolds (cat. A24), soon to be taken up (at least as regards the full-length format) also by Gainsborough. Instead, he concentrated on intimate half or three-quarter length portraits of women, a format which suited him perfectly.

There can be few more unaffected portraits in the whole of British art than *Lady Mary Scott,* which was probably painted in 1762, a year or two before Gainsborough's *Countess Howe*. The sitter is seated so naturally at one corner of a sofa, arms lightly folded,

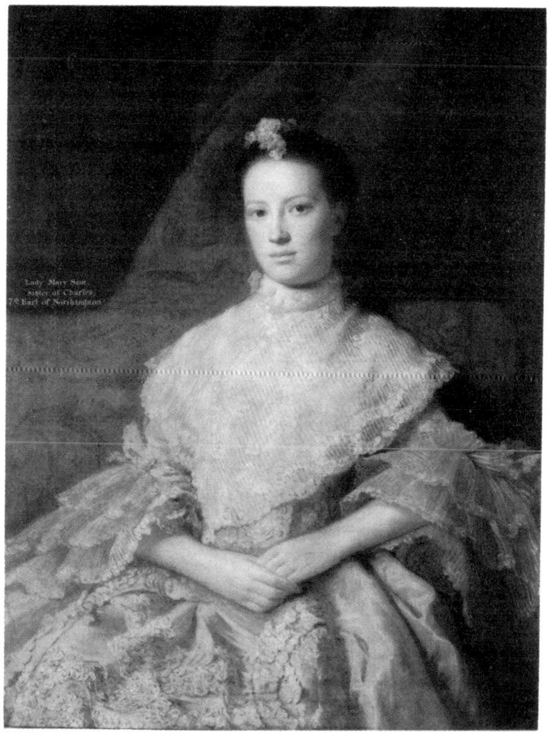

and her contact with the spectator is so immediate, that she might almost be posing for a photograph. Such directness and informality, together with the extreme elegance and simplicity of line, is unique in English portraiture at this period, and Ramsay's work is often compared with French rococo artists such as Nattier or Perroneau. However, although he studied at the French Academy in Rome, Ramsay may well have arrived at his own version of the English rococo portrait quite independently. And behind the apparent simplicity of images such as *Lady Mary Scott* lies the classical tradition of Italian 17th century painting, notably the work of Domenichino, which we know Ramsay deeply admired.

A particular feature of Ramsay's late work is the exquisitely detailed attention which he lavished on his sitters' costume. Soon after the death of Joseph Van Aken in 1749 he gave up his reliance on drapery painters, and much of the charm of paintings such as this, or the famous portrait of his second wife, *Margaret Lindsay*, in the National Gallery of Scotland, lies in Ramsay's use of carefully controlled and largely pastel colours, and his subtle differentiation of the different textures of lace, ruching or silk. In this preoccupation with materials Ramsay comes close to Gainsborough, although the methods they use to achieve their effects are very different. Whereas in *Countess Howe* Gainsborough conjures up his costume in a series of freely painted brush strokes, with loose troughs or zig-zags of shadow painted in on top, Ramsay's brush work is more controlled and refined, careful, but never in the least pedantic.

Like Countess Howe, Lady Mary Scott wears a gown of pastel pink silk, although her dress is very French in its delicacy and exquisite trimmings. The sides of the open gown are decorated with curving robings, and the skirt with silk fly fringe, a sort of braid made of silk cord with knots and bunches of floss silk. The costume is dominated by the vast ruffles (engageantes) which are possibly of fine striped lawn or silk edged with lace; the same material is used for the fichu crossed over her bosom. Lady Mary's necklace is of ruched silk, echoing the tiny flower headdress pinned in her hair. Such headdresses (called *pompons* after Madame de Pompadour) could be of flowers, jewels or feathers. Hogarth in his *Analysis of Beauty* (1753) notes that women of the best taste prefer 'a single feather, flower or jewel. . . on one side of the head';[1] in the 1760's Lady Sarah Lennox wrote to a friend: 'You must wear no cap, and only little, little flowers'.[2] Of all the colours seen in portraiture in the middle decades of the 18th century, shades of pink seem the most popular. Ramsay, in particular – aptly described by Horace Walpole in 1759 as 'formed to paint women' – was fond of the colour, which flattered the fair skins of northern European women. Two further examples are the deep pink worn by his second wife c. 1758, and by *Mrs Bruce of Arnot* (1765, National Gallery of Scotland).

Looking at the two portraits of *Lady Mary Scott* and *Countess Howe*, no-one could doubt that they date to almost exactly the same moment in British art. Apart from the obvious similarities of costume, the portrayal of the smoothly textured heads is almost identical; whereas Gainsborough, however, decided, as the 1760's began, to adopt a Van Dyckian grand manner, and so to enter the lists against Reynolds, Ramsay largely retired from competition, developing instead his own version of the English rococo and creating, as he did so, some of the most serenely lovely images in the whole of British art.

1 W. Hogarth, *The Analysis of Beauty*, 1753, ed. J. Burke, Oxford, 1955.
2 *Life and Letters of Lady Sarah Lennox*, ed. Countess of Ilchester & Lord Stavordale, London, 1901, I, p.177.

A20 *Study for Lady Louisa Connolly, 1759*

Black and white chalk on grey paper, 20×12⅛ (50.8×30.7)

Prov: David Laing; Royal Scottish Academy; transferred to the National Gallery of Scotland, 1910.

Exh: Paintings and Drawings by Allan Ramsay, 1713–1784, *Royal Academy of Arts, 1964 (114).*

Lit: Alastair Smart, The Life and Art of Allan Ramsay, *1952 (pp 84, 106, 109, 191, 193; drawing 109n).*

National Galleries of Scotland (D258, recto)

Allan Ramsay's portrait of *Lady Louisa Connolly*, for which this is a preparatory study, was painted in 1759, shortly after Ramsay's return from his second Italian visit (1754–7). It is one of his few attempts at the grand manner; shortly afterwards he gave up the production of full-length portraits in favour of the smaller-scale, more intimate studies of women which dominate his output in the 1760's (cat. A19).

Lady Louisa Connolly, however, is a pioneering contribution to the renewed vogue for full-length outdoor portraits of women which really began in this year (1759). The use of an outdoor setting for such large-scale canvases had never entirely gone out of fashion in England since it was popularised by Van Dyck. Kneller, Richardson, and later Thomas Hudson, were among the artists to make occasional use of it. In 1752–3 Gavin Hamilton effectively re-introduced the vogue to a new generation of artists in his remarkable portrait of the *Duchess of Hamilton* which, already fully neo-classical in style, was several years ahead of its time. Ramsay's treatment of the theme, however, coincides with Reynolds's first attempt in this vein, in his own portrait of the *Duchess of Hamilton*, painted in 1758-9. This was the first of Reynolds's long series of full-length portraits in the classical vein, and it has many features in common with Ramsay's design. Gainsborough's own first full-length outdoor portrait, *Lady Alston*, would appear slightly later, in the early years of the new

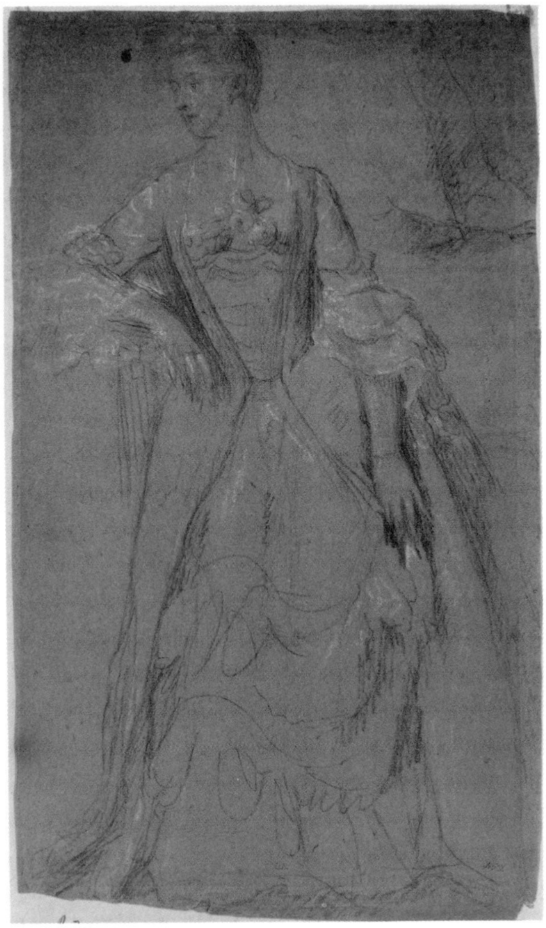

decade, closely followed by *Countess Howe* in c. 1764.

In the finished portrait, Lady Louisa Connolly is placed in a garden setting framed, like Countess Howe, between two groups of trees, and leaning her elbow on a circular pedestal of neo-classical design. The pose is rather more static and conventional than *Countess Howe*, and the portrait has none of the implied movement found in Gainsborough's work; instead there is a rather frozen quality to the pose which, like the prominent neo-classical ornament, may reflect Ramsay's newly awakened interest in the classical past. The slight awkwardness of the sitter's pose in the finished composition suggests that Ramsay was perhaps never entirely happy working in this vein, and as the new decade began he retired from competition, leaving Reynolds, soon to be joined by Gainsborough, in command of the field of full-length portraiture.

In his own careful way, Ramsay pays as much attention as does Gainsborough to the magnificence of his sitter's costume. In the finished canvas, Lady Louisa Connolly is dressed, like Countess Howe, in the height of contemporary fashion, wearing a cinnebar (dark red) dress of rococo design. In the drawing the artist has sketched out the main details and outline of the costume, which he sees as a series of interlocking V-shapes. The gown, for example, has a stomacher bodice – a V-shaped panel pinned between the robings of the dress, and decorated with horizontal lines of ribbon (échelles). The way in which it opens over the skirt forms an inverted V-shape; the artist has left the sides of the gown plain (in the painting there are elaborate undulating robings to the hem), but has indicated with vigorous curves the position of the large pleated flounces on the petticoat.

Ramsay's skill as a draughtsman, acquired, or at least perfected, during his years in Italy, make preliminary studies such as this one, with its strong linear rhythm and bold chalk highlights, a particular delight. Before embarking on a portrait, Ramsay, unlike Gainsborough, would make a preliminary compositional sketch, often with individual studies (for example of the hands) as well. For *Lady Louisa Connolly*, in addition to the present drawing, he produced studies of the right hand, and of the bunch of grapes. These, too, are in the National Gallery of Scotland (nos. 2092, 2093).

After SIR JOSHUA REYNOLDS, 1723-1792
A21 *Mrs. Bonfoy*

Mezzotint by James McArdell, 1755, 13¾×10⅞ (34.9×27.6)

The Trustees of the British Museum, 1830-7-14-44

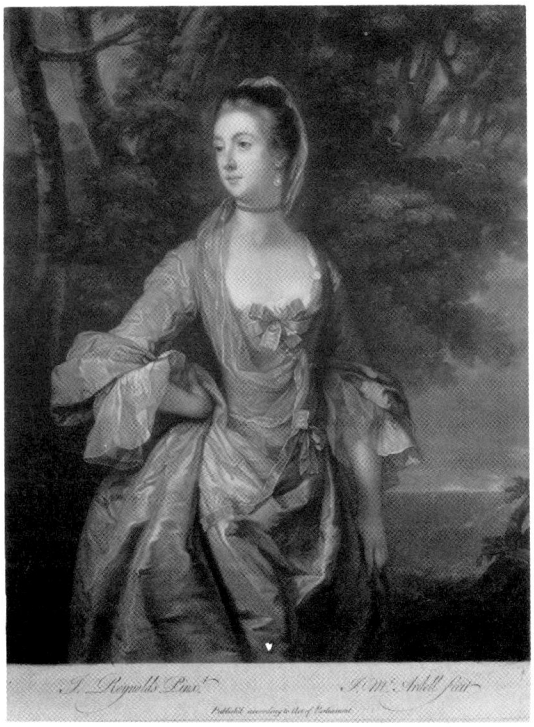

In Reynolds's atmospheric, three-quarter length portraits of the 1750's like *Mrs. Bonfoy,* in which his sitters are still portrayed in more or less contemporary costume, and are placed in an outdoor setting of trees, sea and sky, Reynolds surely anticipated the mood and setting of Gainsborough's much more ambitious full-length outdoor portraits of the 1760's like *Countess Howe*. The two portraits not only share the same rather masculine hand on hip pose. Reynolds, like Gainsborough, has chosen to portray his sitter pausing momentarily as she walks towards us along a wooded shore, hitching up her gown with her hand. Even the slight implied hauteur and assurance of her gaze are distinctly comparable, while for the first time in English portraiture since Van Dyck, there is a blending of sitter and background in terms both of the colouring and of the artist's use of light and shade; together these create an almost romantic sense of mood.

The dramatic hand on hip pose which Reynolds adopted for *Mrs. Bonfoy* derives ultimately from the male portraiture of Van Dyck (fig.6). Reynolds was not the first British 18th century artist to apply this gesture to a female sitter – both Richardson in his *Lady Mary Wortley Montagu* (c.1725) and Allan Ramsay in *The Hon. Rachel Hamilton and her Brother* (1740) had done so before him (see p.23). However, the impact of this boldly assertive pose when applied to the portrait of a woman was evidently not lost on Reynolds, already making a reputation for himself, on his return from Italy two years previously, as an artist of strength and originality. He would virtually repeat the pose, but in reverse, in the lovely *Susanna Beckford* of 1755-6, now in the Tate Gallery, and would also make occasional use of it later in his career, as in the famous *Lady Worsley,* exhibited at the Royal Academy in 1780. One can be reasonably sure that Reynolds judged his use of it in the present portrait to be a success, since this was one of his earliest paintings to be engraved, despite the fact that the sitter, Anne Eliot, was the wife of a naval Captain and not a famous beauty – or courtesan – of the day.

Mrs. Bonfoy is an early experiment by Reynolds in generalizing dress, while keeping the basic lines fashionable. Thus, the long, fairly rigid bodice line is correct for the 1750's, as are the sleeves with their fashionable 'pagoda' cuffs. However, there is no perceptible opening or fastening to the dress; the ribbon at the waist is not convincing; and what happens to the string of pearls as they trail from the ribbon bow at the breast round to the back of the gown? Although Walpole was later (referring to Reynolds's 11th Discourse of 1782) to complain that 'Sir Joshua's draperies represent clothes, never their materials', the artist has, here at least, given us a fashionable silk, possibly a lustring. The portrait is a study in asymmetry; not only does one hand hitch up the skirt in folds at the side, in a pose that has also been noted to follow Van Dyck,[1] but the striped silk scarf falls from the head over one shoulder, and is then caught on the other side of the bodice by that improbable rope of pearls.

1 Reynolds's *Rebecca, Viscountess Folkstone* of 1761 (Earl of Radnor) also makes use of this pose.

After SIR JOSHUA REYNOLDS, 1723-1792
A22 *Nelly O'Brien*

Mezzotint by Charles Phillips, 16¼×13 (41.3×33.0)

The Trustees of the British Museum, 1915-U.-1077

Reynolds's famous portrait of the actress and courtesan *Nelly O'Brien* was probably painted between 1760-62, just before Gainsborough began work on *Countess Howe.* It seems likely that this was the portrait of Nelly exhibited at the Society of Artists in 1763, where Gainsborough may be presumed to have seen it, and Reynolds's combination here of elements from the arcadian or pastoral portrait (cat. A14) with a highly modern image of beauty, arrayed in the height of contemporary fashion, may well have held important lessons for Gainsborough in the year before *Countess Howe.* Both portraits share the same superb sense of balance between the beauty of the sitter, and that of her natural surroundings. A comparison with Gainsborough's earlier portrait of *Lady Alston* (fig 4) shows the ease with which Gainsborough now succeeds in integrating these two aspects of his portrait.

There are of course major differences between the two paintings. In its delightful informality and immediacy, Reynolds's image is the exact opposite of the classicism he deemed appropriate for his full-length portraits (cat. A24); instead it owes much to the more relaxed tradition of French rococo portraiture, whereas Gainsborough has returned in

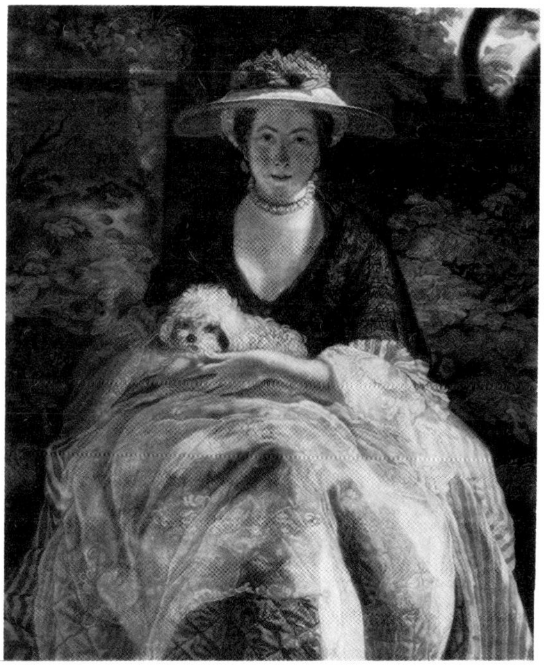

Countess Howe to the grandeur of Van Dyck. One must remember too, that the disparity in the social status of the two sitters would have dictated a different approach for each. It was quite appropriate for Reynolds to show Nelly O'Brien facing the spectator challengingly square-on, looking straight into our eyes. Many of his portraits of actresses and the demi-monde have a delightful directness in consequence of the greater freedom he could employ here. This would not have done for Lady Howe, who, by contrast, is full of dignity and restraint. Reynolds had earlier chosen the same frontal pose for his portrait of another courtesan, *Kitty Fisher,* now at Petworth (1759), but that it was not exclusively reserved for portraits of the demi-monde is shown by its use in the lovely *Lady Caroline Keppel* of 1757/59. What perhaps lends particular enchantment to the present image is Reynolds's combination here of the intimate poses used for these earlier, small-scale portraits with the more ambitious bosky garden setting of *Nelly O'Brien.* The fame of the image made *Nelly O'Brien* a perfect candidate for engraving, although Phillips's mezzotint does scant justice to the original, which is today in the Wallace collection.

The focal point of Nelly O'Brien's costume is the wide expanse of quilted silk which forms the skirt, over which is a fine brocaded silk gauze apron, not unlike that worn by Lady Howe. Quilted skirts were not only practical in the English climate. They also served to give the bulk fashionable in the 1760's – an alternative was to bunch up the overskirt as does *Mrs. Riddell* (cat. A23). In the original portrait, the gown itself is of striped silk, white and green; the same green is picked out in the ribbons of Nelly O'Brien's straw hat, which is worn over a small linen cap, starched or wired to give the effect of wings. The shoulder mantle is of black Chantilly lace; the sleeve ruffles are possibly Brussels. The necklace, unlike Lady Howe's, may be of imitation pearls called French beads; the *Lady's Magazine* (1759) notes that 'a single row of large, round white beads on a black ribband will be found very becoming' (see also cat. A3). The *tout ensemble* is thus a stylish mixture of luxury and simplicity, a mingling of the best taste in dress with touches of individuality, the essence of true chic.

SIR JOSHUA REYNOLDS, 1723-1792

A23 mrs. *Thomas Riddell, 1763* *(col. pl. 4)*

Canvas, 94½×58½ (239×148.5)

Prov: By descent to R.C. Riddell, from whom purchased, 1966.

Exh: Reynolds, *1986 (51).*

Lit: Waterhouse, 1975, pp.23, 47.

Laing Art Gallery, Newcastle-upon-Tyne (Tyne & Wear County Council Museums)

One of the most sympathetic and unusual of all Reynolds's full-length portraits, *Mrs. Riddell* was almost certainly painted in 1763, very close to the date of *Countess Howe.*[1] The subject of both portraits is essentially the same, that of a lady walking in what is almost certainly intended to represent her own landscape park, and Reynolds, like Gainsborough, has positively revelled in the possibilities inherent in the depiction of such a fashionably dressed sitter against a landscape background. If the subject is bold and unconventional enough in itself for the early 1760's, what is even more remarkable is that Reynolds has chosen to portray Mrs. Riddell off-centre, thus creating a deliberate sense of imbalance, while, with masterly subtlety, he also manages to convey his sitter's shyness by the way in which she appears to venture, tentatively, out into the picture space; there is a sense of hesitation as she pauses in front of us, turning slightly towards the spectator, to take stock. As David Mannings has pointed out,[2] the informality of the composition is wholly new in English full-length portraiture, and the painting is much more radically naturalistic in representation than is the supremely confident poise of *Countess Howe*, which is modelled in this respect, as in so many others, on Van Dyck. Reynolds's portrait is also highly searching in its enquiry into human character; this is an introspective, deeply reflective picture, and it is no accident that the portrait was not among his exhibited works.

Despite these differences in treatment, *Mrs. Riddell* and *Countess Howe* provide perhaps the most striking example in all their work of just how similar Gainsborough and Reynolds could be at this point in their careers, at a period when it is more usual to cite instead the many factors which divided them; the 1760's marks the high-water mark of Reynolds's devotion to neo-classicism (cat. A24). Even the technique used in the two portraits is comparable; as Mannings remarks[3], the watercolour-thin handling of paint in the background of *Mrs. Riddell* looks forward to *Countess Howe* (see p.24). Reynolds would more or less repeat the present composition many years later in a sensitive, full-length portrait of the late 1770's, the *Countess of Bute*, where the sitter, unusually, is middle-aged and rather homely. However, *Mrs. Riddell*, together with the lovely *Susanna Gale* in Melbourne (fig. 11), stand apart from his other full-length portraits of the 1760's, as forays into a territory in which Reynolds could compete supremely well, but in which, perhaps, he did not feel entirely at home. These two paintings are sandwiched in time between great formal full-lengths like *Lady Elizabeth Keppel* (Society of Artists, 1762), *Mrs. Hale as Euphrosyne* (1762–4), *Lady Sarah Bunbury* (Society of Artists, 1765) or the *Duchess of Ancaster* (cat. A24). Although Reynolds also produced at this period a number of smaller, informal masterpieces such as *Countess Spencer and her daughter* (1759–61) or *Nelly O'Brien* (cat. A22), these are his only deviations from the grand manner in full-length female portraiture during these years.

Like *Countess Howe, Mrs. Riddell* wears a costume which is elegant without ostentation, rich but restrained dress suitable for the country setting. Both ladies have frilled sleeves and large lace ruffles or *engageantes*, but Lady Howe's white fichu is replaced here by a shoulder mantle of black silk gauze. Instead of the little net cap worn by Lady Howe under her *bergère* hat, Mrs. Riddell wears a gauze scarf to keep her plait in place. Her dress, in contrast to Lady Howe's informal 'nightgown', is a *sacque* with a matching petticoat of white satin; the fabric is ruched and puckered to provide the three-dimensional ornamentation which is an essential element of the rococo in costume. Instead of the more formal version of the *sacque* with back drapery trailing on the ground, here the silk is bunched up into a kind of bustle by means of interior tapes. Not only is this part of the growing informality in dress of the 1760's but it might also be seen as a tribute to the popular costume of Rubens's wife (cat. A13) with its gracefully kilted-up skirt; white, too was a colour favoured by Van Dyck.

1 Unfortunately the sitter book for 1763 is missing, so precise confirmation is lacking.
2 *Reynolds*, 1986, p.218.
3 Ibid.

After SIR JOSHUA REYNOLDS

A24 Mary Panton, Duchess of Ancaster

Mezzotint by John Dixon, 24⅛×15 (61.2×38.1)

The Trustees of the British Museum, 1902-10-11-727

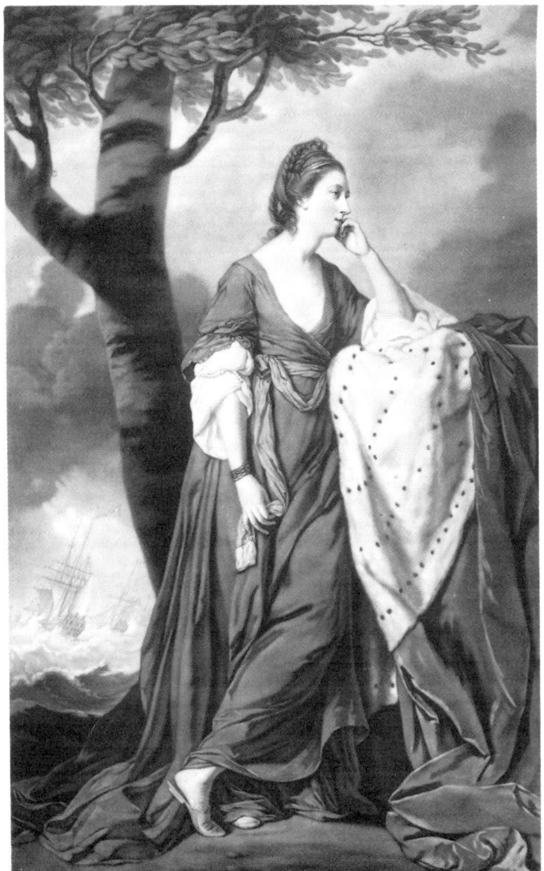

At the moment Gainsborough was embarking on his great triad of full-length portraits of the early 1760's showing women in modern dress *(Mrs. Thicknesse, Lady Alston* and *Countess Howe)*, Reynolds was producing in his own whole-length portraits of women some of the most uncompromisingly classical images of his entire career. The 1760's was the apogee of his devotion to classicism, and there is no doubting the severity of images such as this one; his portrait of *Elizabeth Gunning, Duchess of Hamilton* (Lady Lever Art Gallery), which initiated this phase in 1758-9; or *Lady Sarah Bunbury sacrificing to the Graces* (Art Institute of Chicago), in which the idea is arguably carried to the point of absurdity.

Reynolds's presentation here in 1764 of the Duchess of Ancaster in profile, with her cleanly chiselled features, her hand raised pensively to her face, and her crossed legs, is strongly reminiscent of an antique marble, although Mannings has pointed out that Reynolds portraits such as this one are also strongly suggestive of the allegorical figures on 18th century English tombs.[1] The costume is an early example of Reynolds's theory that in portraiture women should wear 'something of the general air of the antique for the sake of dignity, and. . . something of the modern for the sake of likeness'.[2] In his 'struggle with the hydra Fashion', as Edward Dayes puts it,[3] he has chosen a vaguely 'classical' gown, an imaginary confection possibly based on the loose morning 'bedgown' or dressing gown, and fastened with a fringed sash. On her feet the Duchess wears, not the classical sandals Reynolds sometimes gives his ladies when they pretend to be creatures of mythology, but a pair of fashionable mules, which nevertheless succeed in *looking* thoroughly antique, while she leans on a red velvet coronation mantle with four powderings (rows) of ermine to indicate her ducal rank. The hair is plaited on the crown of the head, in Roman style, and the back hair is slightly unloosed from its fashionable chignon to flow *à l'antique* over her neck.

It might seem that we are poles apart here from Gainsborough's fashion-conscious beauties. Yet Gainsborough and Reynolds can be too conveniently polarised. The similarities in their art at this period of the early to mid-1760's deserve mention as well (see p. 24 and cats. A1, A23). Reynolds, like Gainsborough in *Countess Howe,* has opted here for an outdoor setting, making use of a strongly accented tree trunk to act as an effective counter-poise to the weight and solidity of the figure. Although the seascape to the left of the Duchess is old-fashioned to the extent that it hardly relates to the 'platform' on which she stands, Reynolds, like Gainsborough, is aware of the need to integrate his figure fully into the setting in terms of light and shade.

The Duchess of Ancaster, daughter of Thomas Panton of Newmarket, Master of the King's running horses, was a famous beauty of the day. In his portrait of her, Reynolds surely consciously echoed the pose in Thomas Hudson's earlier full-length portrait of the Duchess in 'Van Dyck' dress, standing in front of the rotunda at Ranelagh. Such a direct comparison would have enabled his clients to see, in this new age of the exhibition picture (the painting was shown at the Society of Artists in 1764), the new 'Public Face' which Reynolds had brought to English portraiture, and the disappearance of the rococo under the onslaught of neo-classicism.

1 *Reynolds*, 1986, p.198.
2 7th Discourse, 1776.
3 *Essays on Painting*, 1805.

THOMAS GAINSBOROUGH, 1727-1788

A25 *Richard, 1st Earl Howe* *(col. pl. 2)*
Canvas, 95 × 60¾ (241.2 × 154.3)

Prov: As for Cat. A1 until c.1880, when purchased by Richard William Penn, 3rd Earl Howe (1822-1900); then by descent in the Howe family to the 7th Earl Howe.

Exh: Art Treasures, *Manchester, 1857(299); South Kensington, 1868; Grosvenor Gallery, 1889(70);* Royal Naval Exhibition, *Chelsea, 1891 (332); Birmingham,* Loan Collection of Portraits, *1900(56);* British Portraits, *Royal Academy, 1956-7(222);* Painting from Hogarth to Turner, *British Council, 1966-7(33).*

Lit: G.W. Fulcher, Life of Thomas Gainsborough, *London, 1856, p.222. Sir Walter Armstrong,* Gainsborough, *1904, p.270. E.K. Waterhouse, 1948-50, p.60, and Waterhouse, 1958, p.75.*

The Trustees of the Howe Settled Estates

As with cat. A1, the painting is discussed in detail in the Introduction on pp.26-29, p.36 and pp.39-41; the salient points are summarised briefly here. Despite the fact that the two portraits of Earl and Countess Howe were almost certainly painted as pendants, in 1763-4 (pp.19-20), the portrait of the Earl is markedly different from that of his wife. Although the setting, in which Lord Howe is positioned against an outcrop of rock, with a view of the coast opening up behind and to one side of him, derives from Van Dyck, in portraits like the *1st Earl of Strafford*[1], the painting is essentially an essay in the cross-legged style which dogged British portraiture from the 1720's for over half a century. The pose has its origins in classical sculpture; although Gainsborough's adaptation of it is very close to an 18th century cast after the antique such as cat. A27, it is more likely that he copied it from one of its countless other appearances on canvas. Perhaps the most famous of these is Thomas Hudson's portrait of *Theodore Jacobsen* in the Foundling Hospital (fig. 10). Gainsborough used the pose right from the beginning of his years in Bath, when he first had to turn his hand to the full-length portraits his new clientele demanded, and *Earl Howe* follows his earlier, and more naturalistic, renderings of this stance in *William Wollaston*(c.1759) and *William Poyntz* (Society of Artists, 1762). A few years later, in c.1768, he would produce almost a mirror image of the present painting in his portrait of another commodore, *Augustus Hervey* (cat. A29). Gainsborough's later portraits show that the pose remained a favourite one throughout his career (see cat. A28).

A cross-legged pose is, by definition, a static one, and Gainsborough's composition looks back in this, as in other respects, to the generation of Thomas Hudson, with its clean-cut lines and clear silhouetting of the figure against a rather simplified background. The dynamism and energy of Reynolds's naval portraits of this period, such as *Viscount Bridport* (1764), are altogether lacking, and it is intriguing to compare Earl Howe's somewhat frozen elegance with Reynolds's earlier 1752 portrait of commodore Keppel (cat. A30), as he moves purposefully along a stormy seashore in a scene of action, shipwreck and danger.

Lord Howe wears the undress or everyday uniform of a commodore, with a double-breasted coat of blue faced with white and trimmed with gold lace or braid, a white waistcoat, and knee breeches. Naval uniform was only introduced in 1748, and it was some years before it was worn with a strict attention to detail; for example, Commodore Keppel's suit is of the right cut – but the wrong colour (see p.36). Lord Howe's uniform, although correct, is close to the fashionable man's suit of the period; the coat, with its wide-swinging folds, and stiffened side-pleats, is typical of the somewhat rococo style of the mid-18th century; the scalloped slit up the cuff derives from informal dress of the time, but would soon become known as a cuff *à la marinière*. The hat is a typically three-cornered affair, worn with a silk cockade; underneath is a wig with a single sloping side curl typical of the late 1750's and early 1760's, and tied with black silk ribbon at the back. The kid gloves, although part of his attire, also remind us of Gainsborough's debt to Van Dyck (p.22, cat. A12).

Unlike the portrait of his wife, *Earl Howe* was painted with few evident changes of mind or *pentimenti*. The only noticeable alterations are the re-positioning of the line of the hat over the forehead so that it lies lower and flatter than it did originally, the lengthening of the stiffened pleats of the coat, and possible adjustments to the positioning of the legs. Although the head itself is highly finished, and represents Gainsborough at his finest, there are perhaps indications that the artist finished his canvas in haste; the areas of 'laying-in' around the head and legs are still clearly visible, while the background is surprisingly empty when compared with the overall attention to detail of *Countess Howe*. Stylistically, the portrait represents a return to a more formal presentation of the sitter, after the relaxed approach of early Bath portraits like *Thomas John Medlycott*, in which the sitter is shown perched on top of a stile.

As the victor of Gibraltar, and 1794, there was a constant demand for portraits of Lord Howe, and the iconography is a lengthy one. The principal portraits are by Copley (cat. A13); the full-length by Gainsborough Dupont at Trinity House (where Howe was an Elder Brother from 1787); by Mather Brown (Penn House); and by Henry Singleton (cat. A32). There are also major group portraits of Howe on the deck of the *Queen Charlotte*, again by Mather Brown (cat. C20), and accepting the French surrender on 1st June 1794 by Samuel Drummond (private collection; details on file at National Portrait Gallery archive). A watercolour by Isaac Cruikshank of *Lord Howe being presented with the sword of state by George III* is in the collection of the City of London.

Miniatures of Howe were produced by François Ferriere (Christie's 24.11.64(104)), by John Smart, 1780,[2] and by Edward Miles (Christie's 31.3.81 (125)), while a profile by Dance illustrates the Farington Diary for May 6th 1796 (National Portrait Gallery, Vol. I, p. 610). There is also a crayon drawing by Hugh Douglas Hamilton (*Walpole Society*, 1912-13, p. 107).

Most of the principal engravings of Lord Howe are included in the exhibition (cats. A26, C4, C20, C23, C24, C36). Among a mass of other engraved material, most of which derives from one of the portraits listed above, one print stands out. This is Ravenet's engraving of Hayman's *The Triumph of Britannia*, (1765), which includes a bust portrait of Howe approximately contemporary with Gainsborough's portrait.[3]

Other portraits which require further research are in the United Services Club (by T. Harrison), the Admiralty, Portsmouth (by G.F. Clarke), and the Marine Society (by P. Meguignon). Graves and Cronin also refer to a 'large' (presumably full-length) Reynolds portrait of Earl Howe in the collection of Lord Fitzhardinge in 1898. This is said to be in Reynolds's 'early days' and is therefore, presumably, of Howe as a fairly young man.'[4] The only portrait of Lord Howe together with his wife, by Arthur Devis, is unfortunately untraced (see p. 19).

There are also a number of sculpted images; as well as the tomb in St. Paul's by Flaxman (fig.2, cat. A40), these include plaster busts by Chantrey at Trinity House and at the Royal Naval Hospital, Greenwich. There is also a large figurehead of Howe, taken from H.M.S. Howe, at The Lee, Great Missenden, Buckinghamshire[5]. On a smaller scale, medallion portraits were made by James Tassie (cat. A33) and by Wedgwood after John de Vaere, while there are medals by William Barnett, (cat. C29) and C.H. Küchler (cat. C30) and others (Brown, 1980, nos. 384-387). Lord Howe's image also found its way into ceramics, appearing for example, on Toby Jugs.

1 Millar, 1982/3, cat. 23.
2 Daphnie Foskett, *John Smart*, 1964, p. 68.
3 Brian Allen, *Francis Hayman*, New Haven and London, 1987, p.65.
4 A. Groves and W. Cronin, *A History of the Works of Sir Joshua Reynolds*, II, 1899, p. 488.
5 Reproduced in *Country Life*, January 21st, 1988.

After THOMAS GAINSBOROUGH

A26 *Richard, Viscount Howe*

Mezzotint by James Watson, 1778, 13½×11⅛ (34.3×28.2)

The Trustees of the British Museum, 1902-10-11-6439

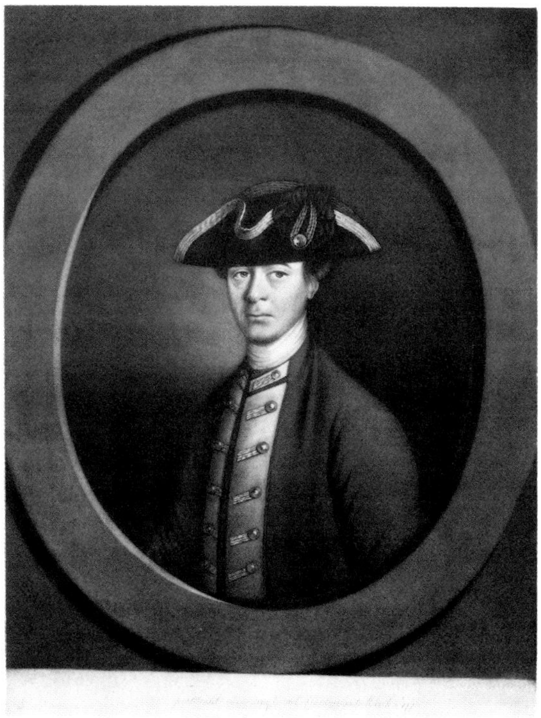

Published at the time the Howe brothers' American campaigns were capturing the headlines, and keeping all England, according to Horace Walpole, in suspense, this fine mezzotint is something of an enigma. It is different enough from the head in Gainsborough's full-length portrait (cat. A25), particularly in the sharply drawn, rather pinched, features, to suggest that Watson's print does not derive from this source. No other portrait by Gainsborough of Earl Howe is, however, recorded, and although there is a second, half-length portrait of him at Penn House which is clearly related to this engraving, this is of a quality to suggest that it is an oil copy after Watson's print, rather than being the original. Another puzzling feature is that although the print is dated 1778, the features plainly suggest the young commodore of fifteen years before, and not the robust fifty-two year old commander of the American campaign, as he appears, for example, in

Corbutt's mezzotint of 1777 (cat. C4). One is left with two possibilities. Either this is a somewhat inaccurate rendering of Gainsborough's 1763 portrait as, indeed, seems on balance most probable, or the portrait at Penn is a copy after a lost Gainsborough original, which would then have been the source for Watson's mezzotint.

Unlike Reynolds, Gainsborough did not favour the making of engravings after his portraits, since he felt that these did only scant justice to the originals. As a result, with the exception of a series of fine engravings after his late works, by his nephew, Gainsborough Dupont, in which Gainsborough was able to control closely the appearance of the final product, his work was only rarely engraved. Watson's engraving of *Earl Howe* should probably be regarded primarily, not as a print after Gainsborough, but as a naval subject, produced to satisfy the popular demand for images of Britain's commanders on sea and land at the time of the American War of Independence. Faced with a need for images, and with the sitter himself still at sea, print sellers and engravers had to turn to an earlier image of Lord Howe when producing this print.

JOHN CHEERE, 1709–1787

A27 *Mercury, c. 1763–7*

Plaster figure, painted ivory, from the Gallery at Croome Court. Height 69 (175.3)

Prov: Partridge and Sons Ltd; purchased 1963

Exh: The Man at Hyde Park Corner, *Temple Newsam, Leeds, and Marble Hill House, Twickenham, 1974 (see cat. 28).*

Lit: Arthur Bolton, The Architecture of Robert & James Adam, *I, pp. 181–3. Francis Haskell and Nicholas Penny,* Taste & the Antique, *New Haven and London, 1981.*

The Iveagh Bequest, Kenwood

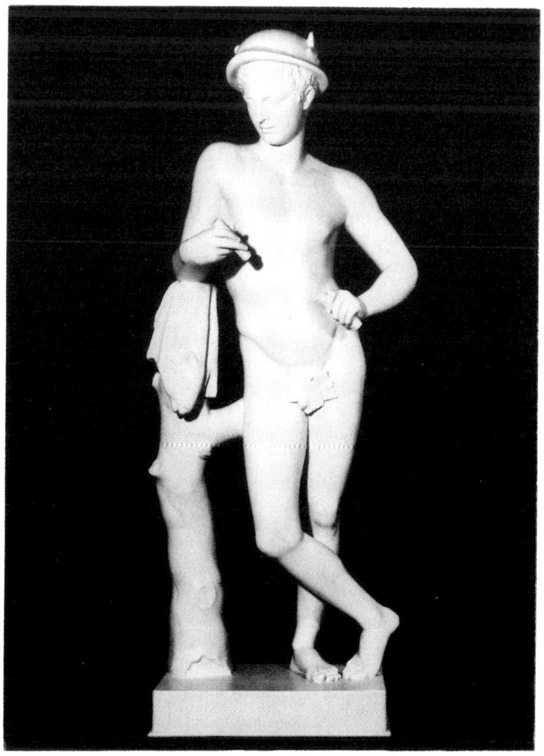

The marble figure of 'Mercury', which is first recorded in the Sculpture Court of the Belvedere in Rome, was among the most famous of the marble statues of antiquity during the Renaissance. After its move to Florence in the mid-16th century it suffered a period of comparative neglect, but the early years of the 18th century again brought it to the attention of artists and sculptors.[1] A large number of copies were produced, although many of these probably derived, not from the original, but from a bronze copy made for François I which is now in the Louvre. Nowhere was the *Mercury* more frequently copied than in England and Ireland, where, from about 1725, plaster casts began to grace the galleries of country houses; Horace Mann, writing in 1756, considered it one of five classical figures peculiarly suited, because of its upright format, for the decoration of such interiors. This particular cast was one of ten figures supplied by John Cheere between 1763 and 1767 to fill the niches in the Gallery at Croome Court, Worcestershire. The room was designed for the 6th Earl of Coventry by Robert Adam in 1763. Other examples survive at Houghton, Chiswick House and Hagley.

The highly mannered cross-legged stance, which is the figure's most salient characteristic, soon passed into painting; from the time of Hogarth onwards, this was to be one of the most enduring conventions of British 18th century portraiture. It seems to have appealed particularly to Gainsborough, who produced throughout his career countless variations on this theme in his full-length portraits of men (cats. A28, 29). When discussing the appearance of the cross-legged pose in classical sculpture, the German scholar, Winckelman, cited the Mercury as an example. Although portraitists like Gainsborough and Hudson would have been aware of its classical connotations, they used it primarily as a convenient compositional device, rather than intending it as a learned reference to antiquity. From the close correspondence of pose between Gainsborough's *Earl Howe* and John Cheere's plaster cast, it is possible that Gainsborough may have studied one of these copies after the antique for himself, rather than simply borrowing the pose from another portrait. The whole swinging outline of the figure is similar, even down to the positioning of the arms, legs and feet, while the tilt and angle of the head echoes the Mercury in reverse. A comparison with Thomas Hudson's well-known portrait of *Theodore Jacobsen* (fig. 10), shows that many eighteenth century artists preferred to adopt a much freer rendering of this antique source.

The principal attribute of Mercury, messenger to the gods, was his winged helmet. However this was added to the classical marble during the Renaissance at the same time as the hands and the attributes he is carrying, and the so-called 'Mercury' may have been originally simply a youth or a satyr.

1 As is pointed out by Haskell and Penny in *Taste & the Antique*, to whom the compiler is indebted for much of the information contained in this entry.

After THOMAS GAINSBOROUGH

A28 *David Garrick*

Mezzotint by Valentine Green, 1769, 23⅞×15⅛ (60.7×38.4)

The Trustees of the British Museum, Cheylesmore 1902-10-11-2269

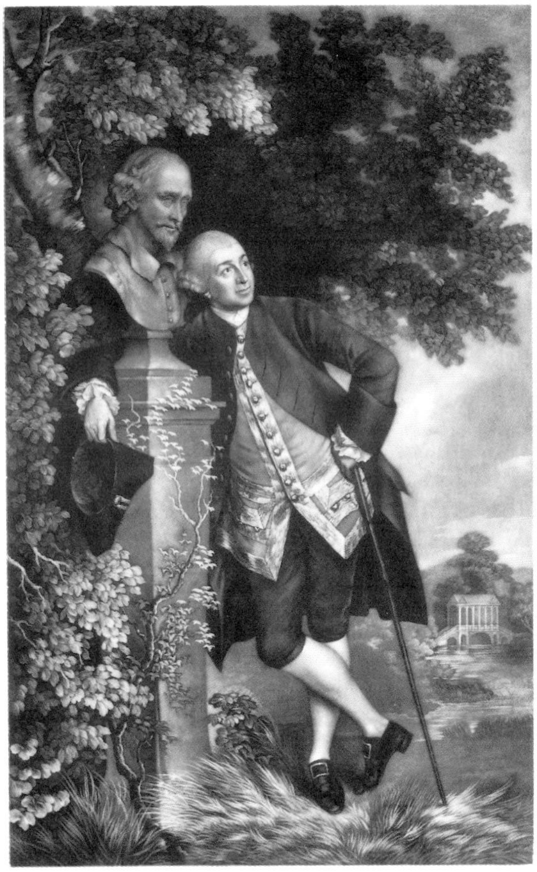

For his portrait of the actor, David Garrick, exhibited at the Society of Artists in 1766, Gainsborough returned once again to the cross-legged pose he had employed in *Earl Howe*. This rather conservative stance might seem somewhat inappropriate for a portrait of the mercurial actor, whose vanity was notorious, and who took an intense personal interest in the numerous portraits of him produced by Hogarth, Reynolds, Zoffany, Batoni and others. However, this is a portrait not of the actor, but rather of the gentleman of leisure, relaxing, probably in the gardens of Prior Park, Bath, with a bust of Shakespeare on a pedestal behind him. Portraits of Garrick show him, not surprisingly, to have been a man with a sense of how to wear clothes to best advantage, and, suited to his role here, he wears a formal coat and matching breeches, with a waistcoat trimmed with braid. He carries the ubiquitous three-cornered hat – in this case a style known as the Kevenhuller – and, a highly fashionable accessory, a cane, and wears a powdered bag wig with two slightly slanting rows of curls or 'buckles' (from the French *boucles*).

Gainsborough used this same cross-legged pose for several of the portraits of country gentlemen he painted during his early years in Bath; for example his William Wollaston (c.1759), lounges in front of a wooden stile, while William Poyntz is propped up against a tree, shotgun in hand. One would like to think that Garrick had perhaps deliberately selected a stance that would cast him in this role. However, Gainsborough used the pose also for naval sitters (Howe himself, cat. A25, and Augustus Hervey, cat. A29) and the considerable frequency with which it occurs in his work of this particular decade suggests that he used it indiscriminately as a favourite compositional device, without any special connotations.

The pose was a standard one with the previous generation of artists, perhaps finding its most considered expression in Thomas Hudson's *Theodore Jacobsen* in the Foundling Hospital (fig. 10). It derives, of course, ultimately from the antique (see cat. A27). Garrick's sloping stance, one hand resting on a pedestal, the other tucked firmly into his pocket, is almost identical to Earl Howe's. However, the portrait as a whole, painted approximately two years later than *Earl Howe*, is much more mobile than the still somewhat static and aloof image of the future admiral. While one can perhaps attribute some of this to the sitters' very different characters – Lord Howe was a man of few words, while Garrick was renowned for his mobility of expression – Gainsborough's portrait of him contains a sense of rhythm and dynamism which his portrait of Howe lacks. This is true also of Gainsborough's female portraits of the second half of the decade, as can be seen when one compares *Countess Grosvenor* (cat. A2) with *Countess Howe* (cat. A1).

Gainsborough's fondness for the cross-legged pose did not end with the 1760's. It appears with remarkable frequency in later portraits, whether their subject be a peer in Coronation robes (*Viscount Folkestone*, Royal Society of Arts, 1776), or in 'Van Dyck' dress, (*11th Duke of Norfolk*, National Portrait Gallery, 1784–6); an army officer on campaign, (*Colonel St Leger*, Royal collection, c.1782); or Gainsborough's own son-in-law, the oboist Johann Christian Fisher (Royal Collection, 1780). One can speculate endlessly as to why Gainsborough reverted so often to this traditional formula in his male portraits; probably the answer lies simply in the fact that, unlike Reynolds, of whose facility for composition Gainsborough was – humourously – envious, his principal interests lay elsewhere.

After THOMAS GAINSBOROUGH

A29 *Augustus John, Lord Hervey, later 3rd Earl of Bristol*

Mezzotint by James Watson, 1773, 20 × 14 (50.8 × 35.6)

The Trustees of the British Museum, 1868-8-8-1665

At the Society of Artists of 1768, Gainsborough exhibited a second full-length portrait of a young naval officer, a contemporary and colleague (or perhaps more accurately, a rival) of Howe's, Lord Hervey. In pose and general arrangement this later portrait is, quite literally, almost a mirror image of Gainsborough's own earlier composition, while the Commodore's uniform worn by both men further enhances the sense of affinity between them. Despite this, the two paintings are, in fact, quite different, and the contrast between them is indicative of the way in which Gainsborough's art was developing as the 1760's advanced.

In his portrait of Lord Hervey, Gainsborough has chosen to displace the figure from centre stage to one side, and he takes full advantage of the space thus left him to include a lively seascape on the left. He has also discarded his earlier placing of the sitter frontally to the spectator; unlike Howe, Hervey is shown in profile, so that even his cocked hat sits at a rakish

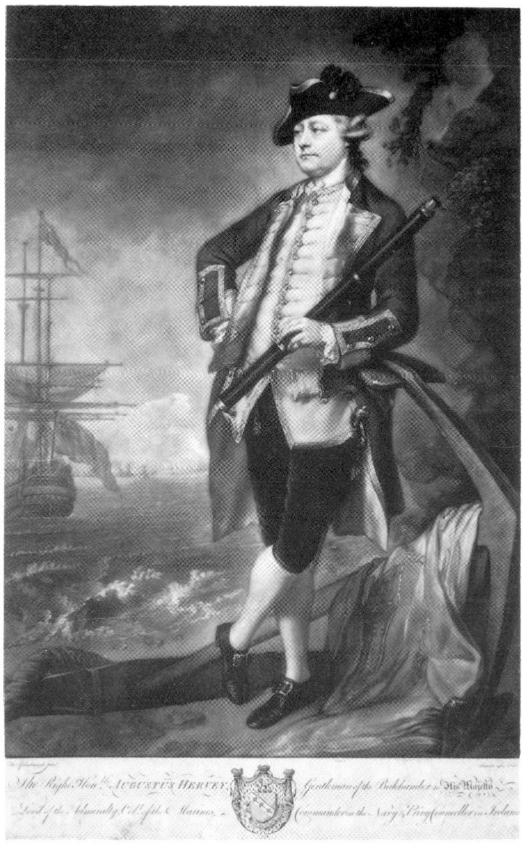

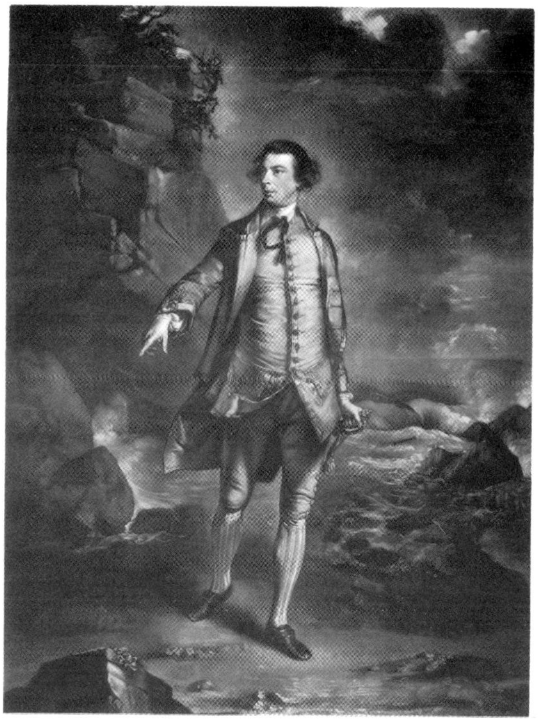

angle. Although the arrangement of hands and arms in the two portraits is superficially rather similar, Hervey sports a telescope in one hand, while the other is placed on his hip in a gesture much more assertive than Howe's. Hervey's face, too, with its shrewd eyes, dimpled chin and rather fleshy appearance is more realistic, and less idealised, than Howe's somewhat impassive, regular features. This is, in fact, a theatrical, rather baroque picture, full, in the original, of vibrant colour and with a tendency to swagger. By contrast *Earl Howe* retains the same sense of ordered balance and calm as its precursors in classical sculpture.

One wonders how Lord Hervey might have reacted to the knowledge that Gainsborough had modelled his portrait on that of *Earl Howe*. In the flesh relations between the two men were by no means always cordial, if Hervey's racy *Journal* of 1753 is to be believed: 'I sailed for Cadiz, where I met the *Dolphin*, Captain Howe. As I was in quarantine for four days I sent my orders to Captain Howe to peruse, but he did not much like I should go to Lisbon and he remain to watch the Sallymen [Moorish Pirates]. On which he sent me orders at first to remain here. This I represented against, and at last in very strong terms, which made a breach entirely between us; but at last he sent me orders to pursue my former orders'.[1] This is by no means the only occasion on which the two men crossed swords.

1 *Augustus Hervey's Journal*, 1746-1759, ed. D. Erskine, p.148.

After SIR JOSHUA REYNOLDS

A30 Commodore Augustus Keppel, 1753-4

Mezzotint by Edward Fisher, 1759, 18⅛ × 13⅞ (45.9 × 35.3)

The Trustees of the British Museum, 1838-7-14-27

Reynolds's portrait of Augustus Keppel, striding purposefully along the seashore in a pose reminiscent of the Apollo Belvedere, was the picture which made Reynolds's name in the year following his return to London from Italy in 1752. It precedes by almost a decade Gainsborough's full-length portrait of another young commodore, Richard Howe (cat. A25), whose career was at least to equal Keppel's in distinction; the two men were almost of an age, and served together on a number of occasions. To a casual observer, however, Reynolds's portrait might well appear to be the later of the two. For whereas Gainsborough has stood by the tried and tested formula of the – inevitably static – cross-legged pose, Reynolds has given us an incisive portrait of action. Keppel strides along the seashore with a gesture of command, while behind him waves break against the rocky shore and a threatening sky lowers overhead. Reynolds had learnt in Italy the meaing of 'sfumato' and his figure is fully absorbed into the stormy setting. By contrast, Gainsborough's subject stands motionless; the portrait depends instead on the almost rococo line of the figure as it projects forward from the background. While in both paintings the sitter is placed against a cliff (a motif derived from Van Dyck portraits of men of action such as the *1st Earl of Strafford* at Petworth and later much favoured by Thomas Hudson, as well as by Reynolds and Gainsborough themselves in their half-length naval portraits), Gainsborough's rocky bluff has, by comparison with Reynolds's, almost the quality of a stage-set. Similarly, the quiet bay portrayed in *Earl Howe* contrasts forcibly with Reynolds's dangerous shore; the wreckage in the distance may refer to an actual shipwreck of Keppel's in 1747.

As is pointed out on p. 36, Reynolds and Gainsborough also differ in their treatment of naval dress. Although Keppel is shown in the correct style of undress uniform, the colours in the portrait are grey, rather than blue. This may have been Keppel's own uniform (he is known to have been interested in the subject). Alternatively, Reynolds may have been 'historical' in his approach; Keppel's shipwreck is supposed to have taken place in 1747, before the introduction of proper uniforms.

As David Mannings has pointed out[1], Reynolds's portrait is almost an object lesson in the 18th century love of the 'sublime'; it not only looks back to Van Dyck, but forward to the romanticism of the age of Byron and the portraits of Sir Thomas Lawrence. It is perhaps rather surprising that Gainsborough, who in *Countess Howe* painted a picture as daring in its way as Keppel, should have chosen this rather more conservative treatment for his portrait of her husband.

Augustus Keppel was one of Reynolds's most important early patrons. The artist accompanied him to the Mediterranean in 1749 and this portrait, painted on Reynolds's return, was probably intended as a thanks offering[2]. It was to be the second in a whole series of images of Keppel which Reynolds would paint throughout his career; the two men were lifelong friends.

1 Reynolds, 1986, p. 182.
2 Ibid.

JOHN SINGLETON COPLEY, 1738-1815

A31 *Richard, 1st Earl Howe*

Canvas, 30×30 (76.2×76.2)

Prov: By descent to the artist's son and then Lyndhurst Sale, Christies, 5.3.1864 (53) bt Anthony; Marquess of Sligo. National Maritime Museum.

Lit: J. D. Proun, 1966, pp. 343, 422-3 and fig. 596.

The National Maritime Museum

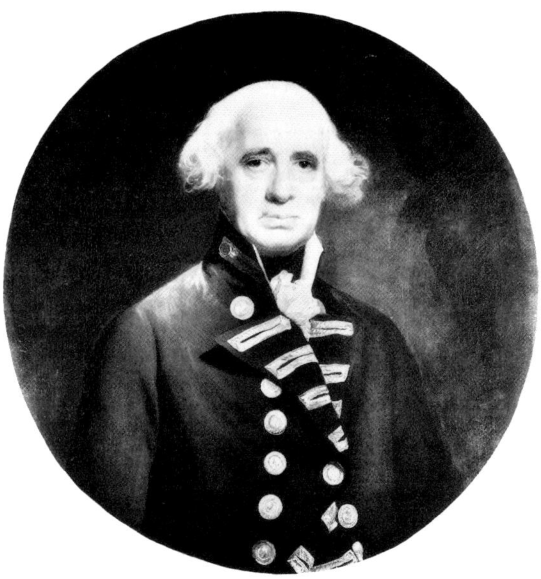

Copley's forceful characterisation of Earl Howe can be seen as the definitive portrait of the Admiral in old age. The portrait was engraved in mezzotint by Robert Dunkarton in 1794, but it was certainly begun, or at least planned, much earlier, in connection with the commission to Copley from the City of London to paint a large history picture on the subject of the Siege and Relief of Gibraltar in 1782 (see p. 83 and cats. C9-11).

In 1783 the Court of Common Council of the City of London resolved that 'an Historical Painting will be the most suitable mode' for it to 'express its respect to the Gallant Conduct of General Elliot, Governor of Gibraltar, Lord Viscount Howe, Commander of the Fleet and the rest of His Majesty's Officers, Solders and Sailors employed in its defence and relief'. The committee consulted Benjamin West and Copley himself, who was now, with the *Death of Chatham* (1779-81) and the *Death of Major Peirson* (1783) behind him, at the height of his reputation as a history painter. Copley's success in winning the commission on March 18th 1783 was principally owing to his suggestion of a dramatic telescoping of the two events of the destruction of the Spanish battering ships, and the Relief of Gibraltar by Howe's fleet, within the compass of one canvas. He agreed to 'undertake the work for one thousand guineas, hoping the Advantages of an Exhibition of the Picture and the publication of a Print from it will compensate him for the time and study required for completing so large a work'. In the event the canvas, (which measures nearly 18×25 ft.) took eight years to complete. During its progress there were wrangles with the officers of the garrison of Gibraltar over the placing of their portraits within the composition, and Copley's solution to this problem obliged him to settle for a more traditional scheme overall, whereby portraits of Lord Howe and his second in command, Admiral Barrington, would be used as flanking medallions to a predella panel containing the *Relief of Gibraltar,* while the main canvas would now be occupied only by the siege. The National Maritime Museum's portrait is, presumably, the one intended to be shown with the *Relief of Gibraltar,* since this is the original of William Sharp's engraving after the whole composition in 1910. However, the *Relief* (which was painted by Dominic Serres) is today known only from the engraving, and it is not certain whether the two portraits were ever handed over to the City, as was the main canvas, which is today in the Guildhall Art Gallery. When Howe sat for his portrait is also unclear, but presumably from about 1787 when Copley was making preliminary portraits of the army officers involved. Copley completed the commission in 1791, when the various parts of the picture were exhibited in a tent in Green Park – the only place large enough to accommodate them! The project ended unhappily in a dispute over his delivery of the portrait to the City after the exhibition and the City's refusal to meet his demands for an increased fee.

The portrait is a perfect illustration of Barrow's description of Howe's 'countenance of a serious cast, strongly marked, and dark; at the same time there was a shyness and awkwardness in his manner, which to a Stranger at first sight gave rather an unfavourable impression'. Sir Roger Barlow, who knew him, refers to his countenance as 'perhaps at first sight somewhat harsh'. Both commentators agree, however, that this was only a surface impression, soon dispelled on closer acquaintance.[1] Lord Howe was, of course, popularly known to his sailors as 'Black Dick', in reference to his complexion.

Copley also painted Lord Howe in full dress uniform; two versions of this composition are known, in the collection of Earl Howe, and the Marquess of Sligo. Copley's compatriot, Mather Brown, also painted a very similar, and almost equally sensitive, bust length portrait of Lord Howe, which is again in the Howe collection at Penn House.

1 Barrow, pp. 402-3.

HENRY SINGLETON, 1766-1839
A32 *Richard, 1st Earl Howe*
Canvas, 22½×15½ (57.1×39.3)
Prov: Fred Harrison; purchased 1859.
National Portrait Gallery, London

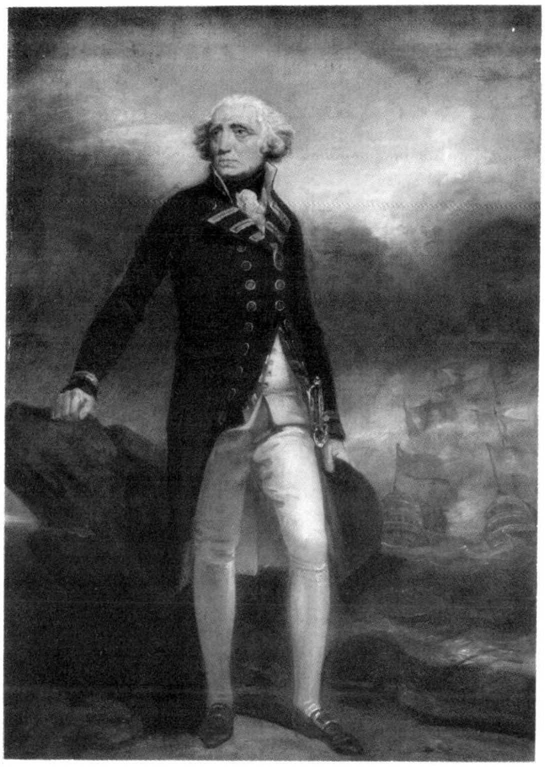

Henry Singleton's portrait of Admiral Lord Howe, engraved in 1799, was presumably painted to commemorate the victory of 1st June, 1794. Behind the sitter, a British and a French ship (perhaps the *Queen Charlotte* and *La Montagne*?) are locked in close combat.

Singleton was principally a – highly prolific – painter of literary, historical and biblical genre scenes, many of which were exhibited at the Royal Academy and later at the British Institution. However, around the years 1790-1800 he seems to have made a minor specialism of naval subjects. In 1799 he showed at the Royal Academy *Lord Nelson boarding the Spanish ships in the engagement off Cape St. Vincent* and *The Engagement of the Glatton, 16th July 1796*. These were followed in 1800 by *The Death of Captain Hood*. The portrait of Earl Howe does not, however, appear among his exhibited works. Singleton also painted a number of portraits of members of the Royal Academy, notably the ambitious *Royal Academicians in General Assembly*, (1795), which is a splendid exercise in the manner of Zoffany's *Tribuna*. Much of the rest of his work hardly lives up to the promise displayed there.

JAMES TASSIE, 1735–1799
A33 Richard, 1st Earl Howe, 1798
Vitreous paste medallion. Height 3½ (9)
Signed: Tassie F. and inscr: Admiral Earl Howe 1798.
Photograph exhibited.

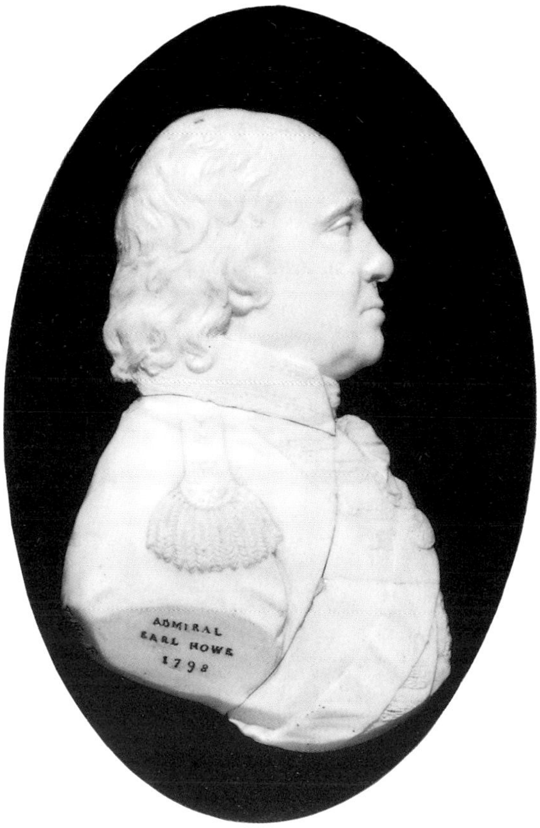

James Tassie's small portrait medallions in glass paste, like the one of Lord Howe exhibited here, were deservedly popular with his contemporaries; his patrons included 'some of the first people in the Kingdom'.[1] The medallion of Lord Howe dates from right at the end of the Admiral's life, in 1798. Probably, like most of Tassie's portraits, it was done from life, although Tassie also occasionally worked from existing portraits.[2] His single sittings lasted only two and a half hours. In this space of time he would complete a preliminary wax, which would be followed by a mould, and then a relief, in plaster of Paris; a further mould in vitreous paste; and, finally, the paste relief itself. As the finished product was considerably cheaper than a portrait by Reynolds or Gainsborough, and yet crafted to a very high standard, Tassie's success is hardly surprising. He guarded jealously his secret formula for the hard, glass-like paste that he had evolved with Dr. Henry Quin in Dublin in the 1760's. This had a great advantage in hardness and permanence over the comparable clay medallions produced by his – part collaborator, part rival – Josiah Wedgwood, and Tassie's portrait of Lord Howe is of a far higher quality than are the Wedgwood medallions of this sitter and the related waxes by John de Vaere, which are dated 1798.[3]

Tassie was better known in his day as a copyist of antique gems, for which there was a big market in the late 18th century. By 1791 his catalogue could boast no less than 15,000 impressions from which casts could be made; this was the largest collection of its kind in Europe.

1 James Holloway, *James Tassie, 1735–1799*, National Galleries of Scotland, 1986, p. 7. The author is indebted to this study for the information on Tassie's career summarised here.
2 It is worth noting the similarity to Barnett's medal (cat. C29).
3 There are examples in the Howe collection, in the National Maritime Museum, and in the National Portrait Gallery.

A34 ***Seal, with engraved portrait of Earl Howe***

Face, 1⁵⁄₁₆ (3.3) × 1¹⁄₁₆ (2.7)

Private collection

Although this fine seal is undated, the bust portrait of Lord Howe is very close, in reverse, to the one found on the medal by William Barnett (cat. C29), and it seems likely that this, too, may have been produced in connection with the victory of 1st June 1794. The letter 'H' can be seen on the gold setting, below the Howe crest.

GEORGE ROMNEY, 1734-1802

A35 ***Louisa, Countess of Altamont, later Marchioness of Sligo, 1788***

Oil on canvas, 29½×24 (74.9×70)

Prov: By descent in the family of the Marquesses of Sligo, Westport House, Ireland; Tate Gallery, 1947.

The Trustees of the Tate Gallery

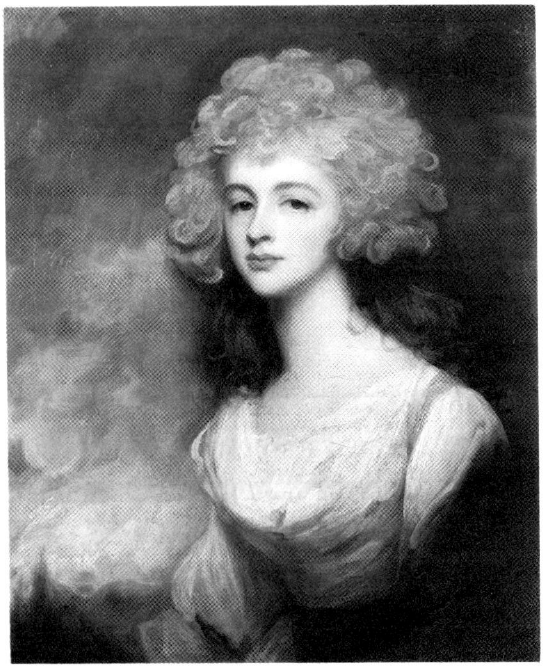

Louisa Catherine was the third and youngest daughter of Lord and Lady Howe. Born on December 9th, 1767, she married in 1787 John, Earl of Altamont (afterwards Marquess of Sligo) and it was to her descendants that many of the Howe family portraits, including the Gainsborough paintings of her mother and father, eventually passed. She also inherited a large number of family papers, which perished early in the 19th century in a fire at Westport House, the family's seat in County Mayo.

Romney's glamorous portrait was painted in the year after her marriage, and shows Lady Altamont in a costume which is drapery at its vaguest, based on the white muslin gown made fashionable in France by Marie-Antoinette and in England by Georgiana, Duchess of Devonshire, from the early 1780's onwards. The hairstyle, with its masses of powdered frizzed hair with loose tresses falling down the back, is *à la Conseilleur;* this was in vogue during the later 1780's. Clearly the Countess inherited her mother's beauty and the family resemblance between the two is striking. Lord Altamont paid for the picture on 3rd August 1788, and it was sent to Bath. The Countess also sat to John Opie; his portrait of her, together with the companion portrait of her husband, is still at Westport House. No portraits appear to have been painted of either of her sisters, although likenesses of all three, together with Sophia and Louisa's husbands and children, can be found in a collection of family drawings and watercolours in Mason's extra-illustrated *Life of Howe* (cat. 37).

Lord Howe's biographers tell us little of Louisa, concentrating instead on the Howe's unmarried daughter, Lady Mary, who was reputed to be their favourite. However, the Kent County Archives contain a fascinating exchange of letters between Lord Howe and his future son-in-law, Lord Altamont, which shows that tempers were frayed almost to breaking point over the marriage settlement; at one point, Howe felt 'under the painful necessity of being obliged to decline the honour of your alliance', insisting on paying for jewellery that Lord Altamont had bought Louisa, and on his daughter's returning her suitor's picture.[1] A compromise was eventually reached, and later we glimpse Louisa and her husband sailing through the French lines in a fog on the eve of the battle of 1st June 1794, on their way to Ireland. Lord Howe later chided his son-in-law on the hazardous nature of this journey[2]. In 1799 concern for Louisa's health led Lady Mary Howe to travel to Ireland to bring her back to London for treatment, but in the event it was Mary who died, and we later find Louisa at her mother's deathbed, with Sophia: 'Her two affectionate & dutiful daughters never left her side till the last scene was closed', wrote Mrs. Howe to the King[3]. Countess Howe left her younger daughter her London house in Grafton Street, and Louisa was still living there in 1812[4].

1 Kent County Archives, c. 267-8.
2 As above.
3 Barrow, p. 395.
4 *Boyle's Court and County Guide and Town Visiting Directory* for 1812, p. 370.

GEORGE MASON

A36 ***The Life of Richard, Earl Howe***

London, 1803

The British Library, 613.k.42

This was the earliest biography of Lord Howe, written shortly after his death by George Mason, who in 1772 had sold his estate at Porter's Lodge, Shenley, in Hertfordshire, to the Howes[1]. The rather slim volume is dedicated to Howe's two surviving daughters, Sophia, Baroness Howe and Louisa, Marchioness of Sligo. Mason admits to having taken much of the material on Howe's early career from the article by Edward L'Epine in the *British Magazine* for June 1783, and much of his account is confined to a simple record of Howe's naval commands and achievements. The tone is, moreover, often gossipy, rather than accurate, and Howe's later biographer, Barrow, writes slightingly of its merits. However, although not a close friend of the family, Mason certainly knew them well enough to provide us with insights into their domestic life, and to write with feeling on the last illness and death of Howe himself, and of his daughter, Lady Mary. This is certainly not a biography in the modern sense of the word, but rather, a memoir; the enjoyment to be obtained from Mason's account lies in the fact that it is coloured by personal recollection.

1 *Victoria Country History*, Vol. 2, p. 155.

GEORGE MASON
A37 *The Life of Richard, Earl Howe*
London, 1803
The British Library, C. 10d.14

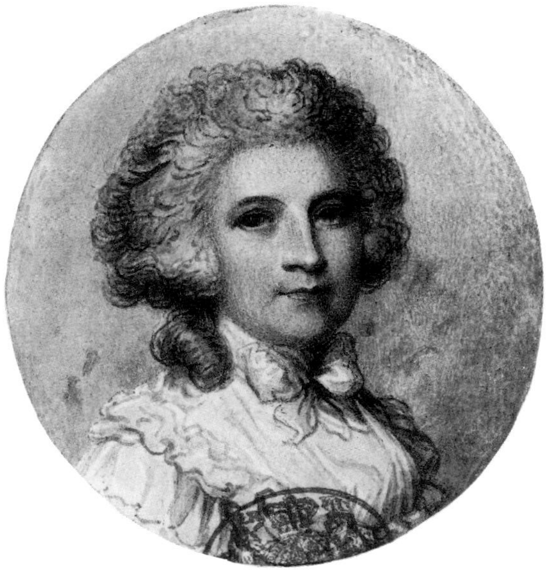

This extra-illustrated edition of Mason's biography (cat. A36) includes drawings and watercolours of members of the Howe and Hartopp families, together with engravings of the various naval commanders under whom Howe served, and other public figures with whom he was associated.

The volume is opened to show a watercolour of *Countess Howe* facing page 19, which contains Mason's account of the Howes' marriage in 1758. Apart from Gainsborough's portrait and one by Francis Cotes in the collection of the Marquess of Sligo at Westport House, which is said to date to c.1758,[1] this is the only surviving likeness of the Countess. Judging by the hairstyle and dress, the miniature must date to the 1780's, when Countess Howe would have been in her fifties. Although the face is rather fuller than in Gainsborough's portrait, the very strong resemblance between the two leaves us in no doubt as to the sitter's identity. The almost identical shaping here of the hooded eyes, long nose, small mouth, and above all the strong sense of character, remind us of the exceptional care Gainsborough always took to establish a likeness.

1 The portrait is not listed in Edward Mead Johnson's monograph, *Francis Cotes,* 1976. Johnson does, however, list as no. 55 a *Mrs Howard,* later Mrs Barnard, signed and dated 1755, whereabouts unknown. From the provenance given, it seems unlikely that this is the same portrait.

SIR JOHN BARROW
A38 *The Life of Richard, Earl Howe*
London, 1838
The British Library, 615.f.13

Barrow's life of Howe is the first account which can be said to merit the term biography. The project is said to have originated at a dinner party in June 1832, when Admiral Codrington, who had served with Howe at the battle of 1st June, suggested to King William IV that it was a great loss to the country that no-one had written a life of Lord Howe. Although many of the Howe family papers had been burnt in a fire at Westport House (see p. 94), Barrow had access to over four hundred letters written by Howe to Sir Roger Curtis from 1776-99, to his private journal and to a series of letters exchanged by the Royal Family with his sister, Caroline Howe. Unfortunately, Barrow fails to give sources for the papers he has consulted, and his account is in places inaccurate, and is often simply a re-working of earlier accounts of Howe's life. Certainly it failed to satisfy Admiral Codrington, who was obliged to refute in his *Memoirs* the accusation in the *Spectator's* review of Barrow's book of 'shyness & want of nerve' on the part of Howe in his later career.

After JOHN THROSBY, 1740-1803
A39 *Langar Hall, the seat of the R^t^ Honble Earl Howe*
Engraving by W. Walker, 1792, for the Antiquities of Nottinghamshire *by Robert Thoroton (edited and enlarged by John Throsby, 1790-96).*
Mrs. Imogen Skirving

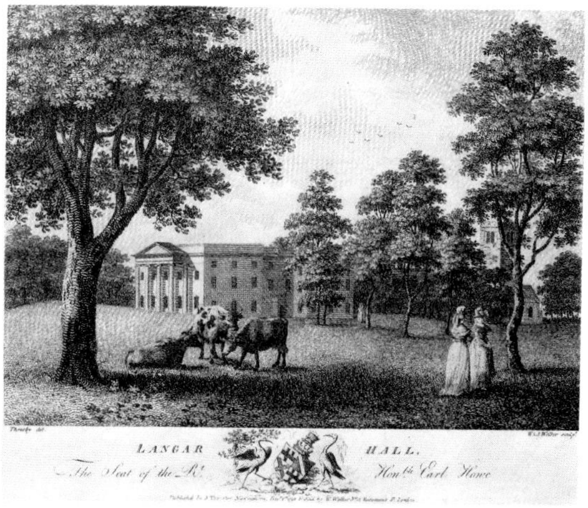

This engraving of Langar Hall shows the house as it appeared in Lord and Lady Howe's lifetime. Although this was the family's principal seat, inherited through marriage with the Scropes, who had been Lords of the Manor there since 1650, Throsby tells us that Lord Howe rarely visited Langar; 'and no wonder, for the roads about it, in many places, must be intolerable in the winter'![1] More likely reasons for his absence are Howe's naval commitments, and his purchase in 1772 of Porter's Lodge in Hertfordshire, where the family lived mostly in later years. Lord Howe also owned property elsewhere in the county, at Epperstone, and Coleston-Basset, as well as Howe House at 19, Castle Gate, Nottingham.

Throsby lamented the lack at Langer of natural beauties such as 'groups of variegated foliage adorning the gentle swells of the earth'; here one beholds only 'the hedge-row, some ill-formed trees, sheep, and dairy cows'. Unfortunately he decided to compensate for this in his engraving by choosing 'that view which gives it an air of grandeur, modern built, where there is the most regularity in its formation'.[2] He has thus obscured the construction of the house, about which little is known, but which was evidently of two distinct periods. The modern Ionic portico must date to the time of Lord and Lady Howes' ownership, and has the effect of re-orientating the building towards the west; in Hollar's 1676 engraving of Langar for Thoroton's *Antiquities of Nottinghamshire,* the two wings, which would later form the side of the 18th century house, are seen to form part of the principal facade. Beyond the house is the church of St. Andrew which, in an arrangement peculiar to Nottinghamshire, nearly abuts the house itself. Throsby tells us that there was internal 'communication' between the two. Probably the family regarded the church very much as a private chapel, if the enormous podium which fills much of the South aisle, and which comprises the family vault, is anything to go by. Here Lord and Lady Howe are buried.

After their deaths, the Howes' eldest daughter, Baroness Howe, sold the Langar estate in 1818 to John Wright, who cut down the timber and left the house to decay. Later a new and smaller house was built on the site; this survives today.

Robert Thoroton's massive history of Nottinghamshire was originally published in 16 A century later the volume was both rare and expensive, and a reprint was needed. In 1790 John Throsby, parish clerk of St. Martin's, Leicester, took on the task. As well as updating information, he also produced a complete new set of illustrations. Unfortunately, Throsby was highly selective in his interests, prefering to concentrate on handsome country seats rather than on Thoroton's broader based, antiquarian investigations. He was, moreover, accurate neither as a transcriber of material nor as a topographer. It seems likely that in taking on the task of revising the *Antiquities* he over-reached himself, since in 1802 a subscription was raised to assist him, given the 'total derangement of his general circumstances' and his 'extreme bodily afflictions'.[3]

1 *The Antiquities of Nottinghamshire* by Robert Thoroton, edited and enlarged by John Throsby. Facsimile edition, 1972, with an introduction by M. W. Barley and K. S. S. Train. Much of the information in this entry is based on their account of Throsby's work.
2 Ibid, Vol. 1, p209.
3 Ibid.

After JOHN FLAXMAN 1755-1826

A40 *The Tomb of Earl Howe in St. Paul's Cathedral*

Engraving by S. Rawle after E. F. Burney in The European Magazine and London Review, *Vol. 74, July-December 1818*

The British Library, P.P.5459.Z

After Lord Howe's death on 5th August 1799, he was buried privately in the family vault in Langar Church in Nottinghamshire (see p. 16). Two months later in the House of Commons, Mr. Dundas proposed the erection of a public monument to Howe. Not only could there be 'but one unanimous sentiment pervading the country as to the propriety of not suffering that noble Lord to go out of the world without publicly testifying the regard due to his memory'.[1] The monument would afford ' . . . to his respectable family . . . a considerable degree of consolation . . . to find that his merits have not been forgotten by his country', while 'to the public it is of importance to keep alive the remembrance of the brilliant services by great and eminent characters'.[1]

The monument (fig. 2) which was erected in the south transept of St. Paul's Cathedral in 1811, was designed by John Flaxman, and is a variant on the type of free-standing monument he had recently evolved for the tomb of another great public figure, the Lord Chief Justice, Lord Mansfield, in Westminster Abbey (1801). It shows Lord Howe standing, full-length, on a raised podium, holding a telescope in one hand and with the British lion lying at his feet. Behind him, seated on a pedestal, is Britannia, while on the left Fame, overlooked by Victory, is reading the names of Howe's two great victories, Gibraltar, and the 1st June 1794. In the background is Howe's flagship, the *Queen Charlotte*. Flaxman would later make use of a similar design for his portrayal of another naval hero, Lord Nelson, whose monument also forms one of the series of Napoleonic war memorials in St. Paul's. Such large public commissions do not appeal to modern taste as much as Flaxman's much more intimate renderings, in his smaller tomb sculpture, of private grief and family life, in which he was able to combine poetic sentiment and realistic characterisation with the purity of the neo-classical style. However, this reaction may be owing, at least in part, to the dullness of execution from which these larger works suffer; unfortunately, having made models of his tombs in clay, Flaxman usually handed over the execution of the marble itself to his assistants.

Many of the Flaxman drawings formerly though to be related to the Earl Howe tomb have now been shown to belong instead to a projected monument to Sir Ralph Abercrombie. There are, however, designs associated with the tomb in the British Museum (1888-5-3-126) and in the Victoria and Albert Museum (8520.6)[2], while a sketch by Flaxman which was sold at Christie's on 12.11.1968(59) shows an earlier idea for the monument. In this, Howe stands in front of a central column inscribed 'June 1 1794', flanked by the figures of Britannia and Victory. There is also an unexecuted modello for a monument to Earl Howe by Thomas Banks, which is now in the Soane Museum.

The erection of the tomb attracted considerable attention in the national press. This engraving was published by the *European Magazine* as a frontispiece to the volume for July-December 1818. Echoing Dundas, the magazine hoped that Howe's 'example will still incite to victory, to heroism and to renown'.

1 Barrow p384-6.
2 We are grateful to Richard Green of York City Art Gallery for allowing us to have sight of Norah Gillow's research on this subject.

Fig. 21
John Flaxman
Tomb of Richard, Earl Howe,
in St. Paul's Cathedral,
1803-11. (detail).

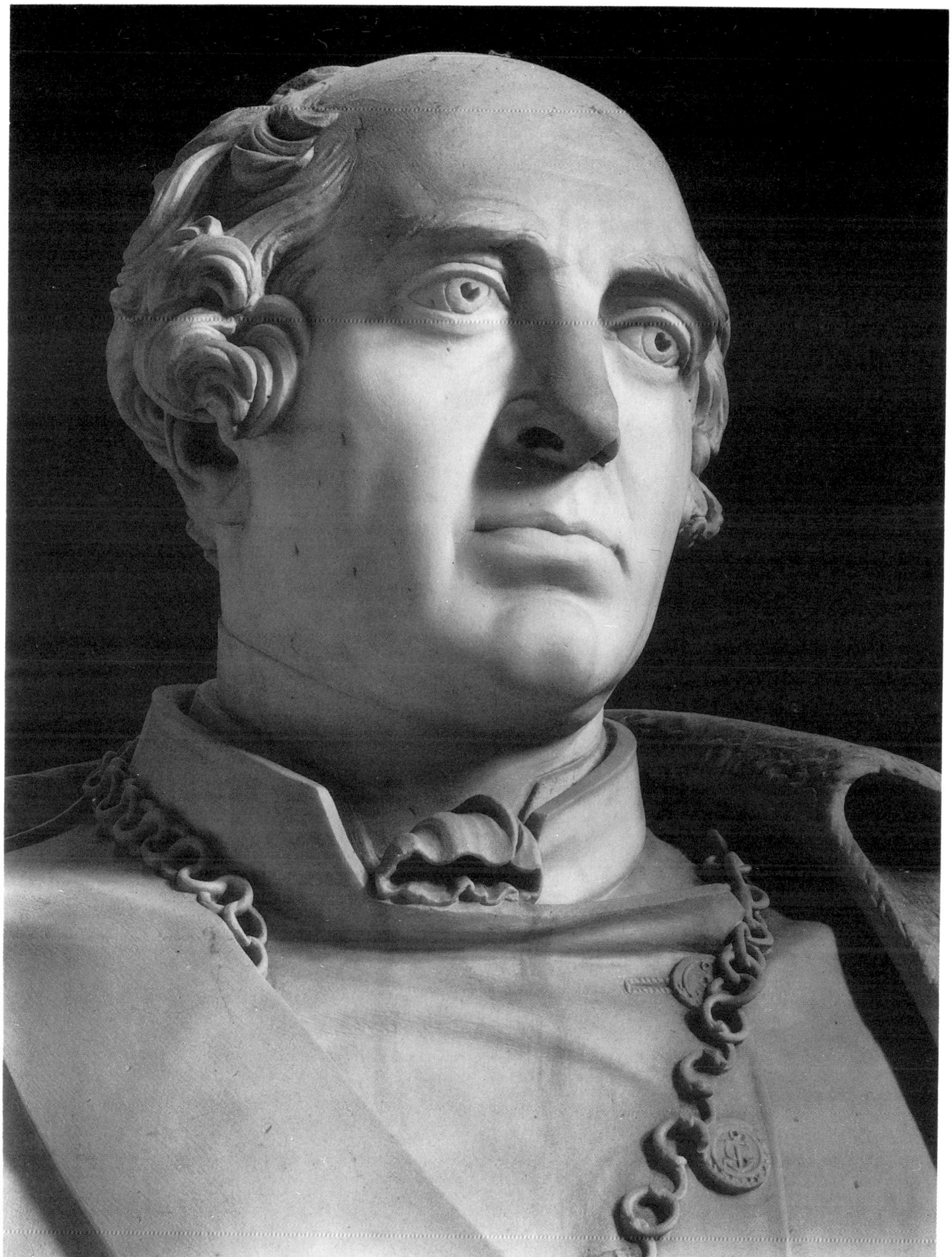

Section B

This section on costume concentrates on the Kenwood portrait of Countess Howe*; sadly, no examples of commodore's uniform of the relevant period have survived, and it was decided that a recreation of Earl Howe's costume could not be justified, given the paucity of evidence available.*

With the costume of Countess Howe *we are more fortunate. A dress and a number of accessories have been traced which relate to – although they are not identical to – those worn in the portrait. Nevertheless, the notion of 'recreating' the dress in any portrait, unless one is lucky enough to have the actual surviving costume to hand, is fraught with difficulties. Even if it were possible to establish exactly the type of dress and the fabrics from which it was made (a fairly rare event, given the artist's process of selectivity and even generalisation of the details of the dress and its materials) it would be unlikley that one could track down a complete outfit resembling the costume in a portrait. Most of all, it would be an impossible task to recapture the atmosphere of the portrait; there is no way in which one can reproduce the elusive but crucial relationship of sitter to costume which is the essence of great portraiture.*

All we aim to do here, therefore, is, first, to show some surviving examples of a comparable dress and accessories and, second, to 're-interpret' the costume worn by Lady Howe with modern fabrics, but, as far as possible, using contemporary 18th century dress making techniques. We have been very fortunate to have the 'replica' dress, apron, fichu and ruffles made by Margaret Dobbie, of the Textiles and Dress Conservation Department at the Victoria and Albert Museum. She has brought her own and the Department's corporate knowledge and experience, notably that of Madeleine Ginsburg, to bear on the task and has throughout been concerned to produce as authentic a likeness as possible. To accompany the dress, a straw hat has been made by Miss Jenny Adey, and a pair of kid gloves supplied by Dents. The shoes are by Francis Wilson.

Unlike the other parts of Lady Howe's ensemble, no jewellery of the type she wears seems to have survived. This has been recreated for us by Christina Rowley at Madame Tussaud's; a brief description of the originals is included below.

The round disc earrings are made of seed pearls, a popular choice in the mid-18th century; in 1759 Lady Caroline Fox writes to the Countess of Kildare: 'I went to Chenevix about pearl earrings; there are none but seed pearl ones round with a little larger in the middle, the price about 2 gns. . . '.[1] *The earrings – which look so modern in our eyes – would have gone out of favour fairly quickly and be thought not worth keeping, and the pearls in the necklace would have been re-designed and re-strung. The necklace itself is of five rows of pearls tied at the back with a white satin ribbon. When the sculptor Joseph Nollekens married in 1771, his bride wore 'a triple row of pearls tied behind with a narrow white satin ribbon'.*[2]

1 *The Correspondence of Emily, Duchess of Leinster*, ed B. Fitzgerald, Dublin, 1949, I, p.244.
This reference was drawn to my attention by Diana Scarisbrick. Another fashionable alternative to real pearls was *coq de perle* or nautilus shell.
2 J. T. Smith, *Nollekens and his Times*, London, 1829, I, p.16.
On jewellery generally, see A. Ribeiro, 'Eighteenth-century Jewellery in England,' in *Connoisseur*, October, 1978.

B1 *Pink silk dress*
Bust: 34 (86.4)
Waist: 28 (71.1)
Length: 59 (149.9)
The National Trust, Killerton, Devon

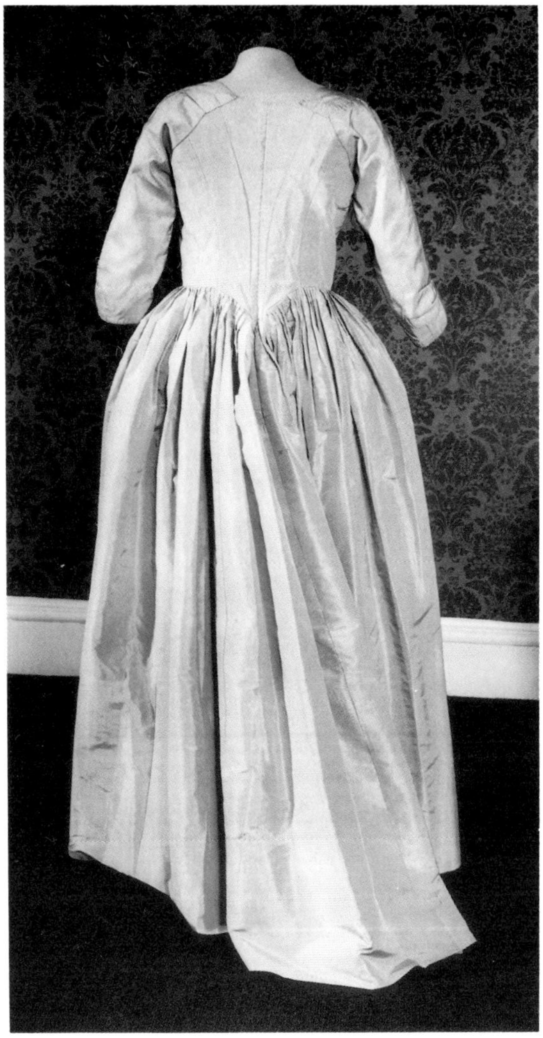

This pink silk open robe, probably dating from the mid-1770's, is displayed together with a pink quilted petticoat, which is probably of a slightly earlier date. Although the dress is somewhat later than that worn by Lady Howe, the construction is basically the same; as in the Gainsborough portrait, it would be worn with a fichu and, probably, an apron.

The dress is a fitted English nightgown, or *robe à l'anglaise,* and it is displayed here from the back to show the construction of the bodice and the elegant sweep of silk so much admired in the 18th century. The back pleats of the bodice are sewn down into a pointed V-line, and the central panel of the dress at the back continues into the skirt without a waist-seam. At the sides and back the skirt is sewn into the waist with tiny pleats to create the bounce and fullness which was part of the fashionable look of the time. The skirt is made from six widths of silk, each 19¼″ wide, with the exception of one piece which is cut slightly narrower. The standard width of silk at this period was about 19-22″.

B2 *Fichu*
Length (top edge): *52 (132)*
Length (other two sides): *33 (83.8)*
Worthing Museum and Art Gallery

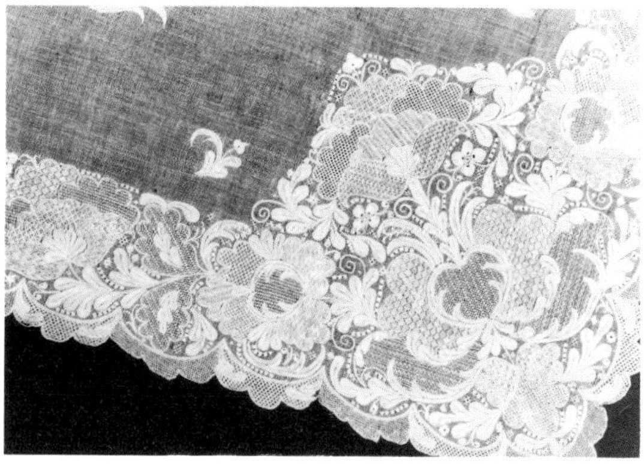

The fichu was a fashionable accessory for informal dress throughout the 18th century. Towards the end of the century it was worn tucked into the front of the bodice, but in the portrait of Lady Howe she wears it crossed over, pinned to the bodice and then tucked in below the apron. This embroidered white fichu of c.1760 is made of muslin. Lady Howe's fichu is of a finer quality and more transparent. It was probably made of silk gauze, but as the material was so fragile, no known examples survive.

B3 *Muslin apron*
Length: *41 (104.1)*
Width at bottom: *68½ (174)*
Museum of Costume, Bath

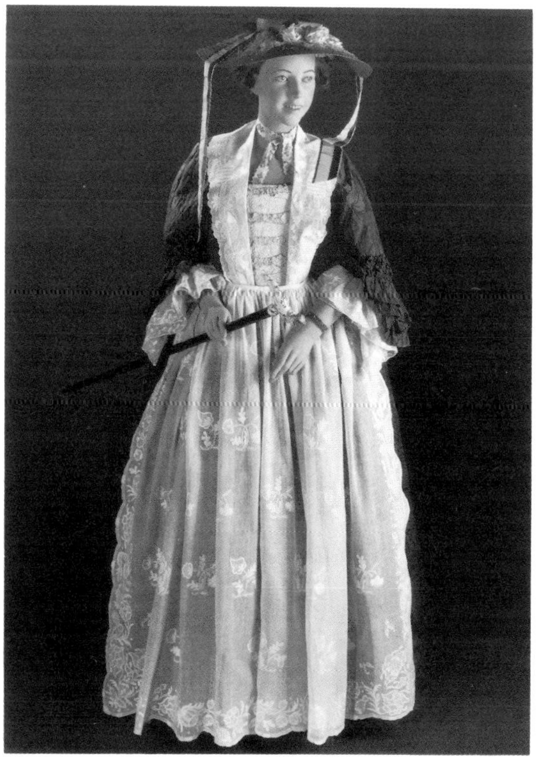

A fine example of a full-length white embroidered muslin apron of c.1760 (the tape waistband is modern). Although Lady Howe's apron is more transparent (it may be of brocaded silk gauze, or silk combined with lace), the size and disposition of the floral sprays are similar to those embroidered on this surviving apron. Aprons were often worn over informal dress, as, for example, the nightgown or *robe à l'anglaise* shown in *Countess Howe*. They may be said to act as a substitute, in terms of decoration, for the ruffles found on more formal dress.

B4 *Engageantes or ruffles,* *c.1760*
Length: *15 approx. (38.1)*
Width: *14 approx. (35.6)*
The Gallery of English Costume, Manchester City Art Galleries

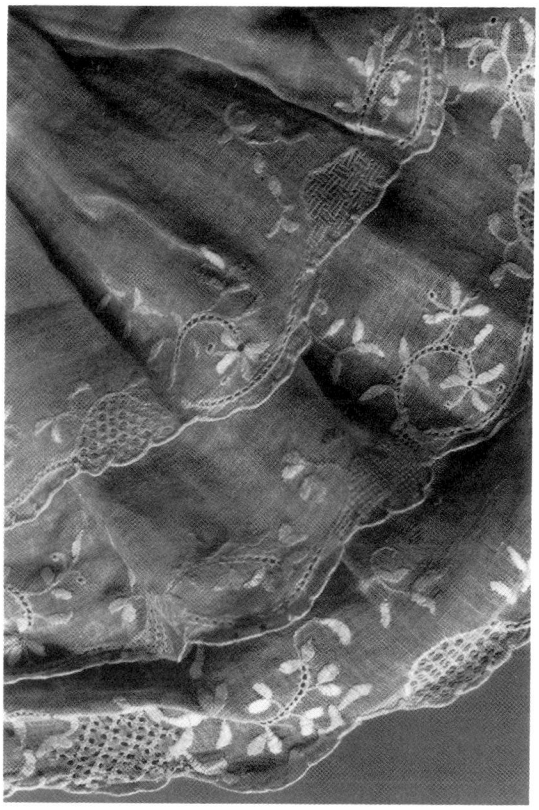

These sleeve ruffles are of fine embroidered white muslin; they consist of three shaped falls of graduated widths, each widening from a narrow top, and gathered together on a narrow linen tape. While Lady Howe's treble ruffles are probably made instead of silk gauze, edged with lace, these surviving ruffles have the same filmy delicacy and date from approximately the same period as the portrait.

B5 ***Straw hat***
Diameter: 15⅞ (40.4)
Grosvenor Museum, Chester

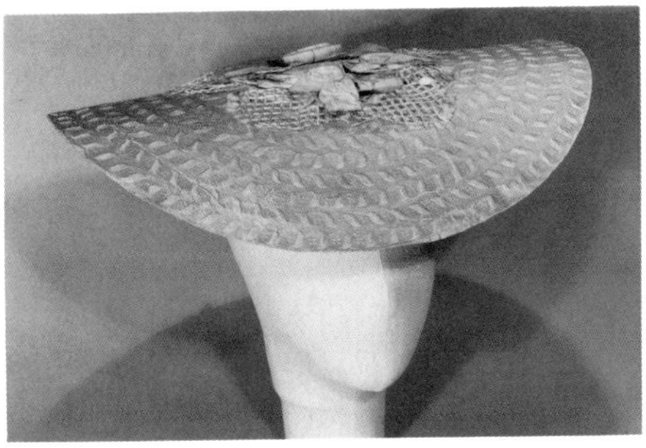

The straw hat shown here is covered in ivory silk and has a stamped pattern on the brim. It is trimmed with ivory and pale blue ribbon. The two ribbons for tying the hat under the chin are missing; they would have matched the ribbon trimming the hat itself. The popularity of such *bergère* hats in the middle decades of the eighteenth century can be seen both from portraiture (cats. A1, A3, A5, A14–17) and from existing examples in museums. It is amazing that any of these often fragile hats should have survived. Most of those which do are made of chip or willow straw imported from Holland; English straw was not apparently used until the late eighteenth century. Unfortunately, no examples of the exceptionally fine 'Leghorn' bonnets, which were made of a fine wheaten straw, are known today; it is probably this type of hat that is worn by Lady Howe. Some hats, like the one exhibited here, were covered in silk or paper embossed to imitate woven straw.

B6 ***Black satin shoe***
Length: 9¾ (24.2)
Height: 4¼ (10.3)
The Trustees of the Victoria and Albert Museum, London

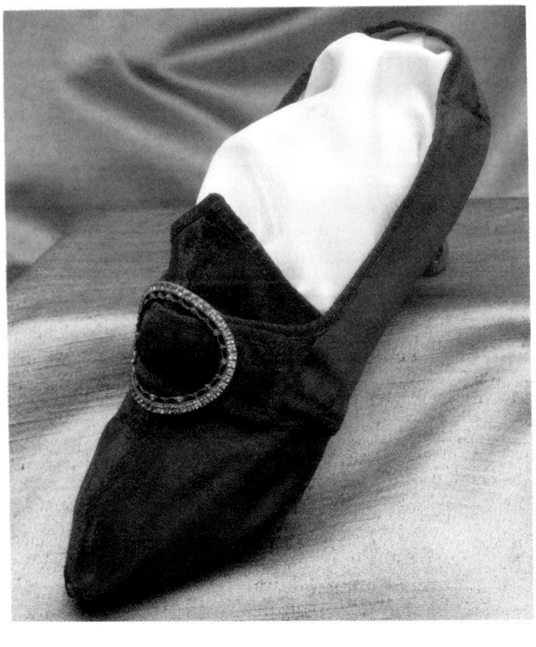

This black satin shoe of the late 1770's is shown with an oval silver buckle set with silver pastes. Plain black shoes with the higher, thick baroque heel of the 1760's, as in the portrait of *Countess Howe,* seem not to have survived as much as shoes of the following decade, like this one, with a lower, wedged Italian heel. The shoe has been mended at the front and back.

B7 ***Pair of shoebuckles***
Brass, 1¹⁵⁄₁₆ × 2⅜ (5.0 × 5.6)
The Iveagh Bequest, Kenwood (Lady Maufe Collection, 29 A & B)

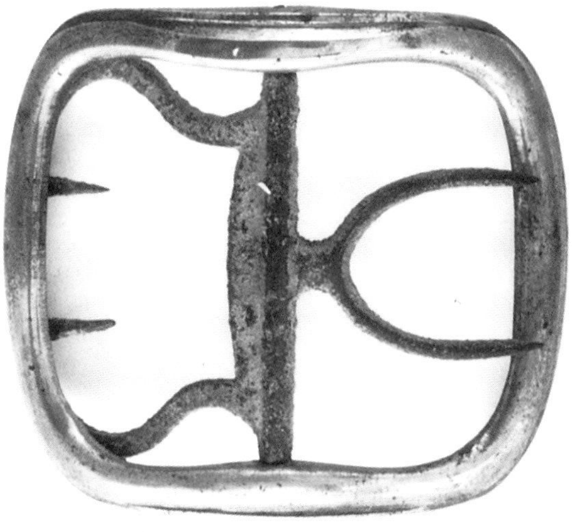

Shoebuckles were worn throughout the eighteenth century as a means of fastening the two straps or latchets of the shoe. This was achieved by means of the roll, with its two small spikes and the tongue, which pierced the upper shoe strap like a miniature pitchfork. The buckle could thus be secured over the instep at the tension required by the wearer. As they were removable, buckles were treated like jewellery. Perhaps the greatest number were in silver, but paste was also highly popular, while less expensive buckles were made in steel, brass, pinchbeck and a range of other materials. Appropriately for informal dress, the buckles worn by Lady Howe seem to be made of one of these cheaper materials, probably pinchbeck, or brass as in the example shown here. The exhibited buckles are, however, simpler than Lady Howe's, which are larger, and rather more curvilinear in form, with some slight decoration. This is in keeping with the rococo style which affected the shoe buckle, like all other forms of the decorative arts, in the middle years of the century.

B8 ***Mercers***
Charles Ryder, Heal 84.224
Atwick & Son, Heal 84.13
The Trustees of the British Museum

Although mercers sold fine quality woollen and mixed cloths, their emphasis was on silks. According to *The London Tradesman* of 1747 (a guide to enable young people to choose a suitable trade or profession), 'the Mercer traficks most with the Ladies. . . (He) deals in Silks, Velvets, Brocades, and an innumerable Train of expensive Trifles for the Ornament of the Fair Sex'. Cheapside had long been a fashionable place for fabrics; here we have a trade card for *Charles Ryder* at the Turk's Head, opposite Foster Lane in Cheapside. In the later 18th century

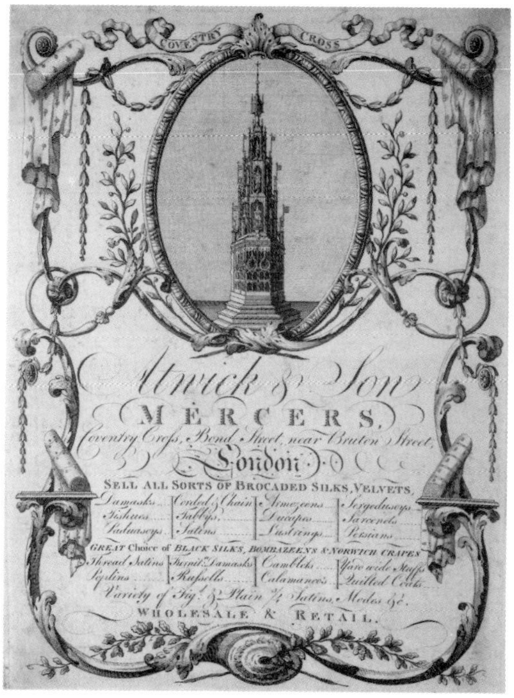

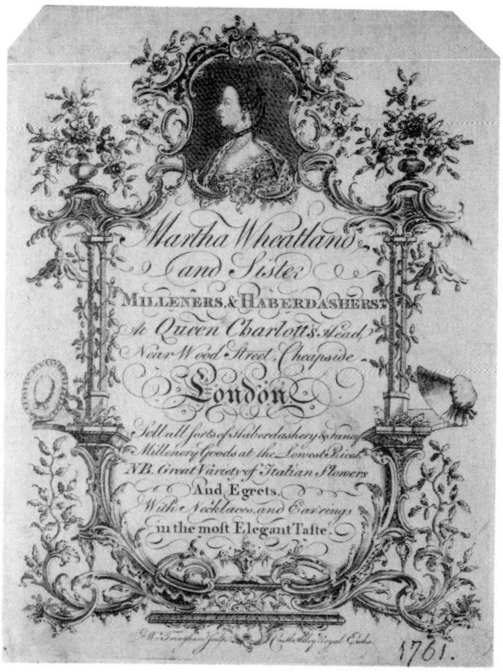

Bond Street became the new fashionable area to shop; see the trade card for *Atwick & Son,* Coventry Cross, Bond Street.

Both these mercers offer a range of fabrics, mainly silks, from the heavier velvets and damasks, to the lighter lustrings, and poplins. Lady Howe might well have purchased her lustring from a mercer such as one of these; the fabric would then have been made up by a dressmaker. Increasingly, however, by the mid-18th century, Mercers were able to offer their customers a making-up service for the fabrics they sold, or even some ready-made items. These included garments where the fit was not crucial, such as cloaks, 'Bed-gowns' and 'Gentlemens, Morning Gowns (i.e. dressing gowns), or items which could be easily altered, like 'Quilted & Hoop Petticoats'. Lady Howe's apron could well have been purchased from such a Mercer. Silks were generally 19″–22″ wide – the widest measure possible on the hand looms of the time. This necessitated more seams than are required in dressmaking today, but it would take the eye of faith to see these in Gainsborough's portrait! The 'Yard wide Stuffs' listed here by *Atwick & Son* probably refer to woollen stuffs or mixed cloths.

B9 *Haberdashers*

J & R Harrop, Banks 70.36

Jeremiah Thody, Banks 70.93

Draper & Coxeter, Banks, 75.11

Martha Wheatland, Heal 86.87

Spilsbury, Banks 70.86

The Trustees of the British Museum

The goods supplied by the haberdasher were essential in the making and the trimming of clothing. Those sold by *Harrop* include various kinds of dress trimmings and linings, 'Best London Pins' (which Lady Howe would have required to pin the bodice of her dress under her fichu), and a range of accessories such as 'Silk & Gauze Handkerchiefs' (i.e. a fichu such as that worn by Lady Howe). *Thody,* a fashionable haberdashers in Cheapside, offers a similar range of goods, including ribbons, muffs, tippets (streamer-like scarves worn knotted round the neck) and fans.

Milliners and haberdashers often sold the same kinds of goods. *Martha Wheatland and Sister* of Cheapside are described as 'Milleners & Haberdashers'. Their goods include hats and bonnets (illustrated on their trade card), 'Italian flowers' (silk flowers used as dress-trimmings), 'Egrets' (heron feathers worn in the hair), and jewellery made of silk and non-precious stones. Milliners, as well as stocking haberdashery wares, also sold linen and lace and made-up accessories such as ruffles, indoor caps, aprons, fichus, etc., several of which can be seen in the Kenwood portrait. *Draper & Coxeter,* for example, offer linen lace and silk (blonde) lace as well as accessories such as aprons and handkerchiefs.

Haberdashers also could offer a pattern-drawing service both for professionals, and for those ladies who wished to do their own needlework. *The London Tradesman* says that the pattern-drawer is employed 'in drawing Patterns for the Callico-Printers, for Embroiderers, Lace-workers, Quilters, and several little Branches belonging to Women's Apparel. They draw Patterns upon Paper, which they sell. . . '. *Spilsbury,* at the Royal Point in York Street, Covent Garden, as well as selling the usual range of haberdashery goods, offers patterns for quilting, for lace including Brussels, and for Dresden (a kind of lace made of fine drawn-work and embroidery).

B10 ***Necklace makers***
James Howard, Heal 67.220
John Howard, Heal 67.222
The Trustees of the British Museum

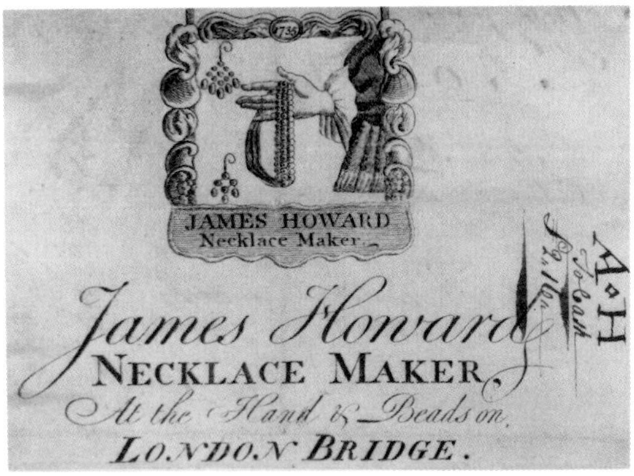

Haberdashers and milliners often included necklaces and earrings among the goods for sale; these would be made of silk or lace, or non-precious materials like paste stones, agates, wax beads, etc. Lady Howe might well have purchased her fairly inexpensive seed-pearl earrings from one of these types of shop. However, for her pearl necklace she might have gone to a specialist necklace maker such as James or John Howard. *James Howard's* trade card, dated 1735, shows how necklaces were strung onto silk (jewelled clasps are rare before 1800); in *Countess Howe* the ribbon fastening the necklace can just be seen behind the rows of pearls. *John Howard's* card, which may date to c.1762, offers a range of inexpensive costume jewellery for formal and informal dress, but the speciality of the firm was artificial pearls made of wax. Lady Howe's pearls look too lustrous, however, to be made of this material.

B11 ***Hats***
Joseph White (bill head), Heal 72.436
Jn°. Higgons, Heal 72.187
The Trustees of the British Museum
Hats were made from a variety of materials in the 18th century, both obvious (silk) and strange (whale-fin, for example), but perhaps the most popular were made of straw; this is borne out by the large number of surviving trade cards in the Banks and Heal collection which advertise such hats. The most prized hats came from Livorno in Tuscany, known to the English as Leghorn, and it is this type of hat which Countess Howe wears in the Kenwood portrait. These hats were made of wheaten straw, cut green, bleached and finely woven. In Piedmont in the early 17th century Thomas Coryat (*Crudities,* 1611) had admired '... most delicate strawen hats... some of them having at least an hundred seames made with silk'. By the mid-18th century these hats were often lined with silk and decorated with ribbons and flowers.
The trade card of *John & Joseph White* – who claimed to run the oldest hat shop in London – probably dates to c.1763 and is therefore almost exactly contemporary with the *Countess Howe* portrait. It shows a very similar straw hat, trimmed, however, with flowers, not ribbon. (The hat is not unlike a surviving example from Castle Howard, York). For further examples see also cats. A15, A16 and A17 The trade card for *Higgons's Warehouse* shows both the flat *bergère* hats of the type worn by Lady Howe, and a

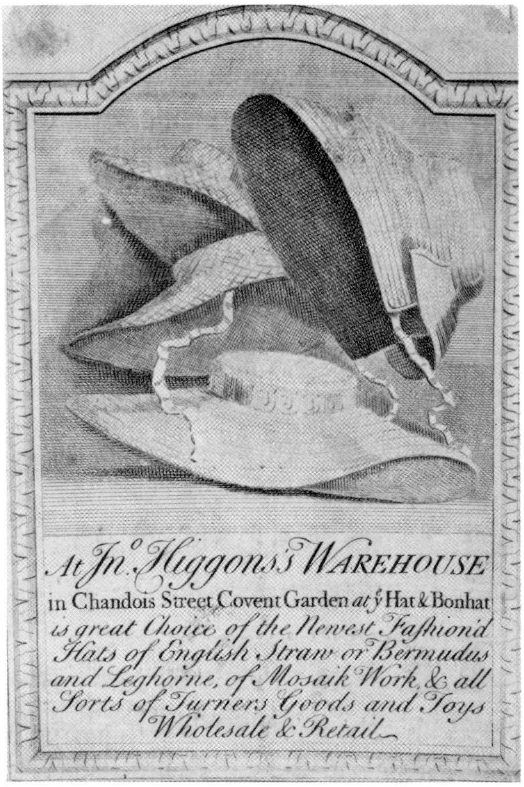

straw bonnet of the kind which came into high fashion towards the end of the 18th century.

B12 ***Gloves***
William Jones, Banks collection, 70.45
The Trustees of the British Museum
The trade card for *William Jones* shows a plain kid glove of the sort worn by Lady Howe. The main aim of gloves as worn by women was to keep the hands white and smooth. The haberdasher *Jeremiah Thody* (cat. B9) advertises 'Gloves of all Sorts, made of Leather peculiar smooth to the Hands... '. These might be what were called 'chicken' or 'chicken-skin' gloves, i.e. the skins of aborted calves which were, according to an advertisement of 1769, 'prepared entirely with Almonds and Spermaceti', with the aim of 'smothing, softning and whitening the Skin'.

B13 ***Shoes***
Richard Mumby, Banks collection 18.61
Leak Richier, Banks collection, 18.67
The Trustees of the British Museum
The trade card for *Richard Mumby,* although somewhat earlier than the portrait of Lady Howe, shows shoes with the same high curved baroque heel. *Leak Richier's* card, on the other hand, shows shoes of the late 1770's similar to the example lent by the Victoria and Albert Museum to this exhibition (cat. B6), with latchets buckled over a lower instep. On the right is a clog or overshoe which was worn for extra protection.

Section C

The Battle of Quiberon Bay, 20th November, 1759

In 1759 Lord Howe served with distinction under Admiral Hawke at the Battle of Quiberon Bay. After blockading Brest, Hawke followed the French Fleet under Admiral Conflans into Quiberon Bay on the Brittany coast, where it was sheltering from a storm, and attacked. Despite the tempestuous weather, which is so evident in Canot's engraving (cat. C1), he succeeded in dispersing the enemy fleet, capturing and destroying several vessels. Lord Howe was in the leading ship, the Magnanime, *which had been captured from the French in 1748, and 'greatly contributed to the conquest, and shared in the honours obtained in Quiberon bay'.[1] He exchanged fire with the* Formidable, *silencing its guns and attacked the* Thesée, *which later sank in heavy seas. The victory was an important one. As the* 'Gentleman's Magazine *put it in its biography of Howe in 1782, 'No man can be ignorant of that memorable battle', and cat. C1 is only one of the many paintings and engravings produced to commemorate it.[2]*

1 *European Magazine*, October, 1782, p.244
2 The National Maritime Museum collection contains eight oil paintings of the battle, including works by Pocock, Luny, Serres, Swaine and Paton(?).

After RICHARD PATON, 1717-1791

C1 *The Glorious Defeat of the French Fleet off Belle-Isle*

Line engraving by P. C. Canot, 1761,
16⅛×24¾ (41×62.7)

The Trustees of the British Museum, 1849-10-3-6

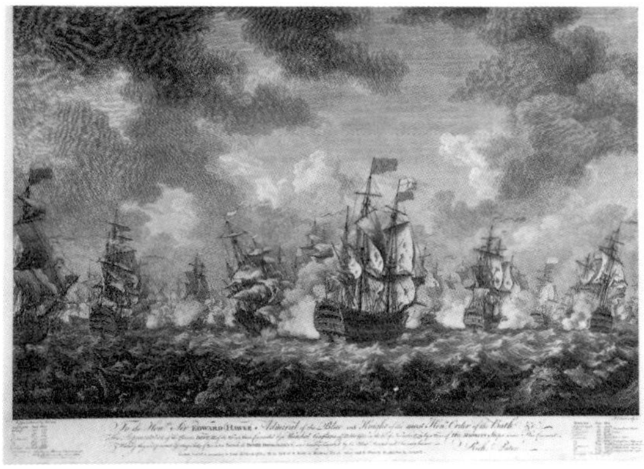

This splendid action view of the battle of Quiberon Bay forms a pair to Canot's engraving of the victory of Lagos Bay against the French, (18th August 1759), won by Admiral Boscawen.

ISAAC SCHOMBERG

C2 *Naval Chronology, Vol I, 1802*

The British Library, 293.k.24-26

Captain Schomberg, who served under Lord Howe on 1st June 1794, published his *Naval Chronology* in five volumes in 1802. It provides an account of the actions in which the English navy took part from the Romans to the present day, and was intended both as a work of reference for 'nautical men', and to refresh their memory of the 'heroic and glorious actions of our ancestors'. The volume is opened at Schomberg's account of the battle of Quiberon Bay, in which Howe's leading role in the action is made apparent.

The American War of Independence, 1775-1781

On 4th July 1776 the American colonies issued the Declaration of Independence. In the same year, Lord Howe was appointed Commander in Chief of the naval forces in North America. His younger brother, Sir William Howe, was already in command of the army there, and the two brothers were commissioned to 'treat with the revolted Americans, and to take measures for the restoration of peace with the colonies' (6th May 1776).[1] Lord Howe was probably a good choice as mediator; he had met Benjamin Franklin in London in 1774, and in a letter to him of June 20th 1776 he refers to his hopes of establishing 'lasting peace and union with the colonies'.[2] Unfortunately, by the time he arrived in America, it was already too late for negotiation, and he was left only to promote the war. Since the colonies had no fleet, his role was limited to providing support for the army, and he assisted in the landing on Long Island and the capture of New York on 15th September 1776, and in the occupation of Philadelphia (1777).

Both brothers rapidly became disillusioned with the state of the war. General Howe offered his resignation in October 1777, claiming that he had not been properly supported, and Lord Howe followed suit on 23rd November. However, in 1778 war broke out again between England and France, and Howe was left to face the large fleet which now arrived in America under the French Admiral d'Estaing. The two fleets met off the coast of Virginia, but despite d'Estaing's numerical advantage, the British were in a strong position, and the French Admiral did not attack. Shortly afterwards, Lord Howe sailed to defend Rhode Island, but d'Estaing arrived before him, and the two fleets faced each other inconclusively until a gale blew them apart. Shortly after this Lord Howe, whose resignation had by now been accepted, resigned his command to Lord Byron and sailed for England.

The Howes had been dismayed at the appointment in April 1778 of a new commission for peace with the Americans, in which they were to share their role as negotiators with Lord Carlisle, Governor Johnstone and William Eden. They felt, moreover, that they had received inadequate support from home, and had no faith in the ministry's comduct of the war. Books and pamphlets were published at home both attacking and defending their conduct (cats. C6, C7). They were also accused of being dilatory in sending despatches home to England. Horace Walpole, who kept up a running commentary on the American wars in his letters, refers with irony to the 'loquacious Howes' or to their 'extreme taciturnity', while on 23rd December 1776 he wrote to Lady Ossory: 'So the Howes did not think their prodigious victory worth writing a line about. They little know that if they did but send us a bantam egg we can hatch an ostrich from it'.[3] So concerned were the Howes about the 'imputations' thrown on them for 'not terminating the American war last campaign',[4] that on their return they succeeded in obtaining a Committee of the House of Commons to investigate the whole conduct of the American war. However, its findings were inconclusive, and in 1779 it adjourned. In its obituary of Lord Howe the Gentleman's Magazine *pointed out that at this critical part of his life, when Howe was 'subject to the censure and praise of contending parties', 'every enterprise in which his squadron was concerned was uniformly successful, and he never failed in obtaining those objects that were within the reach of the naval force he commanded. His defensive conduct, it suggests reasonably, was 'required from the state of his fleet, and the particular situation of the British cause in America'.[5]*

1 *Dictionary of National Biography*, p. 95.
2 *Gentleman's Magazine*, Vol 47, April, 1777, p. 169.
3 Walpole, Vol 32, Letter to Lady Ossory, 23 December, 1776.
4 *Walpole*, Vol. 39, p. 321n.
5 *Gentleman's Magazine*, Vol. 69, II, September, 1799, p. 806.

ENGRAVER UNKNOWN

C3 *Sir William Howe,* 1729-1814

Mezzotint, 1777, 12¾×10 (32.4×25.4)

The Trustees of the British Museum, 1899-7-13-60.

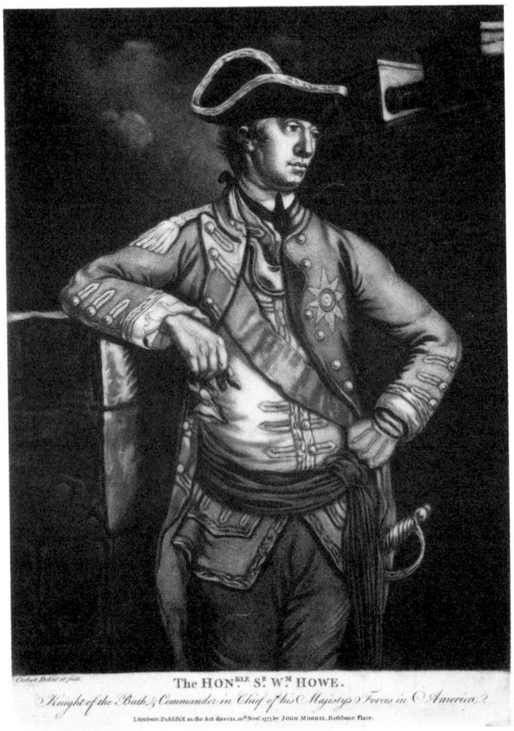

This mezzotint portrait of Sir William Howe, Lord Howe's younger brother, and commander of the land forces in America, is one of a series of engravings depicting leaders on both sides of the American War of Independence, which were published in London from 1775-8. Among those represented are the American commander-in-chief, George Washington, and John Hancock, President of the American Congress. It seems likely that the set was produced at the beginning of the war by an enterprising London publisher, in anticipation of demand, and there is some debate as to whether the portraits might not be fictitious: two portraits of Washington are by an engraver, Campbell, who is unrecorded, while this engraving is said to be by 'C. Corbutt', an alias for the disreputable Charles Purcell, who probably died in 1766, several years before the publication of this print. The poor quality of the engravings themselves might also bear this out. However, whether they are based, as their publishers claimed, on authentic likenesses or not, the prints are a fascinating example of the craving for images which a war such as this one created. The possibility remains that this print is based on an earlier engraving of Howe executed during Corbutt's lifetime.

ENGRAVER UNKNOWN

C4 *Richard, 1st Earl Howe*

Mezzotint, originally published by J. Morris, 1777; the plate re-issued by Laurie & Whittle, 1794, 12¾×10 (32.4×25.4)

The Trustees of the British Museum, 1980-U.1180

This engraved portrait of Lord Howe is something of a mystery. The version exhibited here is a re-worked plate of 1794 which represents Lord Howe as Commander-in-Chief of the Channel Fleet, with his flagship the *Queen Charlotte.* Although the print was

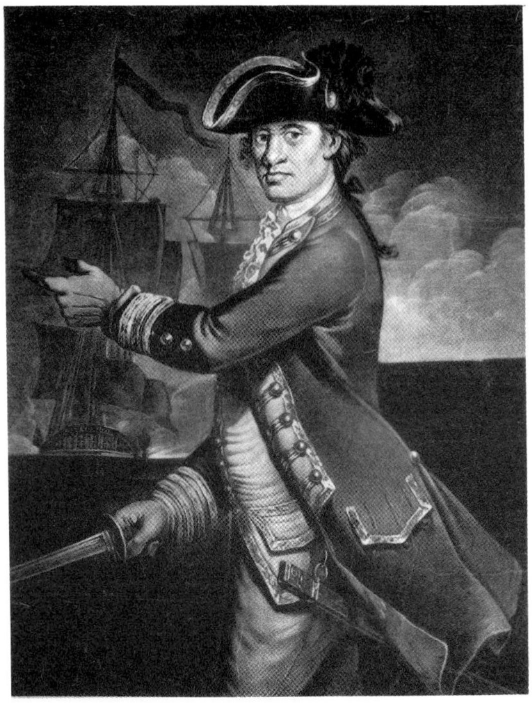

published on 11th June, literally only days after news of Howe's victory reached England, one wonders if it could have been rushed out to commemorate the victory. At all events Lord Howe, as commander of the fleet against the French that summer, was very much in the news. Like the portrait of his brother, Sir William Howe (cat. C3), however, this engraving was originally published by J. Morris in 1777, with the same engraver's name of 'Corbutt'. It seems likely, therefore, that it too formed one of the series produced in connection with the American War of Independence, although Chaloner Smith has not recorded it as such in his *British Mezzotint Portraits.* A further reason for suggesting this is that while the series includes the land commanders on both sides, and the Commander-in-Chief of the American fleet, Commodore Hopkins, the Commander of the British fleet is, apparently, conspicuous by his absence. Whether or not the engraving originally formed one of this group, it must surely, from its date, have been produced in connection with the American war.

Although the engraving is not related to any known portrait of Earl Howe, the features are not dissimilar to those found in Gainsborough's and Copley's portraits of him (cats. A25, A31). This resemblance would tend to support Chaloner Smith's contention that these engravings are, indeed, derived from actual portraits, rather than being fictitious.

C5 *The Defense of Rhode Island,* 1779

Copper Medal, 1 5/16 (3.3)

Inscr: (obverse) De Admiraais Flag ver Admiral Howe 1779

(reverse) D'Vlugtende Americaane^n van Rohde Island Augt. 1778.

Private collection

This medal, produced to commemorate Lord Howe's attempt to defend Rhode Island against the French fleet of Admiral d'Estaign in August 1778, shows, on the obverse, Howe's flagship the *Eagle,* while on the reverse is a bird's eye view of Rhode Island itself.

C6 ***A Letter to the Right Honourable Lord Viscount Howe, on his Naval Conduct in the American War***
London, 1779

The British Library, 103.c.71

One of the highly critical accounts of Lord Howe's conduct of the American war to be published in London in the late 1770's, this letter claims, satirically, to rescue Howe's name from 'the oblivion under which it is likely to remain'. It accuses him of having mishandled peace negotiations as well as the war, particularly through his failure to make use of his power to relinquish taxation over the colonies. As regards the war itself, the author's verdict is that had Lord Howe destroyed enemy shipping, blocked up harbours, and cut off supplies, the outcome would have been very different. Finally, he suggests that Howe 'slipped your cables, and ran from your enemy' – the French fleet of Admiral d'Estaign. However, the suggestion that Howe had a large enough force available to defeat d'Estaign is misleading.

C7 ***Candid and Impartial Narrative of the Transactions of the Fleet under the Command of Lord Howe from the arrival of the Toulon squadron on the coast of America, to the time of His Lordship's departure for England. With observations, By an officer then serving in the fleet.***
London, 1779

The British Library, 103.c.58

Written by one of the officers serving in Lord Howe's American fleet, this account is a defence of his American campaign and is intended, says its author, 'to do justice to a great and good man, by the best mode of justification that can be offered in his favour; a plain state of facts, an impartial account of his actions, submitted to public view'. The writer admits that he 'has not the honour of being in Lord Howe's secrets', but points out that his observations were either formed on the spot, or were suggested to him by 'officers of the first character both in the navy and army'. The public, he considers, has a right to know of the services Howe has rendered to his country, and of the 'ungrateful return he has met with at the hands of some of the servants of the Crown'. He insists that Howe has achieved a 'signal triumph' over the French, while of the British Empire in America he writes, wisely, 'that phantom is vanished'.

C8 ***ANTICIPATION: CONTAINING THE SUBSTANCE OF HIS M——Y'S GRACIOUS SPEECH. To both H—S of P—L—T. on the Opening of the Approaching Session***
London, 2nd edition, 1778.

The British Library, 103.c.54

The pamphlet reports the Parliamentary debate on the American war in 1778, in which Lord Howe, by now returned to England, strongly defended his conduct. Governor George Johnstone, who, with Howe, was one of the five Commissioners appointed to seek reconciliation with the Americans in 1778, attacked him for refitting at New York after the storm at Rhode Island; according to Johnstone, this lost the opportunity of separating the French Admiral d'Estaign from Boston, and, ultimately, the chance of regaining the colonies for Britain. The pamphleteer's report of Howe's reply, in which he stipulates for an enquiry investigating his conduct, is said by his biographer, George Mason, to be a close approximation to his actual style of talking, which resembled his fighting: 'close action was his aim'. In answer to Johnstone, he says: 'That, first, to avoid entering into the motives and principles of his own conduct, as being more proper objects for a particular committee of enquiry, and then to launch out into vague and desultory accusations of any other person, was inconsistent and, he was sorry to add, illiberal. That whatever prejudices those reflections were intended to create against his conduct, he would not then interrupt the business of the day, and the more general subjects of the present debate, but trust to the candour of the house for suspending their opinion, until the whole of his conduct might be minutely investigated by a committee appointed for that purpose; which Committee, he himself should be the first man in that house to solicit, may demand'.

The Siege and Relief of Gibraltar, September-October 1782

From 1779 to 1782 Gibraltar was beseiged by the combined Spanish and French forces. On the morning of 13th September 1782 the Spaniards attacked, bringing up to within 1,000 yards of the rock itself a flotilla of ten specially built floating batteries or 'battering ships'. The Governor of Gibraltar, General Elliott, returned fire and by mid-afternoon smoke was seen rising from two of the ships. 'Before midnight' says General Conway (with slight exaggeration) 'all the famous floating batteries were either burnt or sunk by our red-hot balls'.[1] At 3 a.m. Sir Roger Curtis brought up his gunboats to complete the attack, but was soon instead courageously saving the lives of those abandoning ship. This was despite extreme danger from the battering ships, which now exploded one by one. The British garrison's victory was complete, but the seige remained in force.

On 11th September Lord Howe had sailed from Spithead with 183 sail to relieve Gibraltar. His force consisted of 34 ships of the line and 12 frigates, escorting transport and supply ships. After being delayed by contrary winds, the fleet finally entered the Straits of Gibraltar on 11th October. Only four of the supply boats reached anchor off Gibraltar that night, but, after adroit manoeuvring, Howe managed to get westward of the allied fleet, so that it no longer stood between him and Gibraltar. When the wind changed to the east on 16th October the convoy was able to dock in Gibraltar, landing troops and powder as well as supplies. By the 19th the operation was complete, and Howe repassed the Straits of Gibraltar to the west, closely followed by the allied fleet.

Despite their numerical advantage, the allied attack, when it came on 20th October, was desultory, and the following day the fleet headed for Cadiz, leaving Howe free to return home. Walpole praised Howe's 'grave dignity' in 'marching in face of a very superior navy, maintaining a fortress on their own coast, engaging that navy, obliging it to retire, and walking home himself very deliberately', preferring such a 'sedate triumph' to an all-out battle.[2]

This was the 'action Lord Howe always spoke of, to his dying day, as the greatest he had ever performed, and as the only one, of which he claimed the sole merit to himself'[3]. Coming after the losses and uncertainties of the American war, Gibraltar, as a victory over Britain's traditional enemies, was exceptionally popular with the British public. Walpole undoubtedly spoke for the nation when, after weeks of waiting, he was able to report on 29th October that: 'The great news of the relief of Gibraltar by Lord Howe arrived this day se'nnight'.[4]

1 Walpole, Vol 39 Letter from Conway to Horace Walpole, 30th September 1782.
2 Walpole, Vol. 25. Letter to Mann, 10th November 1782.
3 Mason, p. 50.
4 Walpole, Vol. 25. Letter to Horace Mann, 4th November 1782.

C9 J. K. SHERWIN, 1751-1790

A view of Gibraltar with the Spanish battering ships on fire

Stipple and line engraving, reprinted in 1791 from the original plate of 1784, 16⅞×23⅛ (42.8×58.7)

The Trustees of the British Museum, 1877-6-9-1879

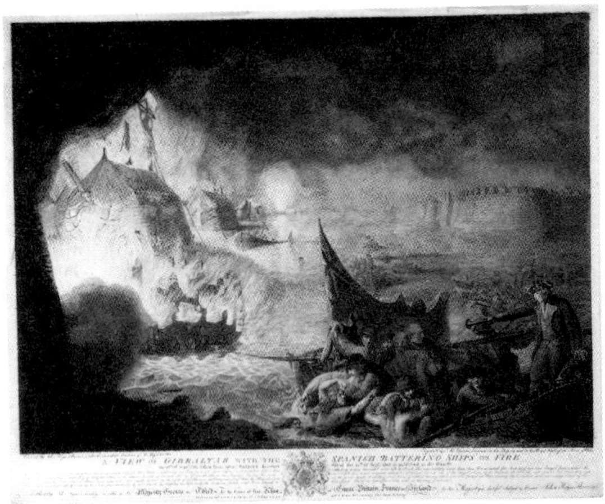

Sherwin's engraving depicts the dramatic events of the night of 13th/14th September as they reached their climax. By the early hours of the morning, the Spanish battering ships were all ablaze. The scene in the harbour was 'highly illuminated; forming, with the constant flashes of our cannon, a mingled scene of sublimity and terror'.[1] The hero of the hour, Sir Roger Curtis, can be seen on the extreme right directing operations from his gunboat; the other boats under his command are spread out behind.

This is evidently the moment when, Curtis tells us, 'numbers of men [were] crying from amidst the flames, some upon pieces of wood in the water... and all imploring assistance'. This formed 'a spectacle of horror not easily to be described' and, abandoning the attack, 'every exertion was made to relieve them'.[2] Curtis was able to report that he had saved the lives of thirteen officers and three hundred and forty-four men. The operation was a hazardous one, in consequence of 'the blowing up of the ships around us, as the fire got to the magazines, and the firing of the cannon of others, as the metal became heated by the flames'. In Curtis's own boat, which sustained a large hole in the bottom, his coxswain was killed, and two others of his crew wounded.

The seige of Gibraltar spawned a large number of engravings, most of which, like this one, concentrate on the destruction of the Spanish battering ships and Curtis's rescue operation. This was also the scene finally chosen by John Singleton Copley for his gigantic (18×25 foot) canvas of the seige of Gibraltar, commissioned by the City of London. Copley had originally intended to combine this scene with a depiction of Howe's Relief of Gibraltar, but this integration of the two scenes proved too difficult, and the relief was eventually relegated to a predella panel, together with portraits of Howe and his second in command, Admiral Barrington (see cat. A31).

1 As observed by Colonel John Drinkwater (quoted in J. D. Proun, *John Singleton Copley*, Vol 2, p. 322.

2 Sir Roger Curtis's own account of the action, printed in the *Gentleman's Magazine*, Vol 52, November, 1782, p. 512.

After RICHARD PATON, 1717-1791

C10 *The Relief of Gibraltar*

Line engraving by Daniel Lerpiniere, 1784

17⅞ × 25¾ (45·4×65·4)

The Trustees of the British Museum, 1877-6-9-1839

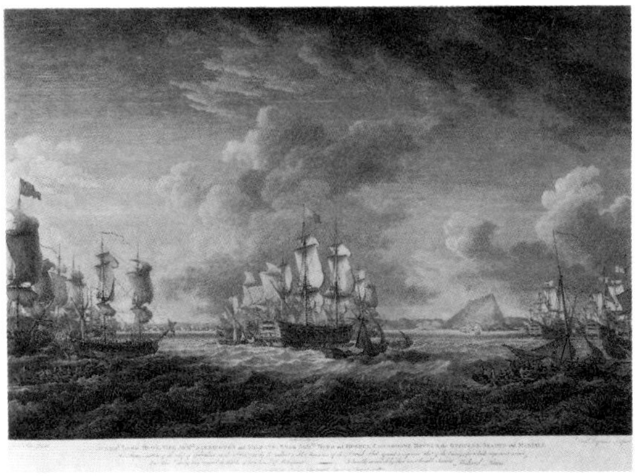

By noon on the 11th October Lord Howe's fleet had entered the Straits of Gibraltar, the transport and store ships leading, and the ships of war following behind ready to break into battle formation. This engraving by Lerpiniere, which derives from an oil painting by Paton now in the National Maritime Museum, shows the convoy's progress towards the Rock itself in the distance. Although it would take another few days manoeuvring before Howe could finally unload all the supply boats, this was effectively the moment when the relief of Gibraltar began.

C11 *Arx Herculea Servata... or Gibraltar delivered. A Poem, in Latin and English. Inscribed to the Right Honorable Admiral Lord Viscount Howe, and to the Right Honorable General Geo. Aug. Eliott, KB*

London, 1783

The British Library, 1570/1478

This high-flown paean of praise in rhyming couplets is addressed to the general who defended Gibraltar, and to the Admiral who relieved the colony. After apostrophising the Spaniards and their battering ships with the words 'O come no nearer – Madmen! tempt not fate', the poet goes on to praise Sir Roger Curtis's rescue mission: 'The hand that crush'd them, now is stretch'd to save,
The plunging wretches from a wat'ry grave'. The pace of the poem then slows to a statelier measure as the writer celebrates Howe's rescue mission:
'But lo! thy Country's fleet's in view
High in the air the British pendants fly,
While Howe securely stems the swelling tide
In full triumphant pomp of naval pride'.
Even the weather is seen to support the
British cause! –
'With Howe, she cries, the elements unite,
In Britain's cause the winds and waters fight'.

Command in the Channel and the Battle of Ushant, 1790-1794

Lord Howe's most famous victory was his last, the 'Glorious First of June' 1794. This was the first naval victory of the Revolutionary and Napoleonic wars with France, which began with the French declaration of war on 11th February 1793. As such, it was immensely popular with the public, and remains one of the greatest of all British naval successes.

In 1793 Howe was in command of the Channel Fleet, with the brief of watching the French, but, largely owing to bad weather, there was no major action that year. On 2nd May 1794 he again put to sea, and waited with twenty-six ships of the line to intercept a convoy bringing much needed grain to France from America. On 19th May Howe heard that the French fleet under Admiral Villaret-Joyeuse had left Brest three days before to escort the merchant ships home. The two fleets finally sighted each other in the North Atlantic, west of Ushant, on 28th May, when the English were to leeward. A skirmish between the English van, led by Admiral Pasley, and the French rear, led to the dismasting of the French Revolutionaire *and the English* Audacious, *both of which had to retire. On the 29th May the English were still to leeward but Howe, in his flagship the* Queen Charlotte, *decided to break through the enemy's line towards the rear. He was followed by the* Bellerophon *and the* Leviathan. *Three French ships were surrounded before the French admiral was able to bring up his fleet in support. The day gave the English the advantage of the wind. The two fleets were now separated by two days of gales, but on the morning of 1st June, with the enemy four miles away, Howe ranged his fleet in line of battle, and signalled his ships each to steer for and engage an opponent.*

Just before 10 a.m. Howe began the action in the centre, with the Queen Charlotte *engaging the French flagship,* La Montagne. *The battle soon became general. At its height, Lieutenant Neville of the Queen's Royal Regiment was killed on the deck of the* Queen Charlotte *(cat. C20). However, about twenty minutes after the* Queen Charlotte *had passed through the line, the* Montagne *and the* Jacobin, *which had come up to support her, retreated, and Howe signalled a general chase. The afternoon was spent in a mopping up operation and in all six ships were taken as prizes. The opportunity to take even more was lost through the over-caution of Sir Roger Curtis, to whom Howe, now an old man and worn out by the events of the day, devolved command at a critical moment. Undoubtedly the epic struggle of the day was the one between the* Brunswick, *which just managed to limp home to port, and the French* Vengeur, *which sank with a large number of its crew still on board.*

Despite the damage he had inflicted on the French fleet – there were 3,000 French casualties as opposed to 290 killed and 858 wounded on the British side, while all of the British ships, with the exception of the Brunswick, *emerged relatively unscathed – Howe failed to achieve his original objective, the prevention of the arrival of the grain ships from America. Nelson, who however deeply admired him, is said to have called a victory not exploited to its full a 'Lord Howe victory'. However, the enormous number of commemorative prints, books and memorabilia which the battle generated (cats. C15 – C31) testify to its electrifying effect on British morale. On 13th June Howe towed the six captured ships into Spithead. On June 26th the King, Queen, and three of the Princesses visited Lord Howe on board the* Queen Charlotte, *in the presence of Countess Howe and her daughter Lady Mary. The King presented Howe with a magnificent diamond-hilted sword (cat. C26) and with a commemorative gold medal and chain (cat. C27); the latter was given also to the other admirals who had served under him, with a smaller-scale version for the captains. Howe also received the Freedom of the Cities of London (cat. C28) and Dublin.*

THOMAS WHITCOMBE, 1763-after 1824

C12 *The Grand Fleet in the order of Sailing under Earl Howe, 1790*

Oil on canvas, 20¼ × 54¾ (51.4 × 136.5)

The Trustees of the Howe Settled Estates

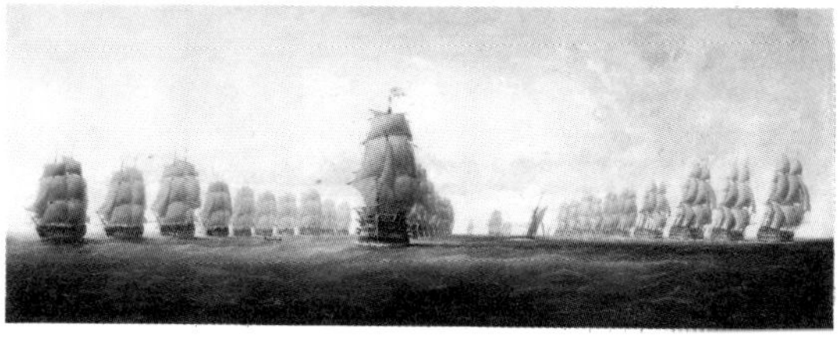

In 1790 war with Spain threatened, and Lord Howe was appointed to command the channel fleet. As a compliment not only to himself, but also to the distinguished flag-officers placed under him, he was given the temporary rank of Admiral of the fleet. During August Howe cruised between Scilly and Ushant arranging continuous naval exercises, and practising his new code of signals. However, in September, the danger of war with Spain receded, and in December Howe struck his flag. He would be placed in charge of the channel fleet again in 1793-4.

Thomas Whitcombe's painting shows Howe's fleet in the order of sailing. The ships are divided into three divisions, the red, blue and white. In all thirty sail of the line are depicted, although Howe is said to have had thirty-five men of war in his fleet on this occasion.[1] The *Queen Charlotte* is at the head of the red division, in the centre foreground; the key on the frame identifies the other ships and their commanders. Many of the officers serving under Howe here would later distinguish themselves at the battle of 1st June 1794.

1 D.N.B., p. 97.

HORACE WALPOLE

C13 *The Yale Edition of Horace Walpole's Correspondence (ed. W.S. Lewis) 1937- Vol. 12, p. 75*

Letter to Mary Berry, 30th November, 1793.

The British Library, 10922.g.

Needless to say, that indefatigable commentator on contemporary affairs, Horace Walpole, has much to tell us, over the years, about Lord Howe and his naval successes and reverses. On the whole Walpole's correspondence suggests that he rather disliked him, although his famous remark 'undaunted as a rock and as silent' pays tribute to Howe's proverbial courage as well as to his 'taciturnity'. Walpole's letter to Mary Berry of 30th November 1793, written as the nation anxiously awaited news of events at sea in the first year of the Revolutionary wars with France, is typical of Walpole's rather satirical approach to his subject, couched in high-flown language which he then deliberately undercuts, and containing his usual accusations of Howe's silence. The letter also provides a vivid and humorous account of the way in which news travelled in the late 18th century, before the advent of radio and television: 'All the town has been running about, asking, guessing, conjecturing and spreading imaginary reports – "Any news of Lord Howe? – What! no news yet!" – Well, this morning a Danish or Dutch ship has told somebody, who has told everybody, who have told the *True Briton*, who has just told me, that Lord Howe has taken five men-of-war, and will be here with them presently. . . '.

C14 *Letters and Secret Orders, 1793*
The Trustees of the Howe Settled Estates

This bound volume contains Lord Howe's instructions to the fleet from on board his flagship, the *Queen Charlotte*, in the first year of the Revolutionary wars with France. The book is opened to a page where Howe gives orders to Captain Pasley of the *Bellerophon* to lead a detachment of five ships in search of some French frigates which have been seen off the coast of Scilly, and to protect various merchant ships from the Mediterranean which are expected to enter the Channel heading for British ports.

After PHILIP JACQUES DE LOUTHERBOURG, 1740-1812

C15 *The Glorious Victory obtained over the French... on the First of June 1794*
Line engraving by James Fittler, 1799, $20\frac{1}{2}\times30\frac{9}{16}$ (52.1×77)
Exhibited together with a key to the British and French ships represented in the print.
The National Maritime Museum

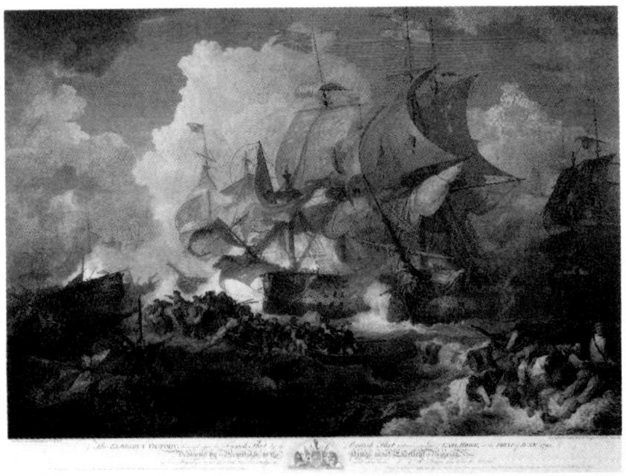

De Loutherbourg's dramatic account of the action of 1st June 1794 is unquestionably the most splendid visual record of the battle. His composition concentrates on the decisive encounter, which began just before 10 a.m., between the two flagships: the *Queen Charlotte,* in the centre, and *La Montagne,* seen here to her left. Howe had passed under the stern of the *Montagne,* and now, broadside on, and at a distance of only a few feet, discharged his guns on her. De Loutherbourg has chosen to depict a moment when the bombardment is well under way, and the *Queen Charlotte* has lost her fore top-mast. The *Montagne* succeeded in preserving its masts and rigging relatively intact, but had its stern and quarter deck stoved in, and many of its guns dismantled. De Loutherbourg is said to have erred in showing the *Queen Charlotte* on the *Montagne's* lee bow; had Howe really been in this position, he could probably have captured the French flagship. On the extreme left the *Vengeur* can be seen going down; many of its crew have taken to smaller boats in the water. Its opponent, the severely damaged *Brunswick,* is shown on the far right. The key which accompanies Fittler's engraving explains the relative positions of the other ships.

The original of this engraving is the vast canvas now in the National Maritime Museum. It was commissioned by the printsellers V & R Green and Von Mechel, as a pendant to de Loutherbourg's highly successful *Siege of Valenciennes* (1793). On his completion of the *Victory of 1st June* in 1795, the two paintings were exhibited together in the Historic Gallery, where, as glorifications on a vast scale of Britain's victories by sea and land, they rapidly became a major attraction. Both paintings were profitably translated into print form. A smaller scale replica on canvas, now in the collection at Penn House, is exhibited here (cat. C16). Cats C17-19 are studies for the finished composition.

PHILIP JACQUES DE LOUTHERBOURG, 1740-1812

C16 *The Battle of 1st June 1794*
Oil on canvas $31\frac{1}{2}\times41\frac{1}{2}$ (80 × 105·4)
Private collection

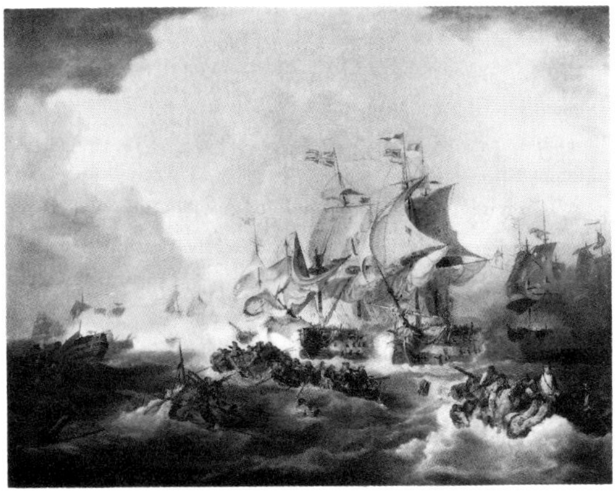

If the vast canvas which de Loutherbourg painted of the *Battle of 1st June* (see cat. C15) must have had a sensational impact when it was exhibited at the Historic Gallery in London in 1795, it was of a scale which made it suitable for display only in the largest of public interiors. It hung for many years in the Royal Naval College at Greenwich. This small-scale replica was presumably painted for Lord Howe and his family. Although the action is simplified in places, lending to the composition a rather more atmospheric quality than is found in the larger work, this is essentially a faithful copy of the original.

C17 *The Queen Charlotte*
Pen and wash drawing, $16\frac{3}{8}\times13\frac{1}{4}$ (41 × 33.6)
The Trustees of the Howe Settled Estates

This highly dramatic wash drawing is a study for Howe's flagship, the *Queen Charlotte,* as she appears at the centre of de Loutherbourg's final canvas, locked in an encounter with the French flagship *La Montagne* (cat. C15). The conflict was a fierce one and the *Queen Charlotte* can be seen with her masts and rigging in considerable disarray. The only apparent difference between drawing and painting is that the ship's stern, clearly visible here, is partially obscured in the finished painting by the fire from the French flagship, which is busy discharging her guns on her English counterpart. The drawing is essentially different in kind from the small-scale watercolours made by de Loutherbourg in Portsmouth (cat. C18), which were intended not as compositional studies, but as a factual record of individual English amd French ships of the line.

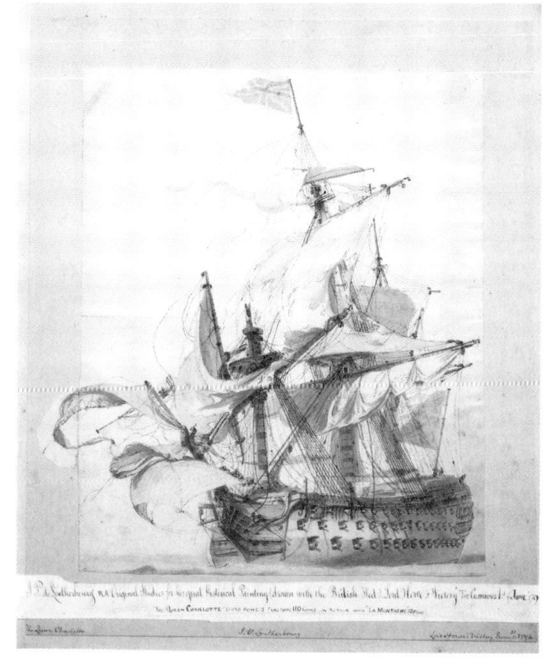

C18 ***Sketches for the picture of Lord Howe's victory, 1st June 1794***

a) Le Juste/L'Amerique 1857-6-13-600

b) Le Sans Pareile 1857-6-13-606

c) The Queen Charlotte 1857-6-13-588

d) Ships in action 1857-6-13-591

Watercolour or indian ink, mostly with pen outlines. Varying from 5⅛–5⅜×7¾–8¼ (13.1–13.6×19.7–20.8)

Prov: Purchased, March 1868

Lit: Binyon, III, p. 77

The Trustees of the British Museum.

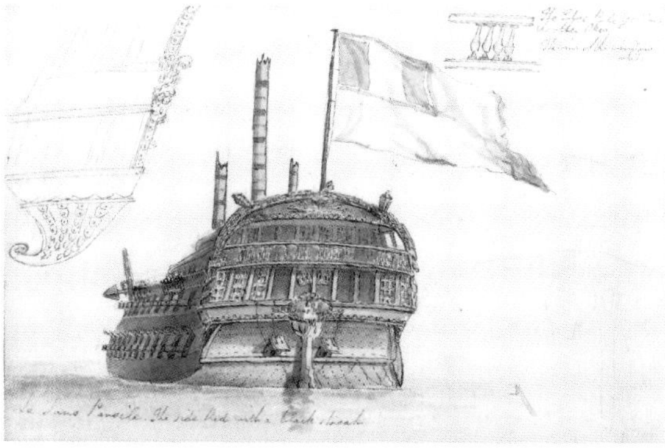

The four sketches exhibited here have been selected from a group of thirty-two studies by de Loutherbourg of the 'Heads, Sterns & Hulls of ships' produced in connection with his painting of Earl Howe's victory on 1st June 1794; also included are studies of uniforms for his *Battle of Valenciennes* (1793). For the land battle, de Loutherbourg had visited the battle-field in Flanders, together with the caricaturist James Gillray. He now spent a great deal of time in Portsmouth making studies of the English, and captured French, men-of-war for his portrayal of the events of 1st June. The painting was intended as a documentary account of the battle, and a high premium was evidently placed on accuracy of detail. Many of the drawings, like the one of the *Sans Pareile* shown here, include the artist's colour notations. The studies include a close-up view of the bow of the *Queen Charlotte,* as seen, centre stage, in the finished painting (cats. C15, C16); a view of the *Sans Pareile,* which appears at a different angle in the final composition; and a view of the captured French ships, *Le Juste* and *L'Amerique*. See also cats. C17, C19 for further preliminary studies.

C19 ***Sketches of Military and Naval Costume, Shipping, etc.***

Album containing ink, wash and pen or pencil drawings

Prov: Purchased, March 1968

Lit: Binyon, III p. 69(20), opened at no. 73.

The Trustees of the British Museum, 201.c.5.

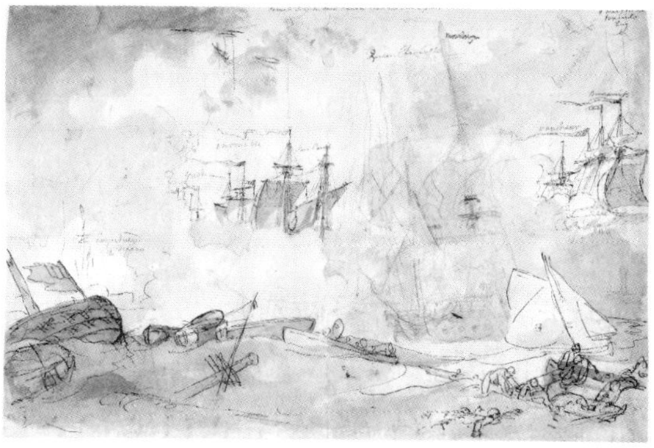

This is an album of studies chiefly for de Loutherbourg's paintings of the *Siege of Valenciennes* and *Lord Howe's Victory*. It is opened at a sketch for the battle of 1st June, which shows de Loutherbourg experimenting with the intended positioning of individual ships within the composition. As in the final canvas, the *Brunswick* can be seen on the extreme right, while the *Queen Charlotte* and the *Montagne* will later be moved further into the centre. The *Sans Pareile* appears behind the *Queen Charlotte,* again as in the finished painting, but the arrangement of the men-of-war to the left of her would later undergo extensive alteration. It is apparently the *Jacobin* and not the *Vengeur* – the only ship actually to go down – which is shown sinking on the left. The album also contains two plans of 'Lord Howe's action off Ushant' at different stages in the conflict; sketches of the *Queen Charlotte* and of the French men-of-war captured during the battle; and a positive mass of studies of shipping, all of which were clearly produced in connection with the *Battle of 1st June*.

After MATHER BROWN, 1761-1831

C20 ***The Celebrated Victory Obtained by the British Fleet on 1st June 1794***

Stipple and line engraving by Daniel Orme, 1795, 17×22½ (43.2×57.1)

Exhibited together with a key to the print.

The Trustees of the British Museum, 1854-10-20-61.

Mather Brown's portrayal of the death of Lieutenant Neville on board the *Queen Charlotte* at the height of the action, as Howe broke through the enemy's line, differs from all other representations of the battle in that it concentrates, not on the manoeuvring of the ships, but on the suffering and achievements of the men who sailed on them. The engraver, Daniel Orme, at whose shop at 14, Old Bond Street, the original painting was exhibited in 1795, boasted that the composition was 'treated in a manner entirely *Novel*, and perfectly distinct from any other Nautical

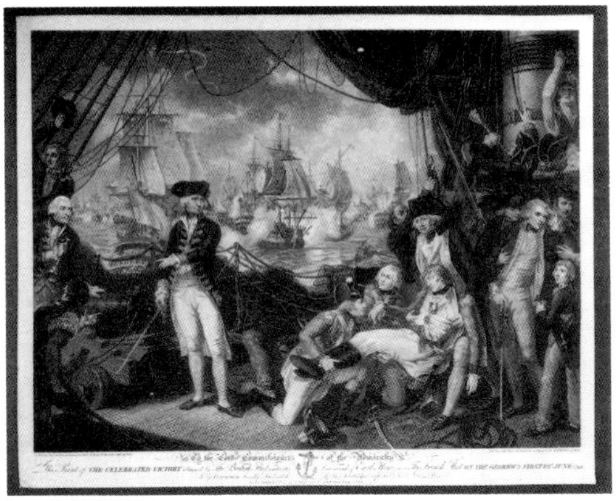

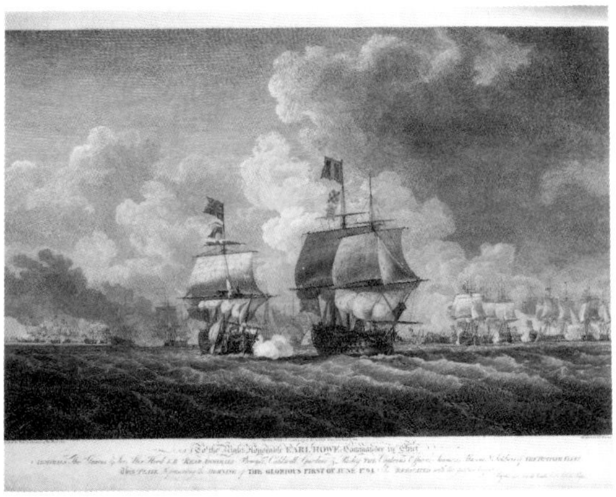

Engagement, hitherto executed; there has never yet been *even* attempted the Introduction of Portraits into a Naval Picture'. He also reveals that Earl Howe had sat expressly for his portrait and that Mather Brown had stayed on board the *Queen Charlotte* after its return to Spithead, painting the officers in Howe's own state cabin and taking detailed measurements of the ship.

The engraving – the original is now in the National Maritime Museum – shows Earl Howe on the Quarter Deck of the Queen Charlotte, with the First Captain of the Fleet, Admiral Sir Roger Curtis, beside him. On the extreme right of the composition, Sir Andrew Snape Douglas clutches his wounded forehead, while in the centre Lieutenant Neville of the Queen's Royal Regiment dies in the arms of his brother officers. Beyond and to the left is the *Jacobin,* which had fired the fatal shot. The other ships represented can be identified from the key to the engraving.

Before its public exhibition, the painting was shown to the King and Queen at Buckingham Palace, who are said to have expressed their approval. Apart from de Loutherbourg's even larger canvas, this was the most ambitious venture by a printseller in connection with the battle of 1st June. As one might expect, it was launched with a certain amount of hyperbole, presented as part of the arts' 'Tribute of Applause' to Howe's great victory.

After ROBERT CLEVELEY, 1747-1809

C21 *The Morning of the Glorious 1st of June, 1794*

Line engraving by B. T. Pouncy, 1796

The Evening of the Glorious 1st of June, 1794

Line engraving by T. Medland, 1796

Both 19⅞×30¾ (50.5×78.1)

The Trustees of the British Museum, Lucas collection, 1917-12-8-4596, 1870-10-8-2784

These splendid engravings are after a pair of oil paintings by the naval artist, Robert Cleveley, which were commissioned by the enterprising printseller, A. C. de Poggi. The paintings were exhibited at de Poggi's premises at 91, New Bond Street in 1796, together with an accompanying *Narrative* of the events of May and June 1794 (cat. C22). Prints were available from de Poggi himself or from Boydell's, at a price of three guineas each or five guineas the pair. De Poggi was able to boast that Earl Howe had 'honoured them with the sanction of his name', and the engravings are dedicated to him and to the fleet.

In support of his claims as to the engraving's accuracy, de Poggi tells us that Cleveley was assisted in this project by several officers of the fleet. The artist had attempted to 'represent those points of time on which the decision and consequence of the battle chiefly depended and which are in themselves strictly historical'. The plate of the 'morning' of 1st June shows the action at 10.40 a.m., about an hour after the *Queen Charlotte* began the action in the centre. The enemy line has been broken at many points, and each ship is either individually engaged with an opponent, or in providing assistance to another. The *Queen Charlotte,* which had lost her fore-top mast and her main-top sail, was unable to recover her position alongside the *Montagne* as she bore away. The plate representing the 'evening' of the battle (in fact at about 2.50 p.m.) shows the respective conditions of the two fleets after the engagement. The French Admiral, Villaret-Joyeuse, is leading eight of his ships in a line, so as to cover the retreat of the *Republicain* and others. Howe, meanwhile, is preventing the escape of seven of the French ships of the line, and directing assistance to the *Vengeur,* which is sinking with many of her crew still on board.

A. C. de POGGI

C22 *A Narrative of the Proceedings of His Majesty's Fleet under the Command of Earl Howe, from the second of May to the second of June, 1794*

London, 1796

The British Library, 194.a.16.

The print seller A. C. de Poggi produced this account of the events of May and June 1794 to accompany the pair of 'capital engravings' after Robert Cleveley (cat. C21) which were on sale at his New Bond Street shop. No doubt he hoped that this background material, which includes Howe's despatches and letters concerning the action, the resolution of thanks to Lord Howe from both Houses of Parliament, and a list of the officers taking part in the action, would assist in their sale.

After ROBERT SMIRKE, 1753-1845

C23 *Commemoration of the Victory of June 1st 1794*

Line engraving, by Bartolozzi, Landseer, Ryder & Stow, 1802, 30×19⅝ (76.2×49.8)

The National Maritime Museum

The plate is one of a set of four engravings by Robert Smirke designed to commemorate the four great English naval victories of the recently ended war with France; the others are the battles of St. Vincent (1797), Camperdown (1797) and the Nile (1798). See also cat. C24.

In the plate of 1st June 1794, Britannia, seated by the shore, is being crowned with laurel by a winged victory; the battle itself takes place almost off-stage,

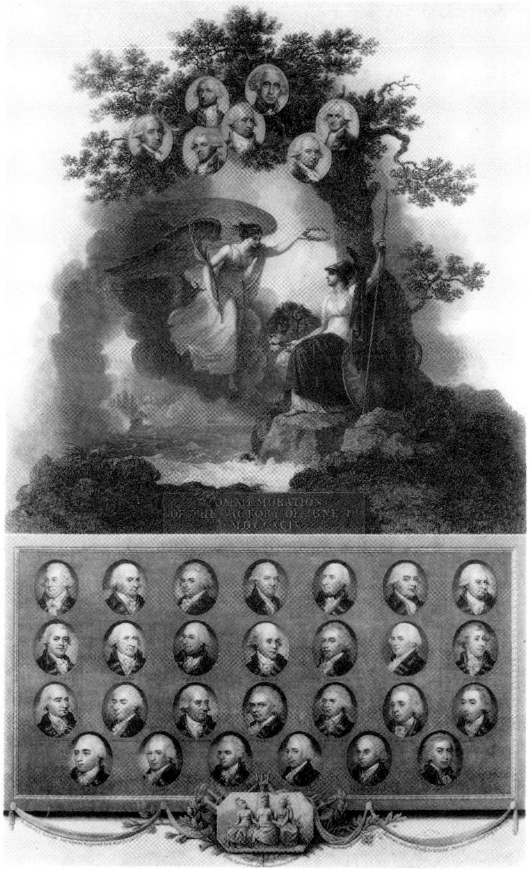

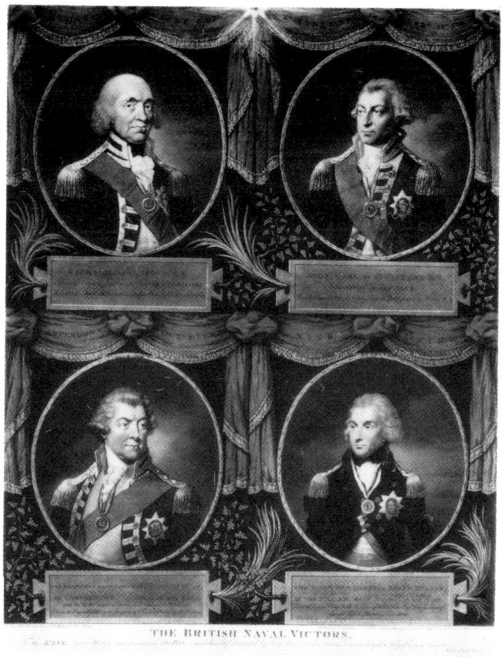

on the left. Above, bust portraits of Howe and his six admirals, Graves, Caldwell, Gardiner, Bowyer, Pasley and Bridport, hang from the branches of an oak tree, while Howe's twenty-seven captains are ranged, rather like a cabinet of miniatures, below. The engraving of the portrait heads was by Bartolozzi, who took the likeness of Howe from John Singleton Copley's portrait of him now in the National Maritime Museum (cat. A31).

These were not the only emblematical engravings of this highly patriotic kind produced to celebrate the successful conclusion of the war with France. A somewhat absurd offering by Piercey Roberts, entitled 'British Admirals. Britannia viewing the conqueror of the Seas' was published in 1800. This, too, sets Britannia on a rock with ships behind her, while a winged victory bears her helmet. On the left is a series of medallion portraits of thirteen admirals, including Lord Howe, inset into the face of a rock. It seems probable that Smirke had the iconography of this rather clumsily arranged engraving in mind when designing his own, much more successful, production, which was published two years later.

After GAINSBOROUGH DUPONT, FRANCIS COTES, R. M. PAYE AND L. F. ABBOTT

C24 *The British Naval Victors*

Mezzotint, by Valentine Green, 1799, 23½×19 (59.7×48.3)

The Trustees of the British Museum, Cheylesmore 1902-10-11-2269.

Published in the year of Lord Howe's death, this mezzotint was produced to commemorate the four great British naval successes of the decade: Howe's Victory of Ushant, 1st June 1 the Earl of St. Vincent's defeat of the Spanish off Cape St. Vincent on February 14th 1797; Viscount Duncan's defeat of the Dutch off Camperdown (October 11th, 1797); and, most recently, Lord Nelson's great victory of the Nile (1st August, 1798). The bust portrait of Howe is taken from Gainsborough Dupont's full length portrait of him at Trinity House, London, which was frequently engraved.

The mezzotint, which was dedicated to the King, is a splendid one, combining fine bust-length portraits – i" Inset to look like miniatures – with swags of drapery, and sprays of oak leaves and laurel as symbols of victory. It is one of a number of group portraits of admirals produced in the late eighteenth century; other groups which include Lord Howe are listed in O'Donoghue's *Engraved British Portraits*, pp.55,79.

J. ADLARD (printer)

C25 *Panorama of the Battle of 1st June 1794*

Line engraving, 16⅛×12⅞ (40.8×32.6)

The Trustees of the British Museum, 1983 U-242

The battle of 1st June was not only reproduced in quality engravings. As this print makes clear, it had also made its way into a new, and potentially even more popular medium, that of the 'moving picture'. There was a great deal of interest in the late eighteenth century in the use of light boxes, peep shows, panoramas, and other devices which could show pictures in movement. Artists such as Gainsborough, and de Louherbourg in his famous *Eidophusikon,* which was the talk of the town when it was shown in London in 1781, made experiments in this vein. In a panorama, a picture is arranged on a cylindrical surface, which then revolves around the spectator. A naval battle, showing the action of ships against the horizon line, would have been an ideal, and indeed a spectacular choice of subject. This particular panorama could be seen at premises in Leicester Square, where, one imagines, crowds of people would have flocked to see this latest curiosity.

C26 ***Sword Presented to Earl Howe by George III, June 26th, 1794***

Hilt in blue enamel and gold, inset with diamonds

Length: $39\frac{1}{2}$ (100.3); hilt 7 (18).

The Trustees of the Howe Settled Estates

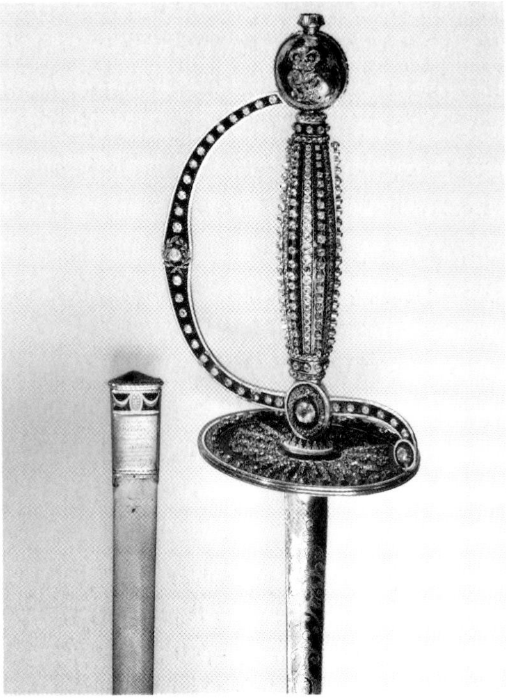

On 20th June the King arrived in Portsmouth, with the Queen and three of the Princesses, to congratulate Lord Howe and his fleet in person. This was an honour for which there was no precedent, and which would not be repeated on the occasion of later British victories.[1] Presumably it was owing to the Royal Family's warm personal regard for Lord Howe and his family. On the evening of their arrival, the Royal Family dined with Countess Howe and her daughter. 'The King and Queen, and the older Princesses... ' wrote Lady Mary Howe, 'appeared almost to share our feelings'.[2]

The following day the Royal Family was rowed out to the *Queen Charlotte* at Spithead. Lady Mary explained that 'Our attendance on the Queen and Princesses prevented Mama and I from seeing the first meeting of the King and my glorious father, which I am told was the most affecting thing possible. My father's knees trembled with emotion when he kissed the King's hand, who presented him with a most magnificent sword set with diamonds... '. The meeting is recorded in H. P. Briggs's later (1828) painting of this scene in the National Maritime Museum (fig 1). The King also presented Lord Howe with a gold chain (cat. C27).

1 Warner, p.43.
2 Op. cit., p.144.

THOMAS (c.1692-1776) and LEWIS (1743-1830) PINGO

C27 ***Gold Medal and Chain presented to Earl Howe by George III, to commemorate 1st June 1794***

Diameter $2\frac{1}{16}$ (5.3)

Inscr: (reverse) Richard Earl Howe. Admiral and Commander in Chief on the 1 of June MDCCXCIV. The French Fleet Defeated

Private collection

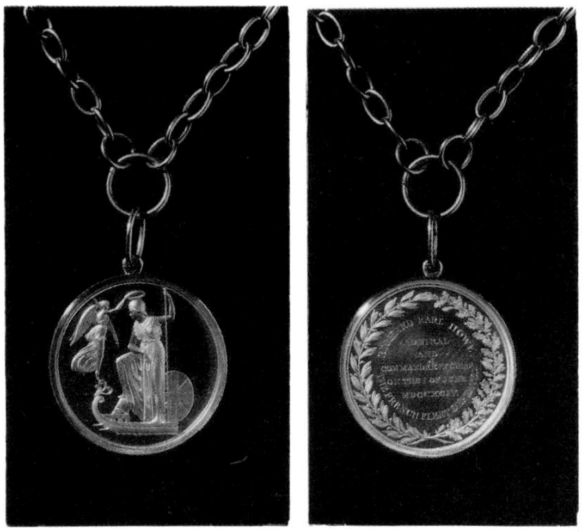

When they met on the deck of the *Queen Charlotte* on 26th June, the King presented to Lord Howe, in addition to the diamond-hilted sword (cat. C26), a 'gold chain, to which is to be hung a medal struck for the occasion; which is also given to the other admirals and captains who have contributed to this victory'.[1] The medal, designed by Thomas, and his son Lewis, Pingo, both of whom were engravers at the Royal Mint, was in two different sizes, one for admirals and a smaller one for captains. The admiral's medal shows on the front, Britannia, crowned by a winged victory, and, on the reverse, a wreath of oak and laurel engraved with the name and rank of the recipient, and the date of the action itself.

This was the first time that a naval battle was followed by the conferring of awards. Prior to this, the only way of honouring a victor was by offering him a baronetage or peerage. The system, once begun, developed in the nineteenth century into the highly elaborate structure we know today. Later medals, however, were worn on a ribbon, and not, as here, on a chain.

1 Letter from Lady Mary Howe; quoted in Warner, p.144.

C28 ***Freedom Box, 1794. Gold with enamel insets***

Length: $4\frac{1}{16}$ (10.4)

Width: $2\frac{7}{8}$ (7.1)

Depth: $1\frac{1}{4}$ (3.1)

Private collection

The inscription on the inside of this gold box explains that a Common Council, held in the Chamber of the Guildhall of the City of London on 18th June, 1794, resolved unanimously to present the Freedom of the City to Earl Howe, 'in testimony of the grateful sense this court entertains of the signal and important Victory obtained by him on the 28th and 29th of May and first of this instant June, over the French Fleet'. Lord Howe was also awarded the Freedom of the City of Dublin.

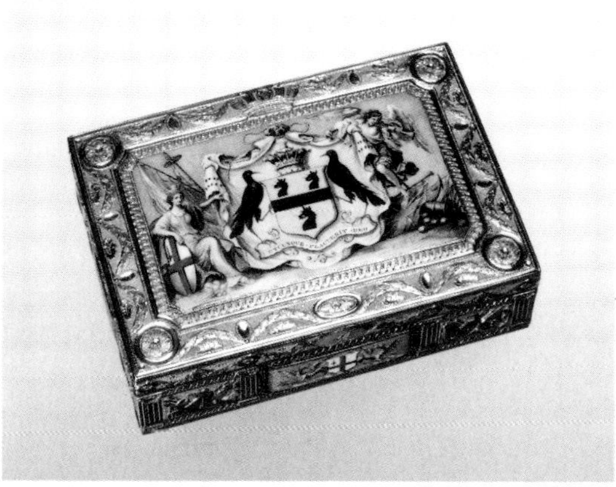

Prints were not the only medium used to celebrate the victory of 1st June, and to supply the strong public demand for commemorative material. Several medals were also struck to mark the occasion. This fine example by William Barnett shows Neptune standing in his chariot in the centre, with Britannia seated to his right, while above a winged victory inscribes on an obelisk the names of the seven admirals who took part in the action. The battle itself is shown in the distance on the left. On the front is a profile portrait of Lord Howe. Barnett's other medals include a portrait of George, Prince of Wales (1794) and, another nautical subject, Captain Cook's expedition to the Southern Seas (1772). There are examples of the present medal in the British Museum, in both silver and bronze.

WILLIAM BARNETT, d. 1824

C29 *Lord Howe's Victory of 1st June 1794*

Silver medal, diameter 2¼ (5.8)

Inscr: (obverse) 'Ric: Comes Howe Vice-Admirallus Angliae & c.' *& signed* 'Barnett' *(reverse)* 'Non Nobis sed Patriae' *and* 'MDCCXCIIII 1st June'

Lit: Brown, 1980, (382)

Private collection

C. H. KÜCHLER

C30 *Lord Howe's Victory of 1st June 1794*

Silver medal, diameter 1⅞ (4.8)

Inscr: (obverse) Ric. Comes Howe Thalassiarcha Britan *(and below)* Patriae Decus et Tutamen *and signed with initials* CHK *(reverse)* Non Sorte Sed Virtute *(below)* Gallor. Classis. Proflig./Die I Junii MDCCXCIV *and signed* C. H. Küchler F.

Lit: Brown, 1980 (383)

Private collection

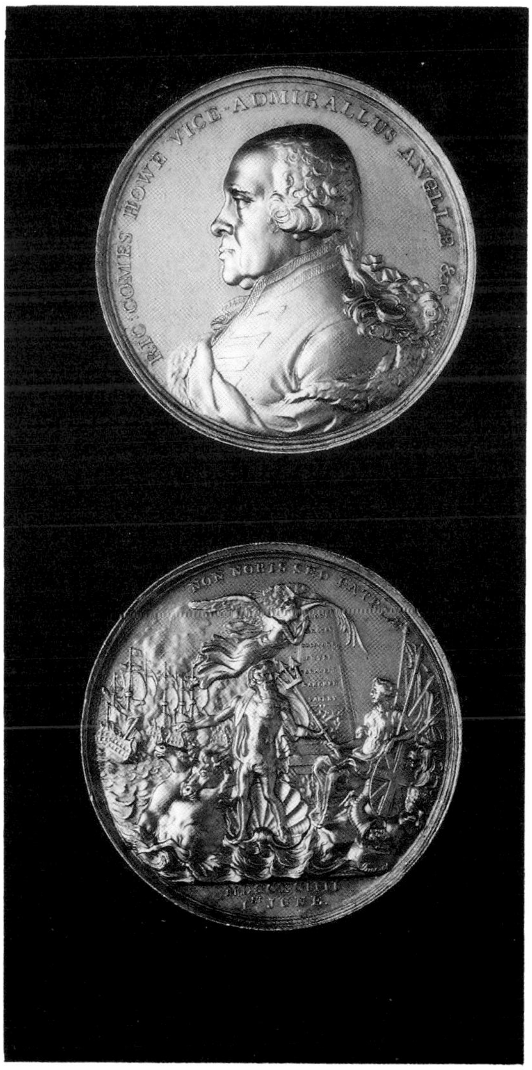

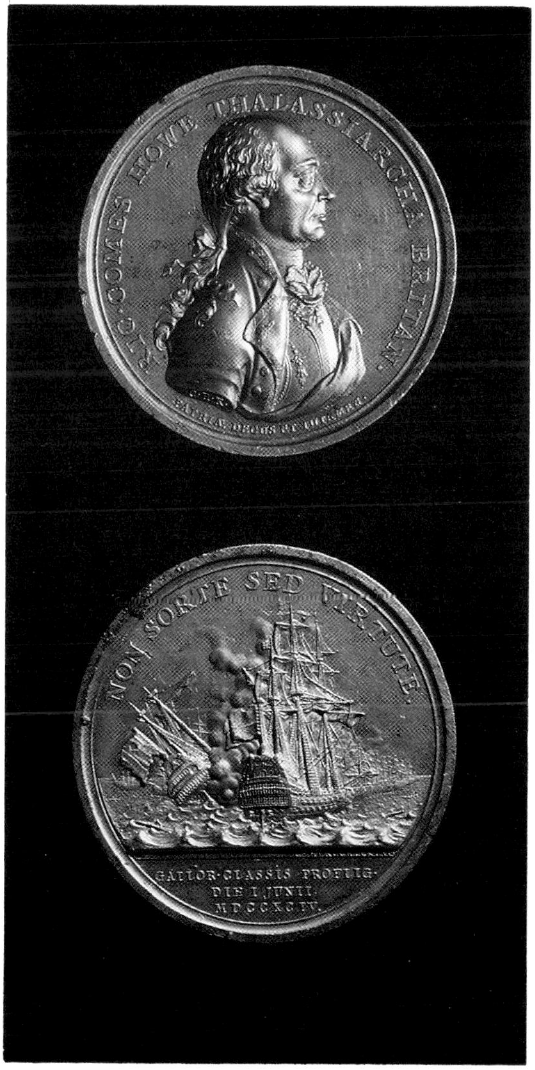

The medal depicts, on the back, a view of the action of 1st June 1794. On the front is a bust length portrait of Lord Howe in profile. As with the medal by William Barnett (cat. C29), the head is not related to any known portrait of Howe. Küchler came to England c.1790 and worked for Matthew Boulton at the Soho Mint, Birmingham.

C31 ***The Glorious Victory of Earl Howe on 1st of June 1794***

Snuff box, porcelain, with black transfer-print of ships on white lid.

Length: 1⅝ (4.1)

Width: 1⁵⁄₁₆ (3.4)

Photograph exhibited

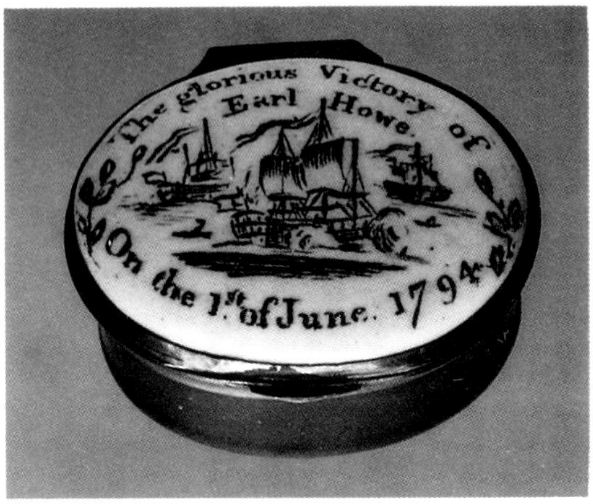

This is one of two very similar snuff boxes in the Howe collection. These should probably be seen, not as individual pieces made for members of the family, but as popular souvenirs of the time – yet another example of the way in which a victory as famous as this one was disseminated.

C32 ***Letter from George III to Countess Howe***

Windsor, June 11th, 1794

The National Maritime Museum

This letter of congratulation, written by the King to Lady Howe after receiving news of her husband's victory, is convincing proof of the close friendship which existed between the Howes and the Royal Family. As the letter is a short one, it is quoted here in full:

'Lady Howe will I trust believe that next to the signal advantage to the great cause in which this country is engaged nothing can give me more satisfaction than that it has been obtained by the skill and bravery of Earl Howe, and I sincerely return thanks to the Almighty without any personal loss to himself. The 1st of June must be recorded as a proud day for him as it will carry down his name to the latest Posterity. I will not add more than that I trust now both your mind and that of Lady Mary will be at ease we must soon hear of his return to Spithead George R.'

C33 ***Letter from George III to Earl Howe***

Windsor, June 8th, 1796

The Trustees of the Howe Settled Estates

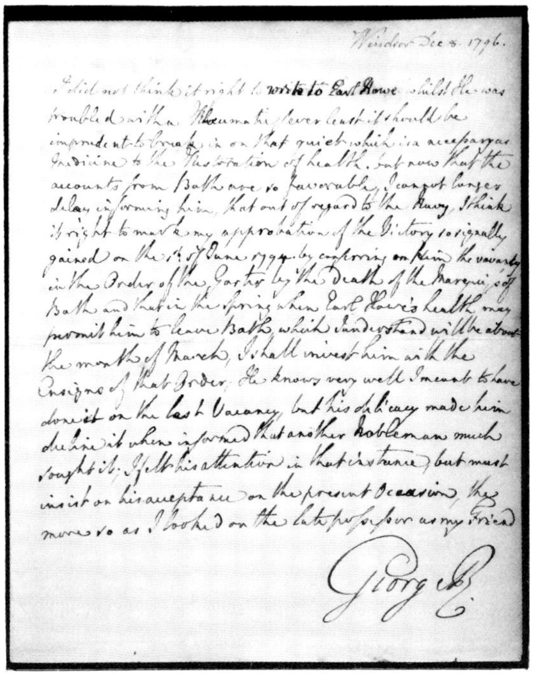

Windsor Dec 8. 1796.

I did not think it right to write to Earl Howe whilst He was troubled with a Rheumatic fever least it should be imprudent to break in on that quiet which is a necessary medicine to the Restoration of health, but now that the accounts from Bath are so favorable, I cannot longer delay informing him, that out of regard to the Navy, I think it right to mark my approbation of the Victory so signally gained on the 1st of June 1794 by conferring on Him the vacancy in the Order of the Garter by the Death of the Marquis of Bath and that in the spring when Earl Howe's health may permit him to leave Bath, which I understand will be about the month of March, I shall invest him with the Ensigns of that Order. He knows very well I meant to have done it on the last Vacancy, but his delicacy made him decline it when informed that another Nobleman much sought it; I felt his attention in that instance, but must insist on his acceptance on the present Occasion, the more so as I looked on the late possessor as my Friend

George R.

When they met on board the *Queen Charlotte* on 26th June 1794, the King had told Lord Howe that he intended to confer on him the Order of the Garter. However, the only vacant place was being sought by the Earl of Chatham, then first Lord of the Admiralty, for the Duke of Portland, and Lord Howe appears to have offered to make way for this candidate. According to Sir Edward Codrington,[1] Howe was incensed at a slight offered by Chatham's brother, the prime minster William Pitt, who suggested that it 'would be for the advantage of the public service that he should forgo the King's promise of the Garter'. Howe is said to have 'coldly declined' the marquisate proffered in its place.

In 1796 there was a new vacancy in the order, and the King now wrote to Lord Howe, reminding him that previously his 'delicacy made him decline it when informed that another Nobleman much sought it', but insisting that he accept on the present occasion, as the King wished 'to mark my approbation of the Victory so signally gained on the 1st of June 1794'. Howe was finally admitted to the Order on 2nd June 1797, when his health allowed him to travel to London.

1 DNB, p.99.

C34 ***Log and Signals Book, 1794***
The Trustees of the Howe Settled Estates
This fascinating document shows, on the left page of each opening, the signals which Lord Howe's flagship the *Queen Charlotte* sent to the other ships in the fleet from 28th May-1st June 1794. The time and number of each signal is recorded, together with the name of the ship or ships to which it was addressed. On the facing page are logged observations such as 'Counted the Enemy 31 sail in all'. The volume is opened at the page on which Howe at 8.45 a.m. on 1st June gives a general signal: 'For the fleet to prepare for battle'. Shortly afterwards, he sends another announcing that, nevertheless, 'People will have time to dine'!

W. GOGGIN (printer)
C35 ***A new song, Called Lord Howe's Glorious Victory over the French***
Limerick, 1800 (?)
The British Library, 11622. df. 51 (6)
This ballad in rhyming couplets on the events of 28th-29th May and 1st June 1794, claims to have been written by a seaman on board the *Orion* ('I am a saucy foremast Jack, to the *Orion* I belong'). The tone is jovial and jingoistic, explaining how 'we made the French dogs fly, Resolved we were to conquer or every man to die'. Despite this, the account is substantially an accurate one, and gives us the events of these three days from a different perspective – that of the ordinary seamen, as they waited for orders to attack, and then as they engaged in close conflict with the individual ships of the enemy line.

C36 ***The European Magazine***
Vol. 27, April, 1795
The British Library, P.P. 5459.2
As the anniversary of the 1st June 1794 approached, the *European Magazine* redeemed a promise to their readers to supply them with an updated likeness of 'our great naval hero'. The bust length stipple engraving of Lord Howe, which forms the frontispiece to the April edition, is taken from Daniel Orme's portrait of him on the deck of the Queen Charlotte (cat. C20), although minus the hat. The *European Magazine* had printed a memoir of Howe in its issue for October, 1782, at the height of public interest in the *Gibraltar* crisis. The April 1795 edition provides a short update on the earlier piece, expatiating on Howe's character, 'which cannot be spoken of in too high terms. Intrepid, active, determined and collected, he has long stood in the first rank in his profession'.

C37 ***The Naval Chronicle***
Vol. I, January, 1799
The British Library, 293. i. 1
This 'Biographical Memoir of Earl Howe' is the first of a series of articles on famous naval commanders which this new periodical, 'dedicated to the interests of the British Navy', planned to offer its readers. Indeed, it occupies pride of place at the beginning of the first volume. The memoir is illustrated with a series of vignettes after Nicholas Pocock, who was present at the battles of 28th-29th May and 1st June, and whose drawings of the events of these few days are amongst the battles' more distinguished artistic products. The collection at the National Maritime Museum includes a bound volume of Pocock's *Notes & Sketches on Board HMS Pegasus* and a series of sensitive watercolours and wash drawings of the battles of 29th May and 1st June (M1012-4 & M1024). The engraving exhibited here is by Wells and shows 'Lord Howe engaging the French Fleet under Admiral Villaret on the 29th May'. Only a few months after the publication of this memoir, Lord Howe was dead, and Volume 2 of the *Naval Chronicle* carried a long obituary notice.

Bibliographical note

Works listed in the Bibliography are cited in abbreviated form in the catalogue, under author's name and date of publication.

I Howe papers

Although Barrow says that many of the Howe papers were burnt in a fire at Westport House, Ireland, in the early nineteenth century, a considerable number of papers have in fact survived. In Britain there are papers in the National Maritime Museum (Letters from George III and Admiral Blankett, family correspondence, signal books, and an annotated copy of *Naval Instructions,* 1772 (HOW 1-11), correspondence with Sir Charles Middleton (MID/ 1/97/2/24) and Lord Hood (HOO); the Public Record Office, Kew (68 letters to William Pitt and the 2nd Earl of Chatham, G.D.8); the British Library (correspondence with Lord Bridport, Sir Frederick Haldinand and Earl Spencer, and over 5,000 letters exchanged by Georgiana, Countess Spencer and Mrs. Caroline Howe); Kent County Archive (correspondence, mainly with Howe's son-in-law, Lord Altamont, U951/C267-8); Hull University Library (22 letters to Lord Hotham DDHO/5/1); Nottingham University Library (letters to 2nd Duke of Newcastle); and the National Register of Archives, Scotland, for the Home family papers. The Historical Manuscripts Commission Report on the Stopford Sackville manuscripts (Vol. 94, II, 1910) lists Howe material among the American War of Independence papers at Drayton. The Howe papers at Penn House also contain Howe's orders to the fleet in 1793, his log and signals book for 1794 and miscellaneous letters. Lord and Lady Howe's wills can be consulted at the Public Record Office in Chancery Lane.

Lord Howe's part in the American War meant that there is considerable interest in his life and career in America, and there are papers in the Pierpont Morgan Library (4 letters); the William L. Clements Library in Boston (the correspondence and papers of the three Howe brothers, *Guide to the M.S. Collections,* 3rd edition, 1978, p.64; included are some family letters and Howe's signal book); Yale University Library (17 orders to Sir John Duckworth); the Lewis Walpole Library, Farmington, Connecticut (Letters to Lord Hotham); and, the largest collection of all, the Huntington Library (408 letters to Sir Roger Curtis, *Guide to British Historical Manuscripts in the Huntington Library,* 1982).

The Howes owned property in Nottinghamshire, Leicestershire, Derbyshire and Hertfordshire, and also had connections with Devon and the City of Bath. The record offices of these counties, and of the City of Bath, all contain important material on the family. *The Antiquities of Nottinghamshire* by Robert Thoroton, revised by John Throsby in 1790-96, facsimile edition by M. W. Barley and K. S. S. Train, 1927, and John Nicholls's *The History and Antiquities of the County of Leicester,* 4 vols, London, 1795-1810/11, are both key sources. There is a useful summary of Lord Howe's connections with Bath in T. Sturge Cottrell, *Richard Howe, Earl Howe,* London and Bath, 1931.

II Lord Howe and his family: printed sources

The two earliest biographies of Lord Howe, neither of them entirely satisfactory, are George Mason's brief *Life of Richard, Earl Howe,* London, 1803 (cat. A36, 37), and Sir John Barrow's identically titled work, London, 1838, (cat. A38). There is also a lengthy section on Howe in the *Memoirs of Sir Edward Codrington,* 1873, ed. Lady Bourchier, Vol. I, pp. 12-40. These were preceded by a number of contemporary articles on Howe, notably in the *British Magazine* by Edward L'Epine for June 1783 (British Library copy destroyed in World War II), the *European Magazine* for October 1782, pp.243-5 (with a 'supplement' in April 1795, pp.219-20, cat. C36), the *Gentleman's Magazine,* Vol. 52, for October 1782, pp.511-514, and the *Naval Chronicle,* Vol. I, for January 1799 (cat. C37). The *Gentleman's Magazine* also included a long obituary notice (Vol. 69, September, 1799, pp.805-808).

Howe's victories of Gibraltar and 1794, and equally his difficult time as Commander-in-Chief of the navy during the American War of Independence, all attracted a large number of tracts, both critical and favourable, in poetry and prose. The most important of these are included in the exhibition (cats. C6-C8, C11, C22 and C35). *The Yale Edition of Horace Walpole's Correspondence,* ed. W. S. Lewis, 1937- , is a postive mine of information on Howe, although the anecdotes are somewhat slanted since the two men obviously did not get on. *Augustus Hervey's Journal* for 1746-59 (ed. D. Erskine, London, 1953) gives us a glimpse of the young Commodore at the outset of his career. Modern sources include Oliver Warner's *The Glorious First of June,* London, 1961; T. S. Anderson, *The Command of the Howe Brothers During the American Revolution,* New York and London, 1936; and Ian Gruber, *The Howe Brothers and the American Revolution,* Chapel Hill, University of North Carolina, 1972. Engravings of Lord Howe's naval battles are listed in Harry Parker, *Naval Battles,* London, 1911.

III Gainsborough his predecessors and contemporaries: selected bibliography.

David Blayney Brown, *Catalogue of the Collection of Drawings,* Ashmolean Museum, Vol IV, Oxford, 1982.

Laurence Brown, *A Catalogue of British Historical Medals,* Vol. I, London, 1980.

Deborah Cherry and Jennifer Harris, 'Eighteenth-Century Portraiture and the Seventeenth-Century Past: Gainsborough and Van Dyck', *Art History,* Vol. 5, No. 3, September 1982, pp. 287-309.

Ellen G. D'Oench, *The Conversation Piece: Arthur Devis & his Contemporaries,* Yale Center for British Art, New Haven, 1980.

Dictionary of National Biography; entries on Richard, Earl Howe and Sir William Howe.

Elizabeth Einberg, *Manners & Morals, Hogarth and British Painting 1700-1760,* The Tate Gallery, London, 1987.

Francis Haskell & Nicholas Penny, *Taste and the Antique, The Lure of Classical Sculpture, 1500-1900,* New Haven & London, 1981.

John Hayes, *The Drawings of Thomas Gainsborough,* London, 1970.

John Hayes, *Gainsborough, Paintings and Drawings,* London, 1975.

John Hayes *Thomas Gainsborough,* The Tate Gallery, London, 1980.

John Hayes, *Gainsborough 1727-1788,* Grand Palais, Paris, 1981.

John Hayes, *The Landscape Paintings of Thomas Gainsborough,* 2 vols, London, 1982.

John Hayes and Lindsay Stainton, *Gainsborough Drawings,* International Exhibitions Foundation, 1983.

James Holloway, *James Tassie 1735-1799,* National Galleries of Scotland, 1986.

David Irwin, *John Flaxman 1755-1826,* London, 1979.

Ellen Miles, *Thomas Hudson, 1701-1779, Portrait Painter and Collector, A bicentenary exhibition,* The Iveagh Bequest, Kenwood, 1979.

Sir Oliver Millar, *Van Dyck in England,* National Portrait Gallery, London, 1982-3.

National Maritime Museum, Greenwich, *Concise Catalogue of Paintings,* HMSO, 1958.

F. M. O'Donoghue, *Engraved British Portraits,* London, 1908.

A. P. Oppé, *The Drawings of Thomas and Paul Sandby. . . at Windsor,* London, 1947.

Nicholas Penny, (ed.), *Reynolds,* Royal Academy of Arts, London, 1986.

J. D. Prown, *John Singleton Copley in England,* Cambridge, Mass., 1966.

Aileen Ribeiro, *A Visual History of Costume, The Eighteenth Century,* London, 1983.

Aileen Ribeiro, *Dress in Eighteenth Century Europe, 1715-1789,* London, 1984.

Aileen Ribeiro: 'Fashion and Fantasy: The Use of Costume in Eighteenth-Century British Portraiture' in *The British Face, A View of Portraiture 1625-1850,* Colnaghi, 1986.

Royal Academy of Arts, London, *Paintings and Drawings by Allan Ramsay, 1713-1784,* 1964.

Stephen V. Sartin, *Polite Society by Arthur Devis 1712-1787,* Harris Museum and Art Gallery, Preston, 1983-4.

Alastair Smart, *The Life and Art of Allan Ramsay,* London, 1952.

John Chaloner Smith, *British Mezzotint Portraits,* 4 vols, 1883.

Lindsay Stainton, *Gainsborough and his Musical Friends,* The Iveagh Bequest, Kenwood, 1977.

Humphry Ward & W. Roberts, *Romney,* 2 Vols, London, 1904.

E. K. Waterhouse, *Reynolds,* London, 1941.

E. K. Waterhouse, 'Preliminary Check List of Poprtraits by Thomas Gainsborough', *The Walpole Society,* Vol. 33, 1948-1950.

E. K. Waterhouse, *Gainsborough,* London, 1958.

E. K. Waterhouse, *Reynolds,* London, 1973.

E. K. Waterhouse, *Painting in Britain 1530-1790,* London, 1978.

E. K. Waterhouse, *The Dictionary of British 18th Century Painters,* Woodbridge, 1981.

Mary Woodall, (ed.), *The Letters of Thomas Gainsborough,* Bradford, 1963.

Lenders to the exhibition

Her Majesty The Queen A17

Bath, Museum of Costume B3

Chester, Grosvenor Museum B5

Edinburgh, National Galleries of Scotland A20

Exeter, National Trust, Killerton B1

Trustees of the Howe Settled Estates A25, C12, C14, C17, C26, C33-34

London, British Library A36-38, A40, C2, C6-8, C11, C13, C22, C35-36

London, The Trustees of The British Museum A3, A9, A12-14, A21-22, A24, A26, A28-30, B8-13, C1, C3-4, C9-10, C18-21, C24-25, C30-31

London, The Iveagh Bequest, Kenwood A1, A27, B7

London, The National Maritime Museum A31, C15, C23, C32

London, National Portrait Gallery A32

London, The Trustees of the Tate Gallery A35

London, The Trustees of the Victoria & Albert Museum B6

London, Witt Print Collection, Courtauld Institute of Art A10

Manchester, City Art Galleries, The Gallery of English Costume B4

Newcastle-upon-Tyne, Laing Art Gallery A23

The Marquess of Northampton A19

Nottingham, Castle Museum and Art Gallery A15

Oxford, The Visitors of the Ashmolean Museum A4, A6-7

Private Collections A8, A16, A34, C5, C27, C28, C29, C30

L. G. Stopford Sackville A11

Mrs Imogen Skirving A39

His Grace the Duke of Westminster DL. A2

Worthing, Museum and Art Gallery B2